MADLY MURDEROUS

John Dunning

ARROW

First published 1985

5 7 9 10 8 6

© John Dunning 1985

First published in the United Kingdom in 1985 by
Hamlyn Paperbacks

Arrow Edition 1988
Random House, 20 Vauxhall Bridge Road, London SW1V 2SA

Random House Australia (Pty) Limited
20 Alfred Street, Milsons Point, Sydney,
New South Wales 2061, Australia

Random House New Zealand Limited
18 Poland Road, Glenfield
Auckland 10, New Zealand

Random House South Africa (Pty) Limited
PO Box 337, Bergvlei, South Africa

Random House UK Limited Reg. No. 954009

A CIP catalogue record for this book
is available from the British Library

ISBN 0 09 935050 0

Printed and bound in Germany by
Elsnerdruck, Berlin

CONTENTS

INTRODUCTION

It may be that even those persons into whose hands the previous books in this series have fallen will be unaware of the commendable efforts of editors and agents to deter me from writing introductions. Unlike editors and agents, readers are not professionally required to read introductions and therefore, sensibly, do not as a general rule.

There are advantages to this state of affairs. As the introduction will be read only by the agent, the editor and very close relatives of the writer, it is possible to write almost anything, thus providing the writer with an outlet for his or her personal prejudices and, at the same time, sparing the reader their inclusion in the less tedious parts of the book.

Naturally, some limits must be observed. A reader may well mistake the introduction for the first chapter, and it will not do for him or her to be confronted with the opinion that he or she is probably as mad as the most psychotic of March hares.

The fact that this opinion can be statistically supported does not help matters in the least. Although the proportion of persons medically and legally insane within Western society is sufficiently large that some are certain to be included in the readership, the more choleric may take offence at being so distinguished and proceed to actions such as may be expected from disturbed spirits. The writer who wishes to avoid disembowelment or similar unpleasantness will, therefore, exercise restraint in composing the introduction.

Not so the body of the work. Here, defendants may be freely described as homicidal maniacs, psychopaths, mental incompetents, idiots, cretins, morons, feeble-minded, lunatics or anything else that will relieve them of the responsibility for their acts. Indeed, this is how they described themselves and how defence attorneys and experts describe them. Insanity is the most favoured excuse of the defendant whose guilt is proven and who does not want to be inconvenienced because of his act.

According to modern Western theories of crime there is no such thing as malice, every member of the human race is essentially good, and criminals do not exist. There are only misguided victims of the system who, with a little psychiatric counselling, can be converted into useful members of society.

Nearly all criminals are in wholehearted agreement with these theories, although they do little to support them. Despite a constant bombardment of statistics by the media to prove that psychology is invariably successful in the rehabilitation of violent offenders, I have been writing true crime stories for barely fifteen years and one valued collaborator has provided me with his third murder case, having been convicted, cured and released twice previously. I confidently await the fourth.

Others, less diligent or more agile in avoiding detection, can boast of two successive murders to their accounts, and the number of repeated lesser offences is legion.

Loathe as I am to criticize the findings of such an unimpeachable institution as the media, I humbly submit that there are quite a few persons who die painful deaths at the hands of these born-again useful members of society.

This does not mean that I would question the principle of non-responsibility by reason of insanity. A great many murders and other crimes are committed by persons who are, beyond all doubt, mentally incompetent. What is more dubious is the theory, more ideological than medical, that such persons can be cured to the point where it is safe for them to mingle with their potential victims.

Granted that some undoubtedly are, but, if even one cure in ten turns out to be imperfect, the risk to society in general and, particularly, children and others incapable of self-defence is, to my mind, unacceptable.

Unfortunately but predictably, the persons effecting the release of supposedly cured, violent criminals are required to accept no more responsibility for their acts than are the criminals.

There is, however, a difference. When a judge, social worker, penologist or psychologist effects the release of a convicted murderer who then proceeds to another murder, he or she does not plead not guilty to having made possible this second crime by reason of insanity, but merely observes that to err is human.

Perfectly true and, for this reason it might, perhaps, be advisable, in situations where error can result in the painful death of others, to be a trifle less arrogantly confident in making decisions.

It is hardly likely that the suggestion will be accepted. The release of criminals into society is normally carried out anonymously, or under such conditions as to make fixing of responsibility difficult or impossible.

Ergo, another suggestion. Might it not be well to arrange that no one has the authority to release a convicted felon?

Even less popular than the first! Modern trends are in precisely the opposite direction. Not only is it possible for persons who need take no responsibility for the act to effect the release of criminals, but in many countries sentencing is so light that the criminal scarcely requires such services. He has already served his sentence and departed before the ideologues have had time to arrange for his release.

Ideally, and ideologically, there should be no sentencing at all. If the accused is not a criminal, but merely a disturbed person, how can he or she be sent to jail? It is far better that he or she be sent to an institution for psychiatric observation and treatment.

This is, astoundingly, often successful. Psychiatrists do not maintain their reputations and clinics do not stay in business by reporting large numbers of failures.

Such treatment is, however, expensive and, as even the resources of the taxpayer have limits, the length of stay is usually brief. The patient is then released as cured of his or her antisocial tendencies and, should another offence occur, assured of success with an insanity plea on the basis of an official record of mental illness.

It helps, of course, if each succeeding offence is slightly more atrocious than the last, although in many cases such heights of atrocity have been reached that it is difficult to extend them, thus leading persons planning an insanity defence to make their crimes more appalling than they might personally have wished. It is popular among defence attorneys in some countries to plead that their mandate must be insane as the crime perpetrated was so dreadful that no sane person could have committed it.

Oddly enough, it appears to occur to no one that such dreadfully insane persons should not be lightly returned to the company of their potential victims because some one believes this ideologically desirable.

From the point of view of the crime writer, the situation is utopian. The choice of crimes, each more frightful than the last, is enormous and unending. There is never any shortage of material and, as even murder is a media event, the murderers compete for publicity by devising ever more ingenious and monstrous means of dispatching their victims.

But, although this has been challenged, crime writers are also human, and it is trying to spend the working hours writing about dangerous psychopaths who have been cured and have celebrated their recovery by torturing to death a child, after having read in the morning newspapers that the government is planning the release of vast numbers of rehabilitated prison inmates. Granted, the true reason may be simply lack of jail space, but this does not help the tortured child.

A crime writer thus finds himself in the position of one who sees numbers of persons being eaten by lions and can do nothing about it, while prominent, self-appointed authorities sit on the sidelines and shout, 'Lions are not dangerous!'

This can lead to frustration and a feeling of unreality. Media, courts, sociologists, psychologists, penologists and politicians all know that dangerous persons are being released into society and that they not infrequently commit new crimes. They do nothing about it and steadfastly maintain the opposite.

Actually, the very theory of law and law enforcement

appears to have undergone a change without the knowledge or consent of the members of society most concerned, namely the victims.

The whole concept of law, and the only one which makes any sense, is the protection of property and the weaker members of society. Without law, the protection of women (with apologies to the Women's Equality Movement) and children falls to the male head of the family in which they are included. If the male is weak, unwilling or dead, the protection is lacking and, even if he is strong and able, he cannot spend all of his time accompanying his wife to the market and his children to school. Within a community, the community itself must assume the task of providing security, or life in such a community is not possible.

This is the situation which is now developing on an international scale. None of the Western European democracies are safe places to live. There are substantial numbers of disturbed persons and, to use an unpopular term, criminals at large. Old persons, children and women are their most favoured victims, and their motives run from simple theft through forced sex to the satisfaction of sadistic perversion.

The number of such dangerous individuals increases steadily. Sentences are light and rarely served in full, and the criminal is so sympathetically treated in the press that there is scarcely any opprobrium attached to the profession. A systematic effort is made to depict criminals as victims of an unjust society, and it is continually repeated that the death penalty and heavy sentences are no deterrent to crime.

True, they may be no deterrent to crime, although this is not quite so indisputable as it is made to seem, but they are a powerful deterrent to the individual criminal, and the essential point which has been lost from sight is that society must offer security to its members whatever the cost. Concern for the rights of the accused is fine and just and humanitarian, but this concern must be superseded by the right of persons not to be murdered, tortured or raped. The accused may plead not guilty by reason of insanity but, if convicted of the act, must be put away permanently where they can do no further harm. Success in an insanity plea should be equivalent to life imprisonment.

Admittedly, this is no more than a stop-gap measure. If the proportion of mentally disturbed persons within society continues to grow at its present rate, the number of psychopaths will exceed the number of relatively sane . . .

What is to be done about this?

Nothing.

The number of persons with criminal tendencies is already so high that a return to more severe forms of law enforcement is probably impossible politically. Although polls in nearly every Western country show a substantial majority in favour of the death penalty, moves to reinstate it are voted down with monotonous regularity by the representatives of that same majority.

As in the traditional advice to rape victims (now offered seriously by many police departments), relax and enjoy it. Living in a society of the insane can be far from dull if reasonable precautions are taken . . .

In this book, you will find a number of such irrational persons and a few who were quite sane but, modern theory to the contrary, simply malicious. Compare them. I think you will find that the more insane they are, the more entertaining.

1

A LINGUISTIC
MISUNDERSTANDING?

One of the more vexing aspects of life is the difficulty in
determining just how insane everybody else is. If they are
only a little insane, they can be entertaining. If a trifle more
so, they can be dangerous. For the denizens of our chrome,
neon and plastic world, the trifle can be a matter of survival.

Obviously, the greater the number of persons with whom
contact is made, the greater the number of those a trifle
beyond the limit, and in the major cities it is probable that the
average resident encounters someone dangerous nearly every
day in the week.

This would be disturbing if it were obvious but, fortunately or unfortunately, these psychopaths often look no
crazier than the nominally sane who, striving to cope with the
pressures of big city life, are often not completely in possession of their faculties. There are days in a city like Paris when
everyone looks as mad as a March hare in a marijuana patch.

But not, of course, in June. June is late spring or early
summer, and there are few places in the world that are more
romantic than Paris in the spring.

At least in theory. It is true that there have been some
unfortunate experiments with architecture; that air, water
and soil are hideously polluted; that the concentration of
motor vehicles is such that it is impossible either to drive or to
park; and that the fortunate are mugged by gangs of relatively
small children while those less so are raped, robbed and
murdered by the preceding generation, but still, it is Paris
and there is nothing like it. Along the Champs Elysées the
trees are in leaf. Flowers are blooming. The forests of the

Bois de Boulogne, filled with picnickers by day and whores by night, are green and, for those who have the time and money to afford it, there is a very pleasant restaurant, accessible only by boat, on the island in the Lac Inférieur which is not really inferior, but merely called that to distinguish it from the Lac Supérieur directly to the south of it.

At approximately seven-thirty in the evening of Saturday, 13 June 1981, a group of diners, seated on the terrace of this restaurant which commands a view of the lake shore some fifty yards away and the path running along it, were treated to a spectacle unusual even for Paris.

A slight Oriental, so small as to merit the appellation of dwarf, was struggling along the Chemin de Ceinture du Lac Inférieur bent nearly double beneath the weight of two large, cheap suitcases. Although the suitcases were equipped with the little wheeled frames used by tourists for dragging their luggage through Europe's porterless railway stations, the gravelled path rendered them largely useless.

The diners watched with the interest but detachment of the Parisian. The general opinion was that this was an Oriental tourist who had gone astray and was wandering about in the Bois de Boulogne looking for the railway station or, perhaps, the Tour Eiffel.

It was thought unusual. Not that there was anything remarkable about an Oriental or a dwarf or even a tourist lost in the Bois de Boulogne, but the combination of all three was not something seen every day and, besides, this was an uncommonly strange-looking tourist. As Orientals went, he had a rather large, fleshy nose, his face was long and hollow-cheeked and his hair was even longer and hung in dank, straight, scanty strands over his high, bulging forehead and around his prominent ears. Far from presenting the approved expression of the inscrutable Oriental, he appeared to be nearly out of his mind with nervousness and excitement and his eyes rolled wildly amidst the streams of sweat pouring down his face.

Beneath the bemused gaze of the diners, the strange figure passed down the path and slowly vanished from sight. The diners returned to their entrées.

By eight-thirty they had not yet arrived at dessert when, further to the north along the Chemin de Ceinture du Lac Inférieur and out of sight of the restaurant, strollers who had either already eaten or who could not afford to do so, came upon the same small Oriental, still struggling along with his suitcases. At the sight of them, he apparently came to the conclusion that the effort was not worth it and, abandoning his property, took to his heels and disappeared into the bushes and the darkness.

The most logical explanation for such behaviour was that the little man was a thief and that the suitcases were filled with booty, possibly even cash. The strollers, therefore, hurried forward to investigate.

At close range, however, they saw that, if this was a thief's booty, he had apparently robbed a butcher shop for thin trails of something red and sticky were running out of the suitcases on to the gravel of the path, and it did not take much imagination to identify this as relatively fresh blood.

Large city dwellers appreciate strong sensations so quite a number of the passers-by remained until the police had arrived in the hope that the suitcases would be opened and provide some spectacle of horror.

They were disappointed. The police did, indeed, open one suitcase and peer inside, but they did not open it enough for anyone else to see anything, and other police officers quickly arrived and sent the sightseers on about their business after having taken their names and addresses.

The suitcases were not, however, removed immediately, as the glimpse taken of the interior had determined that this was a matter for the Sureté, the Paris Criminal Investigations Department. What the officer peeping into the suitcase had seen was a human head; a head with no body and from which nose and lips had been cut away, but definitely a head. As the investigations would show, most of the rest of the body was in the suitcases as well.

But not all. Even the hardened investigators from the Sureté would have been startled had they known where those missing parts now were.

At the moment, they were more interested in knowing

where the little Oriental was. Large numbers of neatly dressed young men flooded the Bois de Boulogne, displayed their identification as agents of the Sureté and asked a great many questions. Vivid descriptions of the wanted man's appearance were received, and they corresponded much more closely with each other than is normally the case. Even in Paris, the suspect's appearance had been sufficiently odd to attract attention.

In a smaller community, such numerous and accurate descriptions might have resulted in a speedy arrest, but within the nine million inhabitants of the Paris agglomeration, even an Oriental dwarf was a single straw in a very large stack. Consequently, the police artist sat about preparing sketches based on witness descriptions which could be distributed to all police units, and a check of the consulates of the Oriental nations was undertaken.

At the same time, efforts were made to trace the suitcases, which were new, and these proved successful. They had been bought only the day before in a department store in the 16th arrondissement of Passy which runs along the edge of the Bois de Boulogne.

Clerks in department stores rarely remember their customers very clearly: there are too many of them. The clerk in this department store remembered the man who had bought the suitcases very well. He had been an Oriental, almost cadaverous looking, and he had been less than five feet tall.

This was of no help to the police. They already knew what the man looked like, and the fact that he had bought the cases in Passy could mean that he lived there or that he had wanted to use them in the Bois de Boulogne. It was still not known where the murder had taken place.

It was known that it was a murder. A single .22 calibre bullet had been recovered from the base of the skull. It had been fired into the nape of the neck at point-blank range and had resulted in instantaneous death.

This and a number of other strange and inexplicable results had been obtained by the autopsy, which had taken place immediately following the transfer of the two suitcases to the police morgue.

4

There opened, they had been found to contain the best part of a young, Caucasian female body cut up and wrapped in plastic rubbish sacks. Laid out on the marble slap of the autopsy table and reassembled like a jigsaw puzzle, it developed that there were a number of pieces missing. The nose was gone. The lips were gone. The breasts were missing, and so was the flesh of both thighs and both buttocks. They had been carefully cut away with something very sharp, probably a razor, and not by a person possessing any professional skill in anatomy, but merely someone who had taken his or her time and gone about the matter methodically and with common sense.

The sex of the murderer was tentatively established as male, for the sex organs of the corpse were recovered intact and contained traces of semen. Whether it had been deposited before or after death, there was no indication of forcible rape and no lesions of the inner walls of the vagina or the labia minor.

On the basis of this evidence, it seemed not improbable that the motive of the crime had been sex, but, as the expert in forensic medicine who had carried out the autopsy remarked, what was not there was more significant than what was. The nose and lips might be an attempt to avoid identification, although the fingerprints had been left intact. Breasts, thighs and buttocks were, however, all fleshy, tender parts which, in an animal, would have provided fine roasts and escalopes. In some ways, it looked as if the girl had been butchered for meat.

No one scoffed at this suggestion. It would not represent the first case of cannibalism in Paris.

The girl was soon identified. A careful check had been made of the reports of missing persons, not only those already received, but any new ones coming in, and on 15 June a group of students from the Université Censier turned in a description of a missing person which coincided with that which the police were seeking.

The victim was an unlikely person to have ended up mainly in two suitcases in the Bois de Boulogne as she was the serious, respectable daughter of a wealthy, retired industrialist in Holland. Aged twenty-five at the time of her death, Renée Hartewelt had completed her studies at the University of Leyden and had come to Paris four months earlier for postgraduate work in French literature and civilization with which she was fascinated. She spoke fluent French, equally fluent German and, of course, Dutch. A gentle, attractive girl with a pleasant personality, she had quickly made friends among the others students, and when she failed to appear for several days they reported her missing.

Although Renée had been well-to-do for a student and could easily have rented an apartment, she had not done so, but had followed the usual student practice of exchanging babysitting services for a maid's room, which was located at number 59 rue Bonaparte in the 6th arrondissement of Luxembourg on the Left Bank in an area infested with students.

In Paris, apartment owners seldom know much about what is going on in the maid's room, almost invariably tucked in under the eaves of the attic and the police hurried to the address in the hope that this might be the scene of the murder.

It was not. The room was in perfect order, and it was obvious that when Renée had gone out to meet her death, she had been expecting to return shortly. No clue whatsoever to the identity of her murderer was found.

This was disappointing. The investigators from the Sureté had hoped to find at least correspondence from or indications of the presence of some male. Female students arriving in Paris often made friends with persons about whom they knew very little. It was inevitable that a certain percentage of these should be mad and, as there was little doubt but that Renée's murderer was, at the least, seriously disturbed, it was possible that her death was the result of such a chance, casual acquaintanceship.

Apparently not, however, Not only was there nothing to indicate a more intimate-type friendship in the room, but her friends at the university reported that she had been little interested in such matters. Unlike many foreign students in France, Renée had really been interested in French culture.

6

Renée's belongings and, eventually, what remained of her body were sent to her parents and the investigation continued.

The investigation was now concentrating on the manner in which the Oriental dwarf had arrived at the Bois de Boulogne with his macabre baggage, and where he had been during the approximate hour which passed between him being seen by the diners at the restaurant on the island and when he had encountered the strollers and fled. It was assumed that he had wanted to dispose of the suitcases in the lake, and there was no explanation of why he had spent over an hour there and had not done so.

The matter was the more mysterious in that no sightings of the dwarf were reported during this hour. Had he murdered the girl in the forest, cut her up there and, after one unsuccessful sortie to dispose of the body, returned to his hiding place to recover from the emotions so evident in his appearance when seen by the diners before trying again?

It seemed extremely unlikely that an Oriental, even if born in France, would have such an intimate knowledge of the Bois de Boulogne, but there was little about this case that was not unlikely, and the police carried out a massive search of the forest, during which they discovered a large number of things, many of them illegal, but nothing connected with the murder or the strange little man.

Eventually, this question of the missing hour would be resolved, but only after the investigation had shifted from the Bois de Boulogne to the manner in which the little man had arrived there. At the moment, all that was known was that there was somewhere in Paris an Oriental dwarf who had apparently raped and murdered a Dutch girl and had cut away certain parts of her body. For what purpose was pure speculation.

The agents of the Sureté did not like this at all. It was bad enough when French girls were raped and murdered in Paris. Such things happening to foreigners could give the city a bad name.

On the other hand, there was, at least, a fair chance that the murderer did not have French nationality. A great many

Orientals, particularly Vietnamese, do, but Renée had been only four months in Paris at the time of her death and, given her studious nature, had probably not had contact with too many persons outside the university. It could, therefore, be hoped that she had been raped and murdered by one of her fellow foreign students. The instructors were, of course, mainly French.

The problem with this line of investigation was that there were a great many foreign students, and it was not a simple matter to trace everyone with whom Renée might have come into contact. The friends which had been interrogated all professed ignorance of any contacts she might have had to an Oriental dwarf.

None the less, the dwarf was a student and, had he not been identified first by other means, he would probably have been successfully traced through the university.

As it was, his identification was established through the testimony of a taxi driver who had been called to an apartment building at 10 rue Erlanger in the 16th arrondissement on the evening of 13 June.

There he had found waiting on the sidewalk in front of the building a very small Oriental man with two large, imitation leather, cardboard suitcases. He had got the suitcases into the trunk with great effort as they were very heavy, and the little Oriental had directed him to the Bois de Boulogne where he had got out not far from the Lac Inférieur and had set off down the path, half dragging, half carrying the suitcases.

Paris cab drivers are not easily impressed, but this fare was sufficiently odd that the driver remembered the incident very well.

So did two other cab drivers. One had picked up the little man and his suitcases in the Bois de Boulogne at a little after seven-thirty and had brought him and them back to the address at 10 rue Erlanger. The other had picked up man and suitcases for the second time at shortly after eight and brought them to the Lac Inférieur.

The mystery of the missing hour was now solved. The diminutive murderer had made two attempts to dispose of the remains of his victim. He had not been in the Bois de Boulogne, but riding to and from it in taxi cabs.

The police now knew that their suspect was a Japanese named Issei Sagawa, that he was a student at Université Censier, and they knew where he lived. They did not, however, rush straight in and arrest him.

France was, by now, a socialist country and this meant, among other things, that a great deal more attention would be given to the rights of the accused than to those of the public. It was, therefore, essential that the police present an absolutely watertight case if they hoped to obtain a conviction, something felt to be desirable as there was little doubt in anyone's mind that Sagawa was dangerously insane and, if acquitted or released on some pretext, could be counted upon to repeat his offence.

Everything which the police had at the moment was based upon the statements of witnesses who had seen Sagawa with the suitcases or, at least, some suitcases. No one could swear that the suitcases had contained the remains of Renée Hartewelt because no one had seen them open except the police, and they had not been in Sagawa's possession at that time. Moreover, there was the usual problem of identification of an Oriental by Westerners, many of whom would admit in court that all Orientals looked alike to them. Granted Sagawa's appearance was unusual, but a clever defence attorney could undoubtedly turn up a half-dozen Oriental dwarves in Paris and run them through the courtroom. In nine million people, there are a half-dozen of anything.

Although there was no explanation of what she had been doing there, it was practically certain that Renée had been murdered in Sagawa's studio apartment at 10 rue Erlanger, and it was possible that traces of the act would be found there. Sagawa had, however, had ample time to clean up and, if he had been as methodical in the other phases of the murder as he had been in the cutting up, he would have carried out the butchery in the bathtub and then cleaned the drains with lye, a common solution to the problem of bloodstains which occurs to a surprising number of murderers.

There were, therefore, a number of things which could

be investigated and which would improve the case before Sagawa was taken into custody.

The first of these remained without result. It would have been important to establish witness accounts of Renée and Sagawa being together, particularly on the day of the murder, but no such witnesses could be located.

The second line of investigation was also unsuccessful. Sagawa was thirty-three years old and it seemed unlikely that he should have turned violently insane only now. If he was crazy enough to rape, murder and cut up a girl, he had presumably been crazy for some time. A criminal record or a record of extensive psychiatric treatment would be useful in establishing his guilt. He would presumably not be convicted as he would be declared incompetent to stand trial by reason of insanity, but, at least, the case would be solved.

This was something difficult to find out as Sagawa had arrived in France only in April of 1977, and any criminal or psychiatric records he might have would be in Japan, as it was quickly established that he had no record of any kind in France.

However, neither did he in Japan. Sagawa, the son of a wealthy Japanese industrialist, had taken his bachelor's and master's degrees at the University of Osaka where he had written his thesis on Shakespeare's *Macbeth*. He had come to Paris for postgraduate work in preparation for a degree of Doctor of Letters and was specializing in the study of the influence of contemporary Japanese writing on French literature. An inveterate academic, he was extremely well versed in English and also spoke some German and French.

Looking at this background report, it was difficult for the agents of the Sureté to believe that they had the right man. How would it be possible to convince a jury that an eighty-eight-pound, four-foot-eleven-inch Japanese academician and intellectual had suddenly decided, at the age of thirty-three, to rape, murder and butcher a twenty-five-year-old Dutch girl who towered over him by a head and outweighed him by thirty pounds?

Only through physical evidence or a confession, and the investigators were much relieved when it was determined that Sagawa had rented a machine for shampooing rugs on the day following the murder. Obviously, there had been, after all, bloodstains, and there was no machine made which would remove them so thoroughly that the technicians from the police laboratories could not find them again.

As it turned out, the police caution was unnecessary. Issei Sagawa had been methodical in his butchery, but he had not been at all careful about covering his tracks. Taken into custody he promptly confessed, and well he might for his studio was filled with evidence.

Neatly wrapped in its case, the .22 calibre rifle which had fired the bullet recovered from Renée's head was found standing in a plastic cupboard together with other of Issei's possessions. He had, he said, bought it immediately upon his arrival in Paris as he had been warned that the city was not safe.

This useful discovery soon paled into insignificance, however, with the examination of the contents of Sagawa's refrigerator. Wrapped in plastic and placed, partly in the freezing compartment for longer storage, and partly in the body of the refrigerator for immediate consumption, were one of Renée's thighs, one of her buttocks and both breasts. Nose, lips, the other thigh and buttock had, said Sagawa, all been eaten, mostly raw, although he had made the buttock into a sort of stew.

Speaking calmly, emotionlessly and almost detachedly, Issei Sagawa recited the details of his crime. It had begun, he said, when he found himself seated next to Renée at one of the lectures at the university. Both had been strongly interested in literature and they had quickly come into conversation. Renée, whose French was better than Issei's, had offered to help him with certain difficult translations and had come twice to his studio for that purpose. Her manner had been friendly, but impersonal. The idea of a romantic liaison between herself and the very small Japanese had apparently never crossed her mind.

It had crossed Sagawa's, and on the afternoon of 11 June after they had finished drinking tea and were seated opposite each other on cushions in Sagawa's studio, he had suddenly made a declaration of love followed by a blunt request for sexual relations.

Renée had shaken her head gently and had said, 'No, no. You must behave yourself.' She was aware that he was in love with her because he had previously told her so, although he had not asked for sex.

Sagawa had then put a Mozart tape on the tape recorder and had asked Renée to read aloud a poem by Schiller. While she was reading it, he had walked around behind her and, taking the rifle from the cupboard, had fired a single shot in the nape of her neck. She had fallen forward, killed instantly.

Sagawa had then removed the dead girl's clothing and had engaged in sexual intercourse with the corpse, following which, he had spread out sheets of plastic and newspapers to catch the blood and, going to fetch a knife, a razor and the scissors, he had begun to systematically butcher the corpse, placing the entrails and the severed parts in plastic rubbish sacks.

This had taken him a long time. He had no saw or hatchet with which to break the larger bones and had to work his way through the joints with the knife. He was, however, in no hurry, and stopped at intervals to take photographs of the work in various stages of progress.

These pictures were recovered by the police, and some two and a half years later a prominent editor would be sent to jail for having printed either them or other pictures made by the police at the time of the autopsy. In any case, they were pictures of the dismembered body of an intelligent, kindly, young woman whose only fault lay in a failure to grasp the extent of dangerously disturbed elements present in modern society. Had she still been alive, she might have been instructed by the behaviour of the editor in printing the pictures of her butchered body or by the reaction of the readers who undoubtedly enjoyed the spectacle very much and, perhaps, had idle daydreams of duplicating it.

That no one has probably represents a grudging acceptance of the fact that Sagawa's act is a hard one to follow. A Japanese dwarf murdering, raping and partially devouring a rather large, blond Dutch girl in Paris is such a spectacular media event that it may be impossible to improve on it.

For, once the details of the crime were known, it became, of course, a media matter and ceased to have any connection with reality. The editor jailed for printing the photographs was actually only doing his job and, if he was jailed, it was more for flouting authority than for any offence against morals or decency. After all, the job of an editor consists of giving the readers the type of material which they enjoy. If he does not do this, he soon ceases to be an editor.

Issei Sagawa was, of course, placed under psychiatric observation and, after a little more than a year, on 13 July 1982 predictably declared incompetent to stand trial by reason of insanity.

Sagawa was helpful in the psychologists' efforts to arrive at this conclusion. He told them in great detail precisely what he had done to Renée, and he insisted that he had known very well what he had been doing. He had even planned it in advance: it was not an impulsive act.

The doctors did not ask him why he had raped and murdered Renée. The question would have been fatuous. Throughout the world, girls, women and even children were being raped and murdered. There was nothing unusual about it at all. What the doctors wanted to know was why he had eaten part of the victim.

A lifelong ambition said Sagawa. He had always dreamed of eating a nice girl.

After this, there was no question in any of the experts' minds as to what would happen to Issei Sagawa. He would not stand trial, he would not be imprisoned, he would be sent to a relatively comfortable institution for the dangerously insane and that was exactly what happened.

There was a question in the mind of some non-experts. How long would he stay there? If past experience is any guide, not long. Modern ideology does not admit to the concept of the incurably insane any more than it admits to the incorrigibly evil. The human being is basically good and rational. If he is temporarily not, he can be made so through the wonders of psychology.

Issei Sagawa's fame was fleeting in France. The media cannot dwell too long on any subject as the attention span of their readers, bombarded with a thousand times the information they can absorb, is short and, anyway, these people were not French.

In Japan things went rather better. Sagawa's father resigned all of his directorships and retired to his, presumably, rather extensive estates. The prime minister issued a statement. There was endless talk of East-West symbolism, ritual murder and other chic theories. Many Japanese were said to be concerned over the reaction of the French to a brilliant Oriental scholar devouring young women in their capital.

This concern did not go unremarked, and one of the popular riders of the literary trend in Japan entered into correspondence with Sagawa and quickly brought out a book based on his letters and other sources.

The book, of course, immediately became a bestseller with over a million copies sold, and plans are now underway for a movie. The name of a famous producer, whose best-known film portrayed with remarkable realism the severing of a young man's genitals after close to two hours of almost uninterrupted sexual intercourse on the screen, has been suggested.

If the film is produced, and it would be amazing if it were not, it will undoubtedly be a smash hit and the murder, rape and butchery of Renée Hartewelt will be seen and savoured by millions.

As madmen go, Issei Sagawa is one of the more entertaining. He has provided recreation for millions, and has made and will make the publishing, movie and, perhaps, television industries enormous profits. He is even making a little money for me.

The only thing is: this was not so entertaining for Renée Hartewelt, was it?

2

LOVE THY NEIGHBOUR

Not all murders are as profitable or as entertaining to as many as that of the Japanese cannibal and the Dutch student in Paris. The vast majority pass with no more than a brief mention in the local press. They are the shabby, little, day-to-day homicides which take place under banal circumstances and in banal places.

Such as the apartment house where you live. Do you sometimes feel a little nervous about going down to the basement to empty the rubbish? It is very quiet down there, isn't it? People in the apartments upstairs would probably not hear you if you were to call out.

Or perhaps they could not hear you anyway. When was the last time you saw that attractive girl who lives down the hall? Has she moved out? Then why were there no movers? Or is she, perhaps, still in there? In what condition?

There is reason to believe that such thoughts occur to quite a few apartment dwellers, particularly in the larger cities and, in West Germany, Düsseldorf, with a population approaching three quarters of a million, is a fairly large city.

It is also a comparatively new city in so far as its buildings go. The visits of the British and American air forces during World War II left little standing.

By 1980, however, all had been replaced and much added, although the quality of the construction sometimes left something to be desired. Like many of its kind, the four storey apartment building at the corner of Tussmann and Derendorf streets on the northern edge of the city was built without soundproofing so that the tenants were frequently troubled with noise, transmitted, but distorted, by the concrete walls.

During early June of that year the sounds were particularly disturbing. There were muffled crashes, wails which could have been the wind, but perhaps were not, groans? screams? doors closing and opening, the sound of feet . . . Nothing really very different than what had been heard often enough before, but still . . .

The dustbins were in the basement and so were the laundry facilities, but it had been over a week now since Mrs Ilse Bauer had done the laundry, and the rubbish had been dropped off in the basement by her husband Walter every morning on his way to work.

Walter was aware, of course, that his young wife was becoming more and more nervous, but there was nothing that he could do and he assumed that she would eventually get over it. It was probably in part because she could not find a job. Like many younger German housewives she would have preferred to work, but jobs were scarce at the moment.

When he arrived home at approximately six-thirty in the evening of 12 June 1980, a Thursday, however, he found that Ilse's anxieties had developed a more specific focus, and where she had previously complained about there being too many noises, she was now concerned that there were not enough.

'There hasn't been a sound out of that apartment for two days now,' she said. 'I think that we should call the police.'

'Maybe they've moved out,' said Walter, heading for the bathroom. He was a heating systems installer and tended to get his hands dirty at work.

'Don't you think that I would have heard them if they were moving out?' said Ilse. 'I'm here all day and, if they were moving, the halls would have been full of furniture. I think something's happened. I was just reading in the newspaper yesterday about a family that was asphyxiated in their sleep when the gas stove sprang a leak.'

'They probably don't even cook with gas,' said Walter, scrubbing his face with the towel. 'All right, all right. I'll go across and ring the bell, but I'm going to feel like an idiot if they open up and ask me what I want.'

'You can save yourself the trouble,' said Ilse. 'I've been

over there to ring the bell four times this afternoon. Nobody answers and there's not a sound inside. They have two small children, you know.'

Walter stood looking uneasily at her for a moment or two, the towel still held in his hands.

'I guess you're right,' he said finally. 'We better call the police.'

The dispatcher at police headquarters sent a patrolcar. It was a routine report and a routine response. Many such calls were received every day in Düsseldorf and they were routinely checked out. Sometimes the police found a suicide, sometimes they found that the tenant had merely skipped out to avoid paying the rent, and occasionally they found a murder victim. More often than not they found nothing. The tenant of the apartment had merely gone off on vacation and had not bothered to tell anyone.

The locks on the apartment doors at number 12 Tussmann Street were not very sophisticated and, the patrolmen, having produced no response by knocking and ringing the doorbell, opened the door with the equipment which they carried for such cases and went in.

There was nothing in the entrance hall, and the doors leading off it were closed. The first door to the right opened into a bedroom, and there was no one in that either, but the second door led to the living room, and here the officers encountered a sight which stopped them dead in their tracks.

Lying sprawled on a fur rug in front of the sofa was the body of a young, blonde woman, naked, her face distorted in an expression of agony, the mouth open as if crying out for mercy, and her sightless eyes staring at the ceiling.

Beyond her, in front of an open door on the opposite side of the room, lay the body of a small boy wearing pyjamas.

The woman, the child, the fur rug and large areas of the floor were covered with dark, reddish-brown dried blood. The woman's body, in particular, was so enveloped in it that she looked as if she were wearing a tight-fitting, brown garment.

Although the patrolcar officers were both comparatively young men and had had no experience in homicide cases, they were well trained in the procedure to be applied and, while one officer remained in the hall outside the apartment, the other ran quickly down to the patrolcar and telephoned the dispatcher who immediately set in motion an operation which he had had all too much opportunity to practice.

Inspector Gerd Risch, the tall, blond, blue-eyed and pink-cheeked chief of the duty homicide squad was alerted and hurried with his assistant to the charge room. The duty medical officer came to join them from the police clinic, and a three-man squad of detection specialists carrying cases of equipment reported in from the police laboratory. Two unmarked cars from the Criminal Investigations Department pulled up in front of the entrance. The inspector, his assistant and the doctor climbed into one, the three men from the police laboratory got into the other, and less than forty minutes from the time that Walter Bauer had made his call to the switchboard at police headquarters, the homicide squad was at the scene.

The patrolmen were sent back to their beat and, while the inspector's assistant went across the hall to speak with the Bauers, the inspector and the doctor entered the apartment for a preliminary examination of the corpses, the laboratory specialists remaining waiting in the hall until it was completed.

Dr Georg Hofmann, a squat, broad-shouldered man with iron-grey hair and eyes and rimless, pince-nez glasses, had not completed his examination of the corpse of the woman when the inspector, who had gone into the room beyond the dead boy, came out to announce that there was a third corpse.

'Baby,' he said. 'It's lying in its crib. Must have been a total madman. He's wiped out the whole family.'

'Not the husband and father though, I see,'' said the doctor. 'Or was there one?'

It was a legitimate question. There are a great many divorced and single women bringing up children in Germany today.

'I don't know,' said the inspector. 'The baby seems to be the only other body. Maybe Juergen will be able to tell us when he comes back from the neighbours.'

Juergen was Detective-Sergeant Juergen Kettenmeyer, a quiet young man with medium-hair and egg-shaped eyes. Although he had not been long in criminal investigations, the inspector regarded him as a highly satisfactory assistant.

The sergeant, when he returned a few moments later, reported that there had, indeed, been a husband and father, a tall, handsome man who wore a beard and moustache. Aside from that the Bauers had known nothing about him.

'They say that there was the usual amount of bickering in a young family like that with children, but they never heard any really serious fights,' said the sergeant. 'Does it look like it was the husband?'

'Probably,' said the inspector. 'The wife and the kids are dead and he's missing. There are a lot of such cases nowadays. Stress in the family. The fellow cracks, butchers the wife and children and clears out. Tell the lab people to start hunting through here for identification. We'll want to get out a pick-up and hold order on the husband as quickly as possible.'

The laboratory men were summoned and began going through the apartment. Dr Hofmann concluded his examination of the woman's corpse and moved to the little boy lying in front of the door and, subsequently, to the baby in what had apparently been the children's bedroom.

'Well?' said the inspector.

'They were all killed at approximately the same time,' said the doctor. 'Two days ago, three days ago. I'll tell you more exactly when I do the autopsy. Murder weapon in all cases was a thin-bladed knife with a single sharp edge. Probably a switchblade. The woman was stabbed ten or fifteen times. The children, fewer. She put up a fight. There are defence cuts on her hands and forearms. She had intercourse very shortly before her death.'

'Raped?' said the inspector.

'Intercourse,' said the doctor. 'There's no evidence that it was rape.'

'Her husband may have come home and found her with her boyfriend,' said the inspector. 'She was a very pretty woman.'

It was true. Although almost every square inch of the body was smeared with blood, there were only a few smudges on the face of the corpse which, despite its expression of pain and horror, was young and pretty.

'I would think that the boyfriend would be here too,' said the doctor. 'If it was the husband, he must have been out of his mind with rage. Of course, he could have made good his escape while the husband was busy killing the wife and children.'

'Undoubtedly something like that,' said the inspector, 'but I'm wondering why the people next door didn't hear more of the final battle.'

'It may have taken place in the evening,' said the sergeant, coming over with two personal identification cards of the type carried by many Europeans. 'They told me that they were out some evenings. These look like the ID cards.'

'He didn't take his papers with him?' said the inspector. 'That's strange.'

He opened the cards and glanced through them. The dead woman was twenty-six-year-old Margaret Deck, married three years and eight months to twenty-eight-year-old Wilhelm Deck, master electrician, and the mother of two-year-old Thomas and baby Christian, whose entire life had amounted to only six weeks.

'Get out the pick-up order on Deck immediately,' said the inspector, handing the identification cards back to the sergeant. 'You can run a check with the residents registry to see where he comes from. People who commit a crime like that often run for wherever they grew up.'

The sergeant went off downstairs to the radio-telephone in the policecar and the inspector headed for the kitchen where the technician in charge of the squad from the police laboratory was making notes on the reports from his men.

'Anything of significance?' said the inspector. 'We're working on the tentative theory that it was the husband.'

'If it was, he was a cold-blooded rascal,' said the technician. 'After he'd finished murdering the victims, he went into the bathroom to wash up, and then to the bedroom where he changed his clothes. Neat habits. He hung the bloody clothing that he was wearing at the time of the murders up in the clothes closet. Then, it looks like he spent the night peacefully in bed and only left the next morning.'

'You have reason to believe that it happened in the evening?' said the inspector.

'They'd had lunch, but not dinner,' said the technician. 'The murderer had a snack after he got through with his work and he had breakfast. My guess would be that the murders took place shortly before dinnertime, or a little later. They may have been fighting around for some time before he actually got down to murdering them.'

'Maybe we'll get a more exact time for the murders after the autopsy,' said the inspector. 'The people next door apparently didn't hear anything, although it would seem to me that she would have yelled her head off.'

'What about the other neighbours?' said the technician. 'Maybe they heard something.'

'We'll check them out of course,' said the inspector, 'but there are only two apartments in this wing. The other two are in the wing on the Derendorf side, and I doubt that they would have heard anything.'

This turned out to be true. The tenants of the other two apartments on the third floor had not only been unable to hear anything from the Deck apartment, they had never even encountered any of the Decks other than once or twice when Wilhelm Deck or his wife had been emptying the family rubbish into the dustbins in the basement at a time when they were there for the same purpose.

However, those living in the building who had had contact with him at all described Deck as a pleasant-appearing man who had been somewhat reserved. His supervisors at the electrical installation firm where he had worked said that he was a good worker, highly competent technically, and that he had had a rather easy-going nature. He had had no trouble of any kind with any of his fellow workers and, in so far as anyone knew, his family life had been uneventful. He had, in any case, never mentioned any quarrels or differences to anyone at the firm.

The continuing investigation also turned up friends of the Deck family. They were all local people from the area around Tussmann Street which was the district in which both Wilhelm and Margaret Deck had grown up. Mrs Deck's parents had, however, died when she was sixteen years old and Wilhelm Deck's parents had been killed in a car accident three years earlier.

All of the friends of the Deck family insisted that the marriage had been a very happy one and that it was utterly impossible that Wilhelm could have murdered his wife and children. Even if he had been capable of such an action, something which no one who had known him believed, he had had not the slightest motive.

The inspector knew better. There had been a motive and he was tall, taller even that Wilhelm Deck, approximately the same age, had rather long, curly hair and a triangular-shaped face. He had been seen speaking with Margaret Deck in the basement on afternoons when her husband was at work by two of the other tenants, and the inspector thought it probable that he had been her lover. The case, in his opinion, thus became one of the very common murders for reasons of sexual jealousy.

While Wilhelm Deck was working and, presumably, tiring himself out too much to be very active in the matrimonial bed at night, his wife had been entertaining a lover in the apartment during the afternoons. It was not an uncommon thing to do and the German media tended to present such actions as modern, liberal and enlightened. Unfortunately, a good many Germans, even comparatively young ones, were not quite as liberal and as enlightened as the media and, if they came home unexpectedly and found their wives engaged in sexual activities with someone else, they tended to react violently.

The inspector thought that Wilhelm Deck had come home unexpectedly to find his wife in the act of having sex with her lover, for the body, when found, had been completely naked and Mrs Deck had taken off her clothing herself because it was not ripped or torn, but folded and hung neatly over the back of a chair in the living room.

Whether Deck had immediately thrown himself upon his wife and murdered her or whether there had been an extended quarrel first, it was not possible to say. In any case, while the Decks were occupied with each other, the lover had made good his escape. Deck had then murdered his family, had washed up and changed clothes, had had some refreshments, and had gone to bed for a good night's rest. In the morning he had got up, dressed and made off.

Where he had got to was not possible to say as yet, but it was apparently a long way from Düsseldorf, for every police officer in the centre of Germany was looking for him and he had not been spotted.

According to the autopsy report, Margaret Deck had been murdered at sometime between six-fifteen and seven o'clock on the afternoon of Tuesday, 10 June 1980. The children had been murdered at approximately the same time, Thomas by stab wounds like his mother and the baby Christian by having his throat cut.

This estimate of the time coincided with the statements made by the Bauers. Walter had worked late that day and had only come home at eight o'clock. Ilse, who had known that he would be working late, had taken advantage of the free afternoon to do a little shopping and to drop in to see an old schoolfriend. She had arrived home only fifteen minutes before her husband.

By this time, Margaret, Thomas and Christian were all dead and any cries for help that they might have made had gone unheard.

Otherwise, the autopsy report stated that Mrs Deck had had not only vaginal, but also oral intercourse with someone very shortly before she had been stabbed to death. In addition to the defence cuts on her hands and forearms where she had attempted to ward off the knife, there were seventeen stab wounds on the body, nearly all of them to the hilt of what had been a knife with a six-inch blade.

Thomas, being smaller, had been stabbed only six times, although one of the cuts was a slash wound so deep that it had nearly disembowelled the little boy.

Christian had only a single stab wound high up on the left

side of the chest just under the collarbone, and his throat had been cut from ear to ear.

In Dr Hofmann's opinion, the mother had been killed first, and the sounds of the struggle had aroused the attention of Thomas who had come into the living room to see what was happening. He had been cut down in his turn, and the murderer had continued on into the bedroom to finish off the baby. The only plausible explanation for the murder of the children was madness, as they were too small to constitute any danger of identification of the murderer.

As it had been established with some certainty that the Decks had had no enemies and as nothing had been stolen, there seemed little question but that Deck was the murderer, and the only problem that remained was to locate him.

As this had, so far, proved to be impossible, the next best thing was to lay hands on Margaret Deck's lover. He was probably not anxious to become involved in the investigation, but he would have no reason to go to such lengths to avoid the police as the murderer himself.

The investigation, therefore, turned to the identification of the tall, young man with the curly hair and the triangular-shaped face who proved to be remarkably difficult to identify. Not many people had seen him and no one knew who he was, where he lived or what he did for a living. All of the times that he had been seen with or near Margaret Deck were within the past few weeks and, if he had indeed been her lover, then the affair had been going on for only a very short time.

It was while interrogating Mrs Deck's female friends that the police came across an unexpected lead. Twenty-five-year-old Ruth Frankenthal listened to the description of the supposed lover and then said that he sounded like a man from whom she had bought a deep freeze only two days before the murder. Margaret Deck, she said, had been with her at the time and had also been in contact with the man, but she was quite certain that he had not been her lover. In fact she did not think that Margaret Deck knew him any better than she did, which was not at all.

To the inspector's surprise, she said that the man lived in

the same building as the Decks, but on the second floor of the Derendorf wing. He had run into Margaret Deck in the basement when they were both emptying their rubbish and had told her he was moving out and wanted to sell some of his things. Would she be interested?

Margaret had gone to look at the furniture and appliances, but had found nothing that she could use. She had then gone to get her friend Ruth Frankenthal, and the two had returned together. Ruth had bought a deep freeze, and the man had helped the two women carry it downstairs and load it into Miss Frankenthal's station wagon. He had then accompanied the two women to Miss Frankenthal's apartment to help get the deep freeze upstairs.

Ruth described him as pleasant and well mannered, and she thought that he was quite taken by Margaret Deck, but she had not had the impression that he knew her at all well.

The inspector, the sergeant and the two detectives from the Criminal Investigations Department proceeded immediately to the apartment where Ruth Frankenthal had bought the deep freeze. A check with the owner of the building had already shown that it was rented to a Mr Robert Stuellgens, a butcher, who had moved in only at the end of March.

No one answered the doorbell at Stuellgen's apartment, so the police officers opened the door and went in.

The apartment was a shambles of broken furniture and scattered personal possessions, all of it smeared and streaked with dark brown traces of dried blood. Lying in it, in the middle of the living room, was the body of a bearded man who would later be identified as Wilhelm Deck. He had been dead since 10 June.

The autopsy which Dr Hofmann performed on the body showed that Deck had been murdered by eighteen stab wounds from the same knife that had killed his wife and children, and that his death had taken place at roughly the same time as theirs. He had put up a tremendous battle, but had apparently been weakened by loss of blood due to an initial stab wound in the back.

The inspector now felt that he had a clear picture of what

had taken place. Deck, correctly or incorrectly, had thought that his wife was having an affair with Stuellgens and, having murdered her and his children, had gone to finish off the lover as well. Stuellgens had, however, managed to get the knife away from him and had stabbed him to death.

This theory was retained for exactly as long as it took to run a check on Stuellgens through the central police registry.

Stuellgens had only been released from prison in January of that year after having served a six-and-a-half-year sentence for strangling and beating a young mother unconscious, raping her and attempting to rape her child.

It was not his first offence. Stuellgens, who came from the city of Essen less than forty miles to the northeast, was only thirty years old, but any time that he had not spent in prison had been devoted to sex offences, mainly dangerously brutal attacks on minor children. He had, of course, been cured of his antisocial tendencies many times.

The picture had, once again, become less than clear, but one thing was certain, Stuellgens had to be located and interrogated as quickly as possible.

This did not prove to be too difficult. As the inspector had remarked, a criminal often headed for home after his crime, and Stuellgen's mother still lived in the Essen suburb of Borbeck. He was arrested there by the Essen police a few days later, hiding in a garden house. He was still carrying the blood-smeared switchblade with which he had murdered the entire Deck family.

Brought back to Düsseldorf, Stuellgens made little effort to deny his guilt or to offer any rational excuse for his acts. Having had a good deal of experience with courts and the police, he was aware that he had little to fear and he, presumably, told the literal truth with respect to his motives.

He had, he said, encountered Mrs Deck in the basement of the apartment house when she was emptying her rubbish. He had thought that she was attractive and had come to the conclusion that he would have sexual intercourse with her.

He had, therefore, taken every opportunity to make contact with her and had made his intentions rather plain. Mrs Deck, an attractive woman who was, undoubtedly, familiar with propositions of this sort, had made equally plain that she was not interested.

Stuellgens final attempt at seduction had been when he made pretence of moving out in order to lure the object of his desires into his apartment to examine the furniture.

Margaret Deck had come to the apartment, but, when he urged her to sit down and have a drink, had abruptly left, returning later with Ruth Frankenthal. Stuellgens, who had had no intention of moving, had been constrained to sell her his deep freeze.

The incident had left him with the conviction that he was not going to be able to persuade Margaret Deck to cooperate by peaceful means and, as it did not occur to him to abandon his project, he had decided to rape her.

Unfortunately, Margaret Deck had a large and athletic husband and, while Stuellgens had little fear of women and children, he was not overly courageous where men were concerned. Deck, he concluded, would have to go.

He had, therefore, waited in the entrance for Deck on the evening of 10 June and, when the unsuspecting electrician had arrived home from work, had asked him to give him a hand in carrying down some furniture as he was moving out.

Deck had goodnaturedly agreed and, as he preceded Stuellgens into the apartment, had been stabbed in the back.

To Stuellgens's dismay, Deck had not been killed instantly, and there had been a savage struggle with Stuellgens hacking at his incredulous victim like the madman he was.

The match had been uneven for Deck was, of course, neither armed nor prepared for such an attack from a virtual stranger, and he was eventually killed.

Stuellgens, rejoicing that his hotly desired goal was now within reach, had walked through the halls of the apartment building with the bloody knife in his hand, had rung the Deck doorbell, and had informed the appalled Margaret Deck of her husband's fate. He had then forced her to strip at knifepoint and had raped her, following which he had demanded that she perform oral sex on him.

Although his objectives had now been achieved, Stuellgens decided that it would be unwise to leave Margaret alive and, after another struggle, ended by stabbing her to death as well.

The struggle had created a certain amount of noise and Thomas, who was in the bedroom, had come out to investigate.

Stuellgens had immediately stabbed him to death and, going into the bedroom to see who else might be there, he found the baby and, after stabbing it once, cut its throat.

In a state of exhilaration at the success of his plans and too excited to sleep, Stuellgens had decided that what he needed was recreation and, having washed and changed into fresh clothing and had a little something to eat from the Deck's refrigerator, went to get some change from Wilhelm Deck's pockets with which he spent an hour or two playing the pinball machines in a nearby café.

He then returned to the Deck apartment and spent the night in the Deck's bed, departing the following morning after breakfast for his mother's place in Essen.

This ingenuous recital earned Stuellgens what he presumably expected – a declaration by psychological experts that he was incompetent to stand trial as he could not distinguish right from wrong. It was said that he had had an unhappy childhood and this had had an unfortunate effect on his personality.

It might, perhaps, be possible for persons who are not experts in psychology to detect that Robert Wilhelm Stuellgens is unable to distinguish right from wrong, but there are probably few non-professional psychologists so optimistic as to believe that he ever will be.

However, the word 'incurable' is not psychologese. Stuellgens is now undergoing treatment which undoubtedly will prove successful, as it so often has in the past.

3

NO GENERATION GAP IN GERMANY

If Robert Wilhelm Stuellgens was the victim of an unhappy
childhood which interfered so seriously with the development of his personality that it led to less than satisfactory
social contacts, he was not alone. To the careless reader of the
popular press, it sometimes seems that all German child-
hoods are unhappy.

This does not mean that they are, necessarily, uneventful.
Even in the most desolate, most isolated villages, there are
fascinating pursuits for the youth who knows where to look
for them. These pursuits are not dependent upon the
weather.

And a very good thing too. Autumn comes early over the
great German moors of the north, and with it comes the fog,
thick, wet, greyish white, so that the scant traffic over the
infrequent roads slows to a near standstill and the sparsely
populated region seems more deserted than ever.

On the southern rim of this lonely region of trackless
swamps lies the Teutoburger Forest, scene of ancient
Germanic tribal battles and an eerie place to live even for local
residents, secretive and sly with the race memory of a
thousand massacres.

At the eastern end of the Teutoburger Forest, Bielefeld,
with a population of some 200,000 persons, is the largest
community and serves as district capital for the smaller towns
and villages around it. One of these, ten miles to the east, as
the crow flies, is the village of Lage and at 9.45 a.m. on 11
September 1969, a strongly built boy emerged from the mist
and entered the single room of the Lage police station.

'There's a dead woman in the old house at Hoerste,' he announced impassively.

The two officers at the desks looked up in startled surprise. 'Dead from what?' said Sergeant Karl Drescher. 'Who are you?'

'Willi Boeke,' said the boy. 'I'm from Leopoldstal. My dad's the cabinetmaker there. I'm his apprentice. I don't know what she's dead from. She's just dead.'

'Go with him and take a look, Paul,' said the sergeant to Constable Paul Brebsen. 'And bring him back here with you.'

The constable got up, put on his heavy, waterroof cape and, followed by the boy, left the station to disappear into the fog.

As the sergeant knew, Hoerste was less than fifteen minutes walk away, an isolated little huddle of houses not even worthy of the name of hamlet, but he did not expect the constable to return in a half-hour. In such think fog progress was slow, as it was easy to go astray even if a man had lived all his life in the area.

He was, therefore, surprised and startled when Brebsen came running back to the station in just slightly over twenty-five minutes.

'She's dead all right!' exclaimed the constable, a little out of breath. 'And, unless I miss my guess, she's been murdered!'

The boy had followed Brebsen into the station and he went over and sat down in the chair near the coal-burning stove. He was wearing only a light jacket and no hat, and he appeared to be soaked through.

'You!' said the sergeant, addressing himself to the boy. 'What do you know about this?'

'Nothing,' said Boeke. 'I was just passing by the old Koetter house on the Brockmann place and I went in to get out of the wet. Nobody lives there. Then I saw the woman. I thought she was asleep or drunk, but when I saw she wasn't breathing, I figured she was dead so I came right over here.'

'What did you find, Paul?' said the sergeant. 'What makes you think she was murdered?'

'Well, how else would she come to be dead in that old house?' said Brebsen. 'It's the old stone cottage over on Fred Brockmann's place. Nobody's lived there for years. The woman's lying in the front room on her back. She's not an old woman either. Thirty maybe. I couldn't see enough to tell whether she had any marks on her, but she's been dead for a while. The body's stone cold.'

'If it doesn't seem to be a natural death it's out of our jurisdiction,' said the sergeant. 'I'll call Bielefeld and they can send somebody down from the criminal police.'

'He picked up the telephone and dialled the number of Inspector Gerd Fleischer, chief of the district homicide division in Bielefeld. 'Sergeant Drescher in Lage,' he said. 'I think we may have a case of homicide down here.'

The inspector listened to the details, motioning with one hand to his assistant to pick up the extension. 'All right,' he said finally. 'We'll have somebody down right away. Keep the boy at the station.'

He hung up the telephone and turned to Detective-Sergeant Harald Gross, a short, blunt-featured man with thick, stooping shoulders. 'Take it, will you, Hary?' he said.

The sergeant nodded and put down the extension. 'I'll call back over the radio and let you know what it is as soon as I find out,' he said. 'Maybe it's only a natural death after all.'

Forty-five minutes later, the green police Volkswagen came bumping slowly through the fog in the direction of Hoerste. Sergeant Gross was at the wheel, and Constable Brebsen and the boy sat in the back seat. 'There it is,' said the boy, leaning over the back of the front seat and pointing. 'There. To the left.'

The sergeant brought the car to a halt before an ancient, stone building with a tile roof and crumbling brick chimney. At the front of the house were two tiny windows and a low door which stood half open. Gross got out a powerful, electric torch from the luggage compartment of the Volkswagen and entered the building, followed by the constable and the boy.

There were only three rooms, all filled with dust and obviously unused for many years. In the largest room, to the right of the front entrance, the woman lay stretched on her

31

back, nearly in the middle of the floor. She was a young, comparatively attractive woman with fashionable permanent-waved hair, and she was wearing a pale blue dress with a white flower pattern. The dress was pulled down modestly over her knees, but, although it was uncomfortably chilly, there was no sign of a coat or sweater. In the sharp white light of the torch, her features appeared calm and reposed as if she had merely gone to sleep.

'You two go back to the car,' ordered the sergeant. 'I don't want anyone tracking things up in here until we see what's happened. If this is a homicide, there may be clues we can make use of.'

The constable and the boy went back outside and the sergeant bent over the boy. A few minutes later, he too came out of the building and went straight to the policecar. 'Gross calling central,' he said into the radio, pushing down the transmitter switch. 'Reporting to Inspector Fleischer in Homicide.'

There was a crackling from the radio and then the inspector's voice. 'Fleischer here,' he said. 'What is it, Hary?'

'Looks like homicide, chief,' said the sergeant.

'She's dead and I think for some time. There seem to be some scratches and bruises on the body. Can't tell the cause of death. I think we'd better have the medical officer out and somebody from the laboratory.'

'Right,' said the inspector. 'I'll get things moving and come out myself. How far is it from Lage?'

'About three quarters of a mile,' said Gross. 'You'd better go to the station in Lage and have them bring you over here. It's very foggy.'

The inspector, however, appeared to have faith in his knowledge of the district and arrived, forty minutes later, direct from Bielefeld with the police medical officer, Dr Joachim Schreiber, in the front seat next to him and two young technicians from the police laboratory in the back.

The doctor and the technicians immediately followed the sergeant into the house, and the inspector walked over to the sergeant's Volkswagen. 'Is this the boy that found the body?' he asked.

'Yes, sir,' said the constable, climbing out of the car and pulling the boy out after him. 'His name's Willi Boeke.'

'How old are you, Willi?' said the inspector. 'And how did you come to find the body?'

For the first time since appearing at the Lage police station, Willi Boeke showed signs of nervousness. Inspector Fleischer was no village constable, but a heavy-set, brisk sort of man with a broad, high forehead and an unmistakable air of authority.

'Fifteen,' said the boy, his voice breaking slightly. 'I just came in to get out of the wet.'

'Um-hum,' said the inspector. 'And what were you doing here in the first place? Do you live in Hoerste?'

'He lives in Leopoldstal,' said Constable Brebsen. 'His father's the cabinetmaker there.'

'I was on my way to Lage . . .' said Willi.

'Why?' said the inspector.

'Well, I – uh – I had something to do there,' said Willi, shifting from one foot to the other. 'I had to get something . . . I had to get some nails for dad.'

'Leopoldstal is closer to Bielefeld than it is to Lage,' observed the inspector. 'Why didn't you go there?'

'I – I don't know,' said the boy, beginning to stammer slightly. 'I guess I didn't know that. I thought it was closer to Lage.'

'Keep that boy in custody,' said the inspector. 'I'll be talking to him some more.' He went into the house and, after looking through the remainder of the rooms, went into the front room where the doctor was still examining the body.

'Any idea what killed her yet?' he asked.

'Hard to say,' said the doctor, standing up and wiping his hands on a piece of surgical gauze. 'The only signs of external violence are a few scratches and bruises. Nothing serious. There are some marks on the throat, but I can't see enough in here to tell whether she may have been strangled. I doubt it though. There aren't any signs of a struggle in the dust on the floor. At the moment, I'd be inclined to suspect something internal – poison or sleeping pills perhaps.'

'In other words, it could have been suicide,' said the

inspector. 'We may be able to confirm that if we can find out who she is. Are there any papers on the body?'

'No,' said the doctor, 'but Hary says he found a handbag in the corner when he got here. I expect he took it out to the car.'

The inspector went outside to where the sergeant, the constable and Willi Boeke were standing beside the cars. It had started to rain, a fine, cold drizzle, but the fog was as heavy as ever. The ambulance which had followed from Bielefeld had arrived, and was standing near the front of the house with the driver and the stretcher bearers crowded into the front seat.

Sergeant Gross had turned the handbag over to one of the detection men, who was in the process of extracting the contents with a pair of wooden tweezers to avoid obliterating possible fingerprints. 'Here's a personal identity card,' he said, holding the folded cardboard identification out to the inspector with his tweezers. 'You've seen the body. It's her picture.'

The inspector squinted at the little passport photo. 'Guldira Kressenzia Knapp,' he said, reading from the entries on the card. 'Maiden name: Busch. Twenty-nine years old. Eight years married.'

'Where is she from, chief?' said Sergeant Gross. 'Maybe I could go see if the family knows anything about this.'

'Springer Street, fourteen,' said the inspector. 'It's in Detmold. Yes, I think it would be a good idea if you went over and talked to the husband. The next of kin will have to be notified in any case and it's possible that it was suicide. See if she's left a farewell note anywhere.'

The sergeant got into his Volkswagen and drove away. Detmold, a somewhat larger town, was six miles further to the east, and south of Lage.

'Can we go back into the building now?' asked the young technician with the glasses. 'Is the doctor finished?'

'Ask him,' said the inspector. 'It's all right with me.'

'We need to know who's been in there,' said the other technician. 'Would everyone who's been in the building step on a sheet of paper here so that we can get a shoeprint?'

The police officers, the doctor and Willi Boeke came forward to leave their wet footprints on the sheets of white paper which the technician laid out on the stone slab in front of the building.

'Gross was in there too,' said the inspector, 'but you'll have to wait for his footprints until he gets back.'

The technician nodded and went on into the building, followed by his partner who was carrying a large box of equipment.

'The wonders of science,' said the inspector. 'Come here, Willi. You and I are going to sit in the back seat of the car and have a little talk. I have the feeling that you're not being entirely open with us.'

The boy came slowly over and climbed into the back seat of the inspector's Volkswagen with obvious reluctance. The inspector got in beside him and closed the door.

'Now,' he said. 'Let's get a few things straight, Willi. I've been a police officer for a very long time and I have talked to a great many people who had something to hide. Usually I can tell when a person like that is lying, and you're lying, Willi, or at least you're not telling us the whole truth. It's going to save both of us a lot of trouble if you come out now with whatever you know, and we're sure to find it out anyway so what about it?'

Willi Boeke remained stubbornly silent for several minutes. 'It was the way I told the constable,' he said finally, but his voice shook and he was obviously on the verge of tears.

'Sure it was, Willi,' said the inspector, 'but there's something more too. You didn't just happen to go into that house to get out of the wet. If you wanted to dry off, you could knock on any door around here and there'd have been a fire to dry out by. Besides, any boy who found a dead woman like that would have been scared out of his wits. He'd have run to the nearest house. That's Brockmann's. Instead, you went all the way into Lage to the police station. Now, why did you do that?'

Tears began to run down the boy's cheeks. He drew a long, shuddering breath that was half a sob. 'I was afraid somebody would think I killed her,' he said.

'Why?' said the inspector. 'Why would anyone think you killed Mrs Knapp?'

'Because we were doing it,' said the boy.

The inspector was not a man who was easily startled, but he jumped as if he had been shot. 'What did you say?' he demanded, turning in the seat to look directly at the boy who squirmed and turned pink. 'I thought you said you were fifteen years old.'

'I am,' said Willi Boeke, more calmly and with a touch of suppressed pride. 'Guldira was older than I am. She was twenty-nine. We've been doing it ever since I was eleven.'

'Listen boy,' said the inspector threateningly, 'if you're lying to me . . .'

'Ask my father,' said Willi Boeke. 'Ask Guldira's husband. They all know about it. They all tried to stop us.'

The inspector brought out a crumpled pack of cigarettes, shook one out and lit it, never taking his eyes from the boy in the seat beside him. He took a deep drag, blew out a long plume of smoke and said, 'All right, Willi, I believe you. So what happened? How did Mrs Knapp die, and what was she doing in that house?'

'It was last Sunday,' said Willi Boeke. 'I went to Detmold to spend the day with Guldira.'

'That would be the seventh of this month,' said the inspector. 'Today's Thursday.'

'That's right,' said Willi. 'It was Sunday the seventh. Heinrich – that's Guldira's husband – was gone, and he took the children with him.'

'Mrs Knapp has children?' said the inspector.

'Two,' said Willi. 'Uli's five and Sarah is six. They're just little kids. Anyway, Heinrich was coming back on Monday at noon so we left Monday morning as we didn't want to be bothered. Then I remembered the old stone house here in Hoerste. We got here Monday afternoon.'

'And then what?' said the inspector.

'We were feeling kind of bad,' said Willi Boeke. 'Everybody was picking on us and wouldn't leave us alone. We decided to put an end to everything.'

'You mean commit suicide?' said the inspector.

The boy nodded. 'We had two hundred sleeping pills. Guldira was going to take half and I was going to take the other half.'

'But you didn't take yours,' said the inspector.

'I took some of them,' said Willi Boeke. 'Then I fell asleep. That was Monday evening. When I woke up, it was Tuesday morning and Guldira was dead. I thought it was the sleeping pills at first, but then I saw she had some scratches and things and I figured that Heinrich had sneaked over when we were unconscious and killed her. I thought I'd probably get blamed for it and I didn't know what to do, so I stayed there until this morning. Then I went to the police in Lage.'

For several minutes the inspector sat smoking silently. Finally, he gave a deep sigh and tossed the cigarette butt out of the car window. 'Willi,' he said, 'in close to twenty-five years of investigation this is the most unlikely story that I have ever heard. It's so unlikely that I'm inclined to believe it. I don't think you could make such a thing up and I hope, for your sake, that you haven't, because if you have, we are going to find it out and then you'll really be in trouble.'

'That's just the way it was, sir,' said Willi Boeke stoutly.

The two technicians had come out of the house, so the inspector got out of the car and went over to them. 'Find anything?' he asked. 'Can the doctor take the body away now?'

'As far as we're concerned,' said the technician with the glasses, 'we didn't find out very much. Somebody's been staying in there for three or four days. The boy I expect as those seem to be his shoeprints. Not many shoeprints from the woman. There are a couple of blankets and some remains of food. No indication of any third party.'

'You can send the body to the morgue now, Joachim,' called the inspector to the doctor who was sitting in the back of the ambulance. 'Give me a complete autopsy report as soon as possible. Check the stomach. She's supposed to have taken sleeping pills.' He turned back to the technician. 'No trace of a third party, eh?' he said. 'What about shoeprints in the dust?'

'We can't be entirely certain,' said the technician. 'There

have been too many people in and out. There could be another set of prints that was obliterated.'

'See if you can raise Gross on the car radio,' said the inspector. 'Tell central that they're to keep calling until they get him. I want to talk to him.'

The technician went over to the inspector's car to carry out the instructions, and the men from the police ambulance went into the house with a stretcher and came out bearing the body of Guldira Knapp covered with a sheet. They put it into the ambulance and stood waiting.

'All clear, inspector?' asked the doctor.

The inspector nodded absently and the doctor climbed into the front seat next to the driver. The stretcher bearers got into the back with the body and the ambulance disappeared into the curtains of fog and rain, its headlights glowing yellow and its siren moaning softly.

'I've got Sergeant Gross on the radio,' announced the technician coming over from the car. 'He's in Detmold.'

The inspector walked to the car and picked up the transmitter. 'Hary?' he said. 'Have you seen Knapp?'

'Just left him,' said Gross's voice from the speaker. 'I'm parked in front of his house.'

'Bring him in,' said the inspector. 'There's some reason to believe that he may have killed his wife. God knows, he had a motive if what that boy says is true. I'll tell you about it when you get to Bielefeld. It's too complicated to explain over the radio.'

He hung up the radio-telephone and went back to the two technicians. 'Okay,' he said. 'If you're finished here for now secure the door and put the seals on it. We'll go back to Bielefeld. Hary is bringing in a suspect and I want to talk to the boy some more.'

The road from Detmold to Bielefeld is a main highway and, as a consequence, Sergeant Gross and Heinrich Knapp were already at the office of the criminal police when the inspector arrived with the two technicians and Willi Boeke.

While the inspector's secretary set about making coffee, the inspector got out of his waterproof, settled himself behind his desk and began the interrogation of Heinrich Knapp, who was seated in front of it.

'To begin with,' he said, 'I have got a rather strange question to ask you. This boy here says he was your wife's lover. Is that true?'

Knapp shot a bitter glance at the boy, who looked away but did not change expression. He was a lean man in his middle thirties with the tanned face and roughened hands of a man who worked a great deal out of doors.

'Yes,' he said sourly. 'It's true.'

'And this has been going on for four years?' said the inspector incredulously. 'My God, man! Why didn't you do something about it?'

'What?' said Knapp. 'Old man Boeke did everything he could to keep the kid away from her. I did everything I could. What more could we do? All Guldira ever said was to go ahead and divorce her. She wanted to marry Willi anyway as soon as he got old enough.'

'Why didn't you?' said the inspector.

'We've got two kids, inspector,' said Knapp. 'I figured any mother is better than no mother at all.'

'Where have you been for the past few days?' said the inspector, changing the subject abruptly. He took a cup of coffee from the secretary and motioned that she should offer some to the two suspects.

'Where I always am,' said Knapp, taking the coffee gratefully. 'Working. Taking care of the kids. Looking after the house. Guldira hasn't been home since Sunday.'

'Do you always take care of the children when your wife isn't there?' said the inspector.

'My brother's wife helps out sometimes,' said Knapp. Suddenly he had become ill at ease and the words came slowly.

'Is she looking after them now?' said the inspector.

Knapp nodded without speaking.

'Good,' said the inspector, 'because I want you to stay here for a little while. I'd like to talk to you and Willi again after I've heard what the doctor has to say. I expect he'll be finished by this afternoon.'

The doctor was quicker than the inspector had anticipated. By three o'clock, a preliminary report lay on the inspector's desk and the doctor himself was seated in the chair that Knapp had recently occupied, prepared to answer any questions that had not been made clear in the report.

'So,' said the inspector, finishing the second and final page and laying the report on the desk, 'she died early Tuesday morning. She was full of sleeping pills, but the actual cause of death was strangulation while she was unconscious. Everything checks exactly with what young Boeke told me in the car.'

He paused, took out a cigarette and, having lit it, sat smoking and looking thoughtfully at the doctor. 'And yet,' he said after a time, 'somehow I don't believe it. I can't picture Knapp sneaking into that house and strangling his wife.'

'Doesn't strike me as reasonable either,' said the doctor. 'I've only talked to Knapp briefly, but, to begin with, he doesn't seem the type. More to the point though, if he was going to kill his wife, why didn't he do it any time within the past four years that this has been going on?'

'Exactly,' said the inspector. 'Hary is out in Detmold now trying to check Knapp's story about being home every evening and so on. I expect we'll find that that's just where he was.'

The inspector was, however, wrong. When Sergeant Gross returned from Detmold it was nearly eight o'clock in the evening, and the inspector had already gone home after releasing both Knapp and Willi Boeke. The sergeant's news was, however, so significant that he went directly to the inspector's house.

'It looks bad for Knapp, chief,' he said with a touch of regret in his voice. 'He was lying to you. He's been home taking care of the kids every night except one. Monday evening he left them with his brother's wife. He picked them up Tuesday afternoon, but I haven't been able to find any trace of where he was or what he was doing during that time. Was Joachim able to determine the time of death?'

'Early Tuesday morning,' said the inspector. 'Well, I'm

afraid you'll have to go pick him up again. I've already released him.'

'Tonight yet?' said Gross.

The inspector considered. 'No,' he said finally. 'Leave it until tomorrow morning. If he does make a run for it it will be practically an admission of guilt. I don't expect he would get very far and, I don't know why, but I don't think he'll clear out.'

This time the inspector was right. When he arrived at his office the following morning, Heinrich Knapp was already there and waiting for him.

'My sister-in-law told me you checked my story last night,' he said. 'I figured you'd want to talk to me again.'

The inspector lit a cigarette and held the pack out to Knapp. 'Tell me honestly, Mr Knapp,' he said. 'Did you kill your wife?'

Knapp shook his head slowly. 'No,' he said, 'I didn't kill her. I guess I may have thought of it sometimes, but I didn't do it. I know it looks bad for me especially after I said I was home on Monday evening, but I didn't do it. I'm innocent.'

'So why did you lie?' asked the inspector. 'Where were you really on Monday night?'

Knapp flushed brick-red. 'I was ashamed,' he said in a low voice. 'I was with a woman.'

'What's her name?' said the inspector.

'Inge,' said Knapp. 'That's all I know. She's a street girl. I picked her up in front of the Black Dog Bar in Detmold and I spent the night with her.' He was squirming with embarrassment and his eyes avoided the inspector's gaze. 'I'm not an old man,' he murmured. 'It's hard when you don't have a wife that's any use to you.'

'I dare say,' said the inspector. 'You understand I'm going to have to hold you this time until your story can be checked? I'm going to turn you over to one of my detectives and I want you to give him as exact a description of this Inge as you can, and any information you can think of as to where we can find her.'

Knapp was turned over to an investigator and the inspector

called in his secretary. 'Where's Sergeant Gross this morning?' he asked. 'Hasn't he come in yet?'

'He called in,' said the secretary, 'while you were talking with Mr Knapp. He said to tell you that he's had a call from the detail-checking-out people in Hoerste and that he'll contact you as soon as he knows what it is.'

The inspector was, however, too impatient to wait for the sergeant to call him, and he immediately instructed the radio central to try and make contact with the officers in Hoerste. Twenty minutes later, Gross came on the radio-telephone.

'I think we've got something significant here, chief,' he said. 'We have eight men out here checking with the local people to see if anyone saw Mr or Mrs Knapp or the Boeke boy, and they've located a woman who runs a little grocery store. I've just talked to her and she says that a boy came into the store on Monday evening and asked for a doctor. She told him that the nearest one was in Lage. He left then. From her description, I'd say that it was Willi Boeke.'

'That may be interesting,' said the inspector, 'but I don't see that it's very significant.'

'She says that the young man had blood on his hands, chief,' said the sergeant. 'As you remember, Mrs Knapp was scratched up a certain amount. Do you want me to pick the boy up and bring him in?'

'Definitely,' said the inspector. 'And bring the woman too. We'll see if she can pick him out of a line-up.'

The owner of the grocery store could. 'That's the boy,' she said. 'He's the one who came into the store.'

The inspector waited for only one more thing, the report from the detective who was trying to find Inge, the girl with whom Heinrich Knapp had allegedly spent Monday night. Shortly before noon he had his confirmation of Knapp's alibi. Inge had not been hard to find. She was a professional prostitute who had her beat in front of the Black Dog and who was well known in the district. She confirmed Knapp's statement.

'Bring the boy into the office,' said the inspector and, when Willi Boeke was seated in the chair before his desk, began immediately with a blunt accusation. 'Willi,' he said. 'You

42

murdered Mrs Knapp. Now, let's not waste any more time. I want the truth.'

Willi Boeke was, however, not prepared to admit to the truth. For two hours he lied, denied and evaded the inspector's questions, but, in the end, he was no match for the experienced police officer. Defiant but flustered, he blurted out the truth.

'We were both supposed to take the pills,' he said, 'but I decided I didn't want to die so I threw mine away. Guldira didn't notice it in the dark. She took hers and sort of passed out. She didn't die though. After a while, I got tired of waiting and I thought I'd put an end to it. I had realized that I didn't want to marry her after all. She was too old for me and she already had two children.'

'And another on the way,' said the inspector. 'Did you know that?'

'Yes,' said Willi Boeke. 'It was mine and I figured I was too young to be a father. I tried to strangle her a little and she sort of came to and fought with me. That's when she got scratched and I got the blood on my hands. After it was over and she wasn't breathing any more, I got scared and I thought I'd better call a doctor. Then when I went to the store, I suddenly realized that I'd be blamed if she was dead, so I went back to the house and stayed there until Thursday morning when I went to Lage.'

'And you spent those nights sleeping beside the body of the woman you'd murdered,' said the inspector.

'Why not?' said Willi Boeke.

Willi Boeke was brought to trial before the juvenile court in Bielefeld on 4 November 1969 and, after having repeated his confession, was remanded to a home for juvenile delinquents where he will remain until his twenty-first birthday. Under German juvenile law it was the maximum sentence that he could receive.

Now, who was crazy here? Not Heinrich Knapp. He was merely trying to do his best for his children under trying circumstances. Guldira Knapp? Possibly. Any woman of twenty-five who falls passionately in love with an eleven-year-old boy is obviously suffering from more than the boredom of life in a small town, and Guldira was, demonstrably, sincere about wanting to commit suicide.

Willi Boeke was not. He did not take his pills but threw them away, and when Guldira's did not work promptly enough he took matters into his own hands. As he said, he wanted to get rid of her. Why? Was it because he feared the responsibilities of fatherhood? Or was it simply because the ecstasies of young love had already palled. The attention span of an adolescent, even regarding romance, is not long.

Nor was his sentence. It would be unfortunate if he were left with the impression that there is little personal risk attached to murder.

4

YOU'LL ENJOY MEETING
MY SISTER

Not that it is any justification for murder, but Willi Boeke's
reluctance to found a family at the age of fifteen is shared by
many Germans a good deal older. At about the time that Willi
and Guldira began their tender romance, the German birth
rate descended below the replacement level and has remained
there ever since. It is estimated that by the year 2100 or so,
there will not be enough Germans left to field a football team.

Many reasons have been advanced for this decline in
fertility. Easily available birth-control drugs and devices. A
materialistic attitude on the part of young Germans who
prefer vacations and cars to kiddies. Fear of war. The large
number of working women, etc.

One theory which has not been advanced but which,
perhaps, deserves consideration is that the current generation of child-bearing age remembers all too well what kind of
a time their parents had with them and are anxious not to be
subjected to the same fate.

Ideologically and from the point of view of media-
advertising revenues, youth liberation may be a wonderful
thing, but it makes relations within the family difficult and
not infrequently painful. When this new freedom for the
immature is combined with the new sexual morality, the
results can be positively lethal. Even in such a place as
conservative and little influenced by international trends as
France.

Of course, it depends a good deal upon where you are in
France. Paris and the Mediterranean coast are mildly given to
whatever excesses are internationally current, but less than a
hundred miles to the north of Paris, in a city such as Lille,

most of the population is extremely conservative.

Not, perhaps, by inclination. Rather, they are practically all out of work and not a few are wondering where their next meal is coming from. Under such conditions it is difficult to keep up with what is currently 'in'.

Even in Lille, however, family misunderstandings do arise, and on Saturday, 2 August 1980, when the ambulance arrived at the apartment house at number sixteen, rue Gosselin in the Lille suburb of Fives at a little after three in the afternoon, it was to find a large knife rammed to the hilt in the middle of thirty-seven-year-old Daniel Renaut's stomach.

The stocky, heavy-muscled truck driver set hunched forward on the sofa, his hands clamped around the handle of the knife and his thick moustache like a streak of charcoal across the deadly pallor of his face. He was sweating heavily, the glistening streams of perspiration running down his forehead, across his cheeks and into the open collar of the scotch-plaid shirt. Lower down, where the saw-edged blade of the knife was imbedded in his vitals, the blood was seeping slowly out to form a large, irregularly shaped dark patch over the pattern of the shirt.

His sister and her fiancé sat on either side of him, supporting him in their arms. As the paramedic and the stretcher bearers burst through the open door of the apartment into the living room, Renaut raised his head, opened his mouth as if he were trying to say something, and went limp as he lost consciousness.

The paramedic took one look at the protruding knife handle and motioned to the stretcher bearers. 'Into the ambulance with him!' he snapped. 'Quickly! We'll be lucky if we get him to the hospital alive.'

As the stretcher bearers eased the unconscious man swiftly and with the efficiency of much practice on to the stretcher and manoeuvred it through the narrow hall and down the stairs, the intern, following alongside, inserted the transfusion needle and lifted high the flask.

'Have you notified the police?' he called to the couple still sitting on the sofa.

The man and the girl shook their heads mutely.

'Notify them,' said the intern, and went off down the stairs.

A few moments later the communications centre at police headquarters in downtown Lille, the formerly great and grimy industrial city in the northwest corner of France, received a call over the radio-telephone from the driver of the ambulance speeding through the streets in the direction of the Lille Emergency Hospital. A man had been seriously wounded with a knife at 16 rue Gosselin in the suburb of Fives. The paramedic had not had the impression that the couple in the apartment were going to take his advice.

Although it was a weekend and the height of the vacation period, the Criminal Investigations Department of the Lille police was fully staffed. Even in the best of times the cities along the Belgian border in the industrial north of France tend to a comparatively high crime rate. Now, with massive unemployment and a plunging standard of living, violent crime was at such a level that nearly all sections needed to be manned around the clock.

On duty in the Criminal Investigations Department on this day was Inspector Bernard Gentry, a tall, handsome man with long, dark-brown sideburns and a permanently harassed expression, his assistant, Detective-Sergeant Pierre Dunoyer, a bear of a man, with a sizeable stomach and a rolling gait, and one of the department's three experts in forensic medicine, Dr Lucien Thibault who looked like an ageing choir boy. While the inspector and the sergeant set off for the rue Gosselin, the doctor headed for the emergency hospital to learn what he could concerning the condition of the victim, the nature of the wound and to make some estimate of what sort of implement had caused it. At the time, no one at police headquarters knew that the knife was still sticking in Daniel Renaut's body.

At the apartment in Fives, the police officers found twenty-five-year-old Martine Renaut, the sister of the injured man, and her fiancé, thirty-year-old Louis Devynck, still sitting side by side on the sofa, holding hands and looking stunned.

In response to the inspector's questions, both said that

they had no idea how Daniel had come to be stabbed, and that he had staggered into the apartment holding his hands over the handle of the knife. They had immediately called the emergency ambulance.

The inspector, who had heard a great many false statements in his life, immediately recognized this as one and instructed the sergeant to take Renaut and Devynck into custody and bring them to police headquarters. If they insisted on being charged, then they would be held on suspicion of wounding with a deadly weapon.

The sergeant led the two suspects down to the policecar, and the inspector took a quick look through the apartment. He found nothing of significance other than that someone, apparently a man, had been sleeping on top of the covers on the bed in one of the two bedrooms. The form of the body on the covers and the dent made by the head in the pillow were plainly visible.

At police headquarters, Martine Renaut and Louis Devynck were taken to separate interrogation rooms for questioning. In general their statements turned out to be identical. They were, however, going to have to repeat them many times, for the inspector had barely arrived back at the station when he received a call from the emergency hospital. It was Dr Thibault, who reported that Daniel Renaut had died while being carried to the operating room. The murder weapon, a bread knife, had been removed from the body, and he was bringing it back for possible identification and testing for fingerprints. The body was being sent to the police morgue for the autopsy.

The inspector did not pass the news of Daniel's death on to the two suspects, but simply resumed questioning. The longer of the two statements was that of Martine Renaut.

Like her brother and Louis Devynck, Martine had been born and raised in Fives, and had spent her entire life in the little apartment at 16 rue Gosselin. The apartment had originally belonged to her parents, Roger and Leontine Renaut, but Roger had died in 1965 and Leontine in 1973. Daniel, the only other child, had married that year and had moved to the little town of Mons-en-Baroeul.

The marriage had not turned out well and in 1977 he had obtained a divorce. Martine had not had much contact with him since he left home as his job as a long-distance truck driver kept him away a great deal of the time.

She had met Louis Devynck, a giant of a man with shoulder-length red hair, in September 1979 and, they having decided to marry in September 1980, he had moved into the apartment with her in January 1980. Devynck was employed as a mechanic in a garage in Lille.

Louis Devynck's statement agreed with that of Martine's in almost all details. His knowledge of her parents and her brother was, however, more sketchy. As he pointed out, all he knew of them was what she had told him. Although a native of Fives he had never met the elder Renauts before their death, and had only seen Daniel on one or two occasions. He had, he said, heard that Daniel drank rather more than was good for him and that he was known as a barroom brawler. He thought that it might be in some such brawl that Daniel had obtained his knife wound.

Although these were straightforward, reasonable and nearly identical statements, the inspector did not believe a word of them, but having insufficient evidence to bring any kind of a sustainable charge, he was left with no alternative other than to release both suspects with the warning that they were not to leave town or change their address without advising him.

Before the couple left police headquarters, the inspector informed Martine that her brother was dead and suggested that she make arrangements after completion of the autopsy for the transfer of the body from the police morgue to a funeral home for burial.

Martine had an unexpectedly violent reaction, broke down completely, became hysterical and had to be transferred to the police clinic for tranquillizing medication which was, however, so ineffective that she was forced to spend the remainder of the night there.

In the meantime, a contingent of plain-clothes investigators under the direction of Sergeant Dunoyer had gone to work in the Fives suburb. The case was now officially classed as homicide, and a correspondingly large assignment of manpower had been made for the purpose of the investigation.

Nothing unusual was discovered that evening other than that Devynck had been correct in his statement that Daniel Renaut drank more than was good for him and was given to brawling in bars. His divorce had apparently had a bad effect on him, for he had not worked regularly since and had spent his time mostly in taverns drinking or importuning casual acquaintances for small loans with which to finance further drinking.

In 1978 he had been a suspect in the robbery of a filling station, but had been released without charges for lack of evidence. It was not clearly determined how he had supported himself, but it was established that Martine and Louis had been lying when they said that they had seen little of Daniel. The neighbours reported that he had been constantly in and out of the apartment at 16 rue Gosselin.

A startling turn in the investigations took place on the following day when the sergeant appeared in the inspector's office with a large, ugly and brutal-looking man named Felix Martins. Mr Martins, said the sergeant, knew the Renauts and claimed that Martine was a prostitute and that her brother was her pimp. He was, he said, one of her customers.

This statement astonished the inspector very much for he thought he knew a prostitute when he saw one, and Martine Renaut did not look to him like a prostitute at all.

None the less, Martins stuck to his story.

'I met Daniel in a bar one night in June of 1978,' he said. 'We'd both been drinking and I was complaining that I didn't have much luck with the girls. He said if I wanted a nice girl he could fix me up with his sister. It would cost ten dollars and I might have to be a little rough with her because she was a masochist and liked to be slapped around. She'd play coy, but if I pushed her around a little, she'd come across.'

'Was Miss Renaut present in the bar when her brother told you this?' said the inspector incredulously. He had heard some remarkable things during the course of his career, but this was beginning to sound like something outstanding.

'No,' said Martins. 'She was home in her apartment at 16 rue Gosselin in Fives waiting for customers. All I had to do was go there, knock on the door and, when she opened up, push on in and say I'd come to get my money's worth. If she put up any objections I was to ignore them.'

'And did she put up any objections?' said the inspector.

'Fought like a tiger,' said Martins. 'She scratched me up pretty bad, but, for ten dollars, it was worth it. What can you get for ten dollars nowadays?'

'Not much for ten dollars, but you can get fifteen years for forcible rape,' said the inspector. 'She didn't bring charges against you?'

'Why should she?' said Martins. 'I told her I'd already given her brother the money and that if she wanted her cut she could ask him for it. After that, she sort of gave up.'

'That story is so weird that it has to be true,' said the inspector after Martins had left the office. 'My God! What was going on there with those people anyway?'

'Renaut appears to have been peddling his sister's hips without her knowledge or consent,' said the sergeant. 'I suspect that if we keep looking, we'll find others.'

He was not mistaken. Over the next few days, the police were able to turn up no less than four men in Lille who admitted to having paid Daniel Renaut for the privilege of having sex with his sister. The fee had been in all cases the same, ten dollars. So, too, had the sales pitch.

Said Jerome Cousty in his statement to the police, 'I was in this bar drinking and Renaut was standing next to me. I was telling him that I had a lot of trouble meeting girls and, when I did, I couldn't get anywhere with them. He said he knew where I could get a nice girl for not much money. She was a little fat, he said, but she was really good stuff and clean.

'I said, "How much?" and he said that ten dollars would be all right. I could give him the money.

'I said that I thought I would like to take a look at her before I paid because, although ten dollars really was a cheap price, I was living from unemployment compensation and I didn't have very much.

'He said that he didn't have her right there in his pocket, but that he could show me a picture. Then he pulled some pictures out of his pocket and gave them to me.

'I thought they would show her naked or something like that, but they were just ordinary photographs. One was in a living room, and the other one was outside at a picnic or something of that sort.

'Like he said, she was a little plump, but she wasn't bad looking and I figured that for ten dollars I couldn't go wrong.

'I lost my money though because she put up such a fight that I wasn't able to do it to her.'

'Didn't you ask for your money back from Daniel Renaut?' said the inspector.

Cousty, a thin, shabby sort of man with a week's growth of beard and very few teeth, nodded his head sadly.

'He said I wasn't forceful enough,' he said. 'Said she liked to be dominated by men. He said if I wasn't satisfied, I could have another go at her for free. It was pretty generous of him.'

'And did you?' said the inspector.

Cousty shook his head again. 'She hurt me pretty bad the first time,' he said. 'Scratched me all up and she hit me in the eye so that I couldn't see for a couple of days. I thought maybe I'd better not. It was better just to lose the ten dollars.'

Cousty said that Renaut had not told him that the girl was his sister, but the other two men, Gabriel Thonnes and Christian Desgagneaux, both claimed that he had.

As in the other cases they had encountered Daniel Renaut by chance in a bar, had spoken of their problems with women, and had been offered Martine's services for ten dollars. Both had been shown pictures of Daniel's sister and both had accepted the offer.

Desgagneaux, a stocky, powerful man, had overcome the girl's resistance by sheer force and, like Felix Martins, had literally raped her. Thonnes, actually the biggest and the strongest of the four, had been kneed so violently in the groin that he had had to beat a retreat, crawling away on hands and knees in great pain. As he was the last of Daniel's clients that the police were able to locate, it appeared that Martine had been becoming more efficient in defending herself.

'There are probably others, possibly a good many,' said the sergeant, 'whom we have not been able to locate or who are unwilling to admit that they were involved, and the only question that comes to my mind is why she didn't murder him before. She's obviously not a prostitute, and she was very definitely not in agreement with her brother's schemes for making money out of her.'

'Some of the clients must have realized it too,' said the inspector. 'That girl put up a savage resistance. Anyone with any brains at all would realize that she was not faking it for the sake of masochistic kicks. It's significant that all of the four who made statements are very simple men from the lowest class of society and nearly illiterate. Renaut could tell them something like that and they'd believe it.'

'Well, whatever the case, it's one of the most plausible motives for murder that I've ever heard,' said the sergeant. 'Do you want me to bring her in now and see what we can do about getting the confession?'

'Yes, I expect we have to,' said the inspector. 'I just hope that that red-haired boyfriend of hers doesn't try to provide her with an alibi.'

The inspector's hopes were in vain. Louis Devynck did provide his fiancée with an alibi, the best possible alibi.

He confessed to the murder.

'*Merde!*' swore the inspector. 'He's not guilty! He's protecting her!'

Louis Devynck continued calmly to dictate his confession. He had had the trouble with Daniel ever since he took up with Martine, he said. The man had continually hit him up for larger and smaller sums of money and, if he showed any disinclination to hand it over, had made coarse references to his paying the price for sleeping with Daniel's sister.

If insults did not work, then Daniel had come around and punched Martine in the head when Louis was absent working at his job. This had always produced results. Louis did not want Martine hurt and had paid.

On the afternoon of 2 August he had been at home in the apartment as it was Saturday and he was not working. Daniel had arrived at about three o'clock and had demanded twenty-five dollars, saying that he owed it to some men and that they were going to beat him up if he didn't pay.

Louis had refused saying that he had enough of paying,

and that if Daniel got beat up for not paying his debts it served him right.

Daniel had seized the mustard pot off the table and had made threatening motions with it as if he were going to attack the other man.

Devynck had responded by snatching up the bread knife which was also lying on the table.

Suddenly, Daniel had rushed at him with the mustard pot raised as if to strike a blow.

Devynck had no recollection of actually making a stabbing movement, but he must have been holding the knife out in front of him for, the next thing he knew, it was sticking in Renaut's stomach and the man was staggering backwards toward the sofa with his hands clasped over the handle.

Martine had not been in the room at the time, but Louis had called her, telling her that she should summon the emergency ambulance. She had immediately done so. He and she had then sat down on either side of the wounded man to support and comfort him until the ambulance arrived.

Although the inspector did not believe this confession, there were details in it that made it impossible to refute.

To begin with, the police already knew that the murder weapon came from the apartment in the rue Gosselin. The combination of food and grease traces on the handle matched precisely those found on other kitchen utensils in Martine Renaut's kitchen, and no other bread knife, basic for a French kitchen, had been found there.

Secondly, a broken mustard pot had been recovered from the garbage can and traces of mustard had been found on Renaut's clothing and hands, as well as similar traces on the living-room carpet and the sofa.

At the time the significance of the mustard stains was not clear and it was not known whether they were connected with the murder. Now, however, the confession by Louis Devynck brought out their importance and clearly demonstrated one thing. Whether guilty or not, Louis Devynck was in possession of precise knowledge of the details of the crime. It would be difficult to convince a jury that his confession was false and that he was not the murderer.

'And yet that is exactly what we are going to have to do unless we want to see an innocent man sent to prison,' said the inspector. 'I'm as certain that it was really Martine who was holding the knife as I have ever been of anything, but, if Devynck sticks to his confession, I don't see how we're going to prove it.'

'Well, maybe it was Devynck,' said the sergeant. 'After all, he had a strong motive too. Renaut was milking him for everything that he was worth and beating up his fiancée to boot. In either case, it was more manslaughter than murder. I don't think that either Devynck or Martine Renaut actually set out to murder Daniel. There was a quarrel, a brawl of some kind, Renaut grabbed up the mustard pot and made threatening gestures with it, and either Martine or Devynck picked up the kitchen knife to defend themselves. A jury isn't going to give either one of them very much for that.'

'They'd come down on him a good deal heavier than they would on her,' said the inspector. 'And he doesn't deserve it. He's merely being noble. The fact is, with his size and strength, he didn't need a knife to defend himself. He could have taken the mustard pot away from Renaut and stuffed it in his ear. The use of the knife was by someone smaller and weaker than Renaut trying to defend themselves, and that was Martine. She's guilty, and the thing that astounds me the most is why she doesn't admit it. I've told her myself that she's risking very little if she makes a confession, but she hasn't cooperated.'

'Yes, that is strange,' said the sergeant. 'She seems like a decent, respectable woman, and my impression is that she's genuinely attached to Devynck. I can't imagine why she would let him go to jail in her place, particularly when she'd get, at the most, a light sentence.'

The inspector could not imagine it either, but he was determined to avoid sending an innocent man to jail if he could help it, and he reluctantly decided on the use of harsher methods with the recalcitrant girl.

'Bring in Martine and bring in the four men who admit to having paid Daniel ten dollars for the privilege of having sexual relations with her,' said the inspector to the sergeant.

'We've got to shake her up a little. Get her off balance so that she'll make some kind of an admission rather than the denials that she's sticking with now.'

The sergeant did as he was told. Martine Renaut was brought to police headquarters where she was confronted with Jerome Cousty, Felix Martins, Gabriel Thonnes and Christian Desgagneaux.

She promptly went into a hysterical fit and was carried screaming and crying to the police clinic. She did not admit to anything.

'Pity that Louis Devynck isn't as emotional as Martine,' said the sergeant, returning to the inspector's office after having seen the girl to the clinic. 'If he got upset like that, he'd undoubtedly admit something, maybe the truth even.'

'Maybe we should try a confrontation between him and the four customers,' said the inspector, half jokingly. 'At this point, I'm about ready to try anything.'

There was a short, thoughtful silence in the office and then the sergeant said, 'Does he know about the customers and Daniel's money-making schemes? He didn't say a word about it in his confession. And yet you'd think that would be one of his strongest motives.'

'Maybe he doesn't want to embarrass her,' said the inspector. 'Maybe . . .'

'Maybe he doesn't know about them,' finished the sergeant. 'Maybe she never told him.'

'And she doesn't want him to know now,' said the inspector. 'If she were charged and tried . . .'

'. . . the story of her brother's activities on her behalf would become known,' said the sergeant. 'That's why she doesn't confess.'

'Yes,' said the inspector. 'That's why she doesn't confess.'

'But if Devynck already knew,' said the inspector, 'she wouldn't have any reason to hold back her confession any longer. How do we tell him?'

'Maybe we could let both of them listen to the tapes of the four customers' statements together,' suggested the sergeant. 'We could then separate them again for questioning. That way there wouldn't be any question but that everyone concerned was in possession of all the details.'

'All right, that sounds like a reasonable idea,' said the inspector, 'but I want complete security. There's no telling how either she or he will react to this and Devynck is a big man. I think it would be a good idea to have him handcuffed to something solid while he's listening to the tapes.'

The precaution was taken but proved unnecessary. Louis Devynck was a big and powerful man, but he was also gentle. His reaction to the taped statements of the four men to whom Daniel Renaut had sold his sister was not rage but sorrow.

Martine's reaction was almost one of relief.

'I was in a horrible position,' she said. 'If I didn't confess, Louis would have to go to jail in my place and, if I did, he would find out about all the dirty things that Daniel had done to me. I was afraid that he wouldn't want to have anything to do with me after that, and I didn't want to lose him.'

She need not have worried. Devynck was utterly convinced of her blamelessness in the matter, and even after she had confessed to the stabbing, continued to attempt to take the responsibility on to himself,

'He was not even present at the time,' said Martine. 'He had been working hard all week, and he was taking a nap in the bedroom at around three o'clock when Daniel appeared at the apartment. As usual he wanted money, and he said that three men were out to get him unless he could pay them the twenty-five dollars he owed them.

'I told him to keep quiet, that Louis was sleeping, and that he was not going to give him any more money. If he needed money, he should get a job and earn some.

'Daniel was furious and said a lot of filthy things about me and Louis. He started to shout that this was his home, that he had been born and raised here and that Louis was the intruder and should get out. He said he was moving in and that I could easily support both him and myself if I would be a little more reasonable with the friends he sent around.

'I lost my temper completely and started yelling at him too, but it only made him madder and he grabbed up a mustard pot from the table and started toward me.

'I picked up the bread knife and held it out in front of myself, but he kept on coming and he was sneering about how I thought I was going to defend myself with a bread knife.

57

'Louis had woken up and had come to the door of the bedroom, and I was not sure how much he had heard of what Daniel said.

'All of a sudden, he seemed to be right on top of me, and then I heard the mustard pot smash on the floor and he was reeling backwards holding his stomach. It was only when I looked at my hands and saw that I was not holding the knife any longer that I realized what had happened.

'I wasn't able to speak or do anything, but Louis immediately called the emergency ambulance.

'I'm sorry that I killed Daniel, but he was doing terrible things to me and I was afraid of him. Louis is completely innocent. He had nothing to do with it. He only came into the room a second or two before Daniel got stabbed.'

Martine Renaut was charged with unintentional homicide and ordered to be held for trial. Although she spent nearly nine months in pre-trial detention, it was the only time that she did serve, for, on 12 June 1981, she was found guilty of unintentional homicide with extremely extenuating circumstances and sentenced to four years' imprisonment suspended. She and Louis Devynck were married ten days after the conclusion of the trial.

It is difficult to say who was crazy in this case. However, for the sake of complete impartiality, it is probably best to include everybody.

Martine was certainly crazy to put up with her brother's exploitation of her admittedly plump but attractive body. Louis was crazy to keep paying off his future brother-in-law when a punch in the nose would have been more appropriate. Daniel was crazy to think that he could continue supporting himself by peddling his unwilling sister.

And the customers? Some were obviously none too bright, although there is a widespread belief within the male population that girls who get raped secretly enjoy it. They, perhaps, sincerely believed that Martine was having the time of her life.

Others were probably crazy like a fox. Considering inflation and the depreciation of the currency, ten dollars really was a very reasonable price.

58

5

WHY RAPE STRANGERS WHEN YOU HAVE A SISTER?

As there is no evidence that Daniel Renaut entered into retailing his sister before the death of their parents, it may be assumed that Martine had a reasonably happy childhood.

Even if she did not, she, at least, survived it. In the West German town of Menden, which is not one of the most attractive places in the world to live as it is on the edge of the great industrial and mining district of the Ruhr, Gabriele Goerke, more commonly known as Gaby, did not even make it through adolescence. At the time of her death she was just fifteen years old.

Nor had she been having it any too good for the year and a half preceding that Wednesday 8 July 1981 when she was sexually assaulted, strangled and buried in the forest not far from her home.

Gaby was, at the time, no longer living in her home, but in an orphans' asylum as were her thirteen- and eleven-year-old brothers, Georg and Peter, and her nine-year-old sister Petra. None of the children were, however, really orphans as both of their parents were still alive, but too preoccupied with the development of their own personalities to concern themselves with children.

Sigrid Goerke, a woman who took the counsels of the Women's Liberation promoters seriously, had just turned forty and, coming to the conclusion that her husband and five children did not constitute a meaningful relationship, liberated herself and went off to seek love, fame, fortune and anything else that was going.

Albert, her husband, took this badly. He was three years

older than his wife and had considered his domestic affairs more or less settled. Now, he suddenly found himself a single parent with a family of five. He could not even remarry immediately as Sigrid had not bothered to obtain a divorce and no one knew where she was.

There is a classic response to such situations and Albert made it. He started hitting the bottle. In no time at all, he was transformed from a hard-working, sober head of a family to a lolling drunk, and was promptly fired from his job.

The juvenile authorities stepped in and four of the Goerke children were sent to the orphanage. The oldest, Ralf, escaped by taking a drastic step. He married a seventeen-year-old girl the day after his eighteenth birthday, and having thus become responsible for her support could not be sent to the orphans' home. It was an arrangement satisfactory to all parties. Annette, the young bride, remained in school, and Ralf supported them both with his job as a heating plant installer.

Ralf was, therefore, in the clear and no longer concerned with the fortunes of the Goerke family, Sigrid was missing and Albert was drunk. This left Gaby, a pretty, affectionate teenager to hold what remained of the family together as well as she could. This she did conscientiously and, as the children were not separated in the orphanage, a sort of family life without parents began to emerge.

She was, therefore, greatly missed and, at her funeral on 12 July 1981, all of the Goerkes wept bitterly, and so did many of the nearly one hundred neighbours and well-wishers who attended. These non-family members who wept were women. The men did not weep, for their eyes, hot and bright with anger, were searching the crowd for strange faces. Lying in the trunks of several of the cars parked outside the cemetery gates were clubs and lengths of stout rope which they were hoping to be able to put to use.

If the man responsible for this funeral turned up and could be identified, there would be another funeral immediately.

The atmosphere was tense and Inspector Walter Fink of the Menden police Criminal Investigations Department was far from certain that his men, in plain clothes and scattered throughout the crowd, would be able to control the situation if a likely suspect turned up. After all, this series of attacks on girls had been going on for over six months, and not a few were beginning to feel it was time to take matters into their own hands.

The inspector, a slight, neatly dressed man with a conservative haircut and the general appearance of a civil servant which was what he was, doubted that the killer would be rash enough to turn up at the funeral. If he was a local man he could hardly fail to know the temper and intentions of his fellow citizens, who had been growing increasingly restive ever since Friday, 30 January of the same year when seventeen-year-old Gerda Schaefer had acquired the dubious distinction of becoming the first-known victim in the worst series of sex crimes that the little town of fifty thousand had ever known.

Gerda also enjoyed a more desirable distinction. She was, in so far as was known, the only case in which the victim had escaped unscathed. It was thought that this was, perhaps, because it was the first attempt and the technique had not yet been perfected.

Gerda, a pretty, blonde girl who would have looked younger than her age had it not been for her rather startling physical development, had left school the preceding year and was employed as a salesgirl in one of the downtown shops.

The shop closed at six o'clock, and at approximately twenty minutes past six Gerda had been taking a short cut through a section of the forest park on the west side of the city.

She was within two hundred yards of her parents' home when something big and black loomed up out of the darkness behind her and a large, rough hand was slapped over the lower part of her face in what would become locally famous as the strangler's grip.

The strangler's grip was simple but effective. The last three fingers of the right hand were clasped tightly across the girl's mouth so that she could not open it or cry out, and the thumb and index finger grasped the nose, pressing the nostrils together and cutting off the victim's breath. At the same time the elbow of the same arm pressed heavily against the girl's breast, holding her so tightly against her attacker's chest that she could scarcely move.

The prey thus immobilized, the rapist began with his left hand to unfasten Gerda's slacks and push them down over her hips. Her underpants followed and Gerda felt the cold air of the winter night on her naked thighs and belly.

But not on her buttocks. The man had dropped his own trousers and his hot flesh was pressing against her from behind.

He was, presumably, as later events would indicate, trying to enter her vaginally from the rear, but Gerda, who for a modern German girl of her age had had but little experience in such matters, thought that she was about to be raped anally, and this produced such a state of panic that, for a few moments, she was gifted with superhuman strength.

Wrenching herself out of the man's grip, she started to run, tripped on the slacks which had fallen down around her ankles and sprawled full length in the snow.

She would have been lost had not her attacker suffered the same fate. As would later be determined from the marks in the snow, he too had tripped over his pants and had fallen full length.

In the meantime, Gerda had scrambled to her feet and was running for home, holding up her slacks with both hands and screaming at the top of her voice.

The screams did it. By the time the people from the nearest houses came boiling out into the street, the would-be rapist had pulled up his trousers and was long since gone.

He had not lost his head either. He had run directly to the clean-swept, paved surface of the nearby road, and therefore it was impossible to tell which direction he had taken.

Gerda Schaefer was unharmed other than some damage to her nervous system and the Menden police, who were informed and carried out an immediate investigation, came to the conclusion that the attacker had been a transient. He could hardly be a local man for any local men with such tendencies were known and in the police files. Their whereabouts were checked for the time of the attack, and it was determined that none of them could have been reponsible for it.

In March the 13th fell on a Friday, an unlucky day for the police, but even more so for sixteen-year-old Ilse Diederich.

Unlike Gerda Schaefer, Ilse was still in school, but, like her, she was very pretty with long, brown hair reaching nearly to her waist and a figure which sometimes caused male observers to trip over their own feet. Being a modern, liberated girl, she was not a virgin.

Ilse was not passing through a stretch of forest but walking along a narrow, deserted street in the heart of town at approximately four-thirty in the afternoon on her way home from school.

The strangler had apparently been hiding in a small court-yard leading off the street and, as Ilse passed the entrance, he emerged, ran swiftly and silently up behind her, and applied his strangler's grip with such force that the girl briefly lost consciousness.

Although delightfully well built, Ilse was not a large girl and he lifted her easily, carried her into the courtyard, hoisted up her skirt, pulled down her panties and raped her, entering vaginally but from the rear.

As far as Ilse could estimate later, the whole process lasted only a few minutes, and she had scarcely had time to grasp what was happening when she found herself sitting on the cobbles of the courtyard with her pants down and the rapist gone.

As he had held her nose and mouth shut through the attack, it was a few minutes before she could regain her breath, but then she began to yell, not so much because she was frightened but because she was indignant. She had had a confused impression of her assailant and she thought that he was one of her classmates.

As it turned out, he was not. Every male pupil in Ilse's school was interrogated and their whereabouts for the time of the rape checked. By good fortune all of them could be cleared. Ilse had been mistaken.

Aside from a slightly sore nose and mouth, Ilse was not injured, but the rape had been fully consummated. An examination by her family physician produced evidence of forceable entry in the form of a number of minor haircuts on the labia major, and enough semen within the vagina to establish that the rapist belonged to blood group A.

The news of the rape went quickly through the little town and aroused great indignation, but less concern with the general public than it did with the police. The Schaefer case had not received much publicity, and few persons knew that the details of the attack were very similar to those concerning the rape of Ilse Diederich. The police did.

'I think it's obvious that what we have here is the beginning of a series,' said Inspector Fink, mulling over matters with his assistant, Detective-Sergeant Boris Schmidt, in the small office which they shared.

'Well, it shouldn't go on very long,' said the sergeant, who was big, bull-shouldered and had a rather ruddy complexion. 'A stranger in Menden stands out like a cow in a coffee shop.'

'I doubt now that it is a stranger,' said the inspector. 'A stranger wouldn't know the downtown area well enough to know about that courtyard, or to know that the buildings around it are used for warehouses and that there's normally hardly anyone there. One thing's certain though. We know he's young; so young that the Diederich girl took him for one of her classmates. We can run a check on whether anyone has an overgrown sixteen- or seventeen-year-old boy visiting them, but I suspect, in the end, we'll find that he's local himself. Assuming, of course, that we ever find him at all.'

'We certainly should,' said the sergeant. 'Menden isn't that big. Practically everybody here knows everybody else. Somebody will notice something suspicious and report in.'

'Then, I wish they'd do it quickly,' said the inspector, 'because he's got away with it twice now and he's sure to try again.'

The inspector was a good prophet. On the evening of Tuesday, 21 April, eighteen-year-old Liselotte Goebels went to the cinema. The film finished a little before eleven o'clock and Liselotte set off for home.

Menden is a town where there is not a great deal of night life and there were few persons on the street. Oddly, it was just while several persons were in sight, although not nearby, that the strangler stepped out of the shadows of a yard surrounding a private home and took her in his now famous grip.

Liselotte, who had heard all about the Menden strangler and who was anxious to resume breathing, offered no resistance.

Encouraged by this, the strangler pulled her behind a screen of bushes forming a hedge along one side of the house, shifted his grip rather awkwardly, and, having lifted her skirt, raped her from the front after Liselotte had pulled down her own pants. She was a practical-minded girl and, as she later told Inspector Fink, it was bad enough being raped without having your clothes ruined as well.

Although she reported the incident to the police, the rather matter-of-fact tone of the report caused the inspector to wonder how many other such cases there might have been that were not reported at all. Rape has become so common in many parts of the world today that, unless the victim is actually injured, it is often not reported.

Perhaps, just because she had retained such a cool head throughout the procedure, Liselotte provided the best description of the rapist to date. He was, she said, taller than average, above six feet or very close to it. Slim and athletically built, without beard or moustache, he wore the sort of soup-bowl, trimmed-mop haircut affected by some teenagers. He was, she thought, very young as he had been amazingly quick on the trigger, barely penetrating her before he arrived at his climax.

The description was largely an expansion and refinement of descriptions which had already been received from Gerda Schaefer and Ilse Diederich. There was no question but that it had been the same man in all three cases, although the police were scarcely better off than they had been before.

Menden is a small place, but it is not small enough for the police to arrest and check the alibis of every tall youth with a soup-bowl haircut.

'So we wait for the next one,' said Sergeant Schmidt. 'How many do you think he'll manage before he makes a slip?'

'Who knows?' said the inspector, shrugging his shoulders. 'There have been series like this that went on for years and, in some cases, the fellow was never caught. He died of old age or lost interest in sex or something, and the series just stopped of itself.'

'If you can rely on the descriptions,' said the sergeant, 'you and I will both be retired before this one dies of old age or loses interest in sex either. Well, at least he doesn't seem to have injured anyone very seriously so far.'

'He will,' said the inspector grimly. 'He will.'

Once again, the inspector proved to be a good prophet. On 15 May which, like the dates of two of the three preceding crimes, with a Friday, seventeen-year-old Maryse Lang was raped and strangled unconscious at approximately six-fifteen in the evening as she was walking home from work. Unlike the other victims in the series, she fought savagely with her assailant.

Miss Lang, a pretty, rather fragile-looking girl, was a member of a strict religious sect and she was not supposed to engage in sexual activity of any kind until after marriage, if then. In theory, death was to be preferred before dishonour.

It had come very close to being both. There was now no living soul in Menden who did not know that there was a dangerous rapist in their midst, and the police had repeatedly warned that victims were to offer no resistance, but to try to memorize whatever details they could of their attacker's appearance which might help in tracing his identity. The theory was that a victim was better off raped and alive than raped and dead.

Maryse Lang had disagreed, and she had nearly paid for it with her life. When she had begun to kick and struggle, and had actually managed to get her mouth open enough to bite one of the rapist's fingers, he had ceased his efforts to remove her underwear and had brought up his left forearm across her throat, holding it there with such force that the circulation of blood to the brain was cut off and she lost consciousness.

When she came to the rapist was gone, her underpants were around one ankle, and her throat was so bruised that she could speak in nothing louder than a sort of squeaky whisper.

There was no question but that she had been raped. Prior to the attack she had been a virgin, and her thighs and pubic area were covered with the blood from her burst hymen.

Maryse pulled on her pants, straightened her skirt and staggered off to the police station, a bare three hundred yards away, to file her charges in a painful whisper.

It was necessary for her to be hospitalized the following day, as she had received such a shock from her experience that she was developing suicidal tendencies.

Maryse Lang was unable to offer any description of her attacker at all. Whether this was because she had actually not seen him or because her frightened mind had pushed the details of the encounter down into her subconscious where it was no longer available could not be said, but her doctor suspected that it was the latter.

'Well, he's hurt one,' said Sergeant Schmidt. 'You've been one hundred per cent right so far. What's going to happen now?'

'He's going to kill somebody,' said the inspector.

And on Wednesday, 8 July 1981 he did.

It was suspected or, at least, feared that same evening when Gaby Goerke failed to return to the orphanage for dinner. The orphanage was not a closed institution and the children were allowed to go out alone if they were old enough, or in the company of other children if they were not.

Gaby had gone out at approximately five o'clock in the afternoon without mentioning where she was going to anyone, and it had been assumed by those who saw her go that she was going for a walk. The weather was warm, sunny, the height of the West German summer, and not only Gaby but a great many other people were taking walks in the woods which surround Menden.

When, however, Gaby failed to return to the home in time for dinner which was at seven o'clock, her brothers and sister became exceedingly anxious and asked permission to go and look for her.

The permission was granted and not only the Goerke children, but many of the other children and a number of the adult supervisors set off into the woods searching for some trace of the missing girl.

Gaby had been popular and she had not been the sort of girl who could be expected to run away from the orphanage, certainly not as long as her brothers and sister were there. When, by nine o'clock, no trace of her had been found, the director of the orphanage called the police.

Inspector Fink and Sergeant Schmidt were, of course, off duty at this hour, but they hurried to the orphanage from their homes and spoke to the children there. They were in hopes that Gaby might have given some hint that she was planning on spending the night with a boyfriend. The girls of her own age in the orphanage claimed that, from what she had told them confidentially, this would not have been impossible.

She had, however, mentioned no such thing, and had actually acted rather strangely and secretively, although she was normally a girl who confided freely in her friends.

The inspector thought that the reports of strange and secret behaviour were probably the result of the fact that she was now missing. Had she not been, the strangeness and secretiveness would not have occurred to anyone.

What frightened him, however, and what had brought him out of his home in the middle of the evening, was the knowledge that at least four other girls had been attacked in Menden during the past six months and, although Gaby was a year younger than the youngest-known victim so far, it was all too possible that she had become the fifth in the series. She was pretty, well built, and the strangler had never yet asked to see one of his victim's birth certificates.

Moreover, it was now known that he was capable of violence; dangerous violence which could end in the death of the victim. It would not have required much more pressure on Maryse Lang's throat to have sent her to the morgue rather than the hospital.

The only optimistic aspect was that it seemed hardly likely that Gaby would have resisted. She was almost certainly not a virgin, and she did not belong to any religious sect which had strong feelings about sexual intercourse. She knew about the

68

Menden strangler and she knew the advice of the police. She was a self-possessed girl who was not easily frightened. It was scarcely probable that she would have fought with the strangler and, in so far as anyone knew, he did not deliberately harm a victim who did not resist.

It was by now completely dark and the searchers had all returned to the orphanage. They had found no trace of Gaby, but some of the children said they had seen a strange, shaggy man running through the woods.

Had the inspector believed this story, he would have sent police parties out into the woods yet that night, but he did not. If Gaby Goerke had fallen a victim to the strangler, it had been hours before any of the search parties went out, and it was extremely improbable that the murderer would still have been running about out there.

In the past, his practice had been to leave the scene as rapidly as possible.

The inspector, therefore, suspended operations until first light the following morning which, it being summer, was at around six-thirty. At this time, parties of police and firemen plus members of civilian volunteers moved out into the woods and began systematically searching for the missing girl.

At eight-thirty, breakfast at the orphanage having been finished, the older children were given permission to join in the search and it was the children who, on the afternoon of Thursday, 9 July, found her.

Gaby lay buried beneath six inches of soft earth and leaf mould less than a hundred yards from her old home. One of the boys running back toward the orphanage had put his foot squarely into the soft earth of her grave and had gone head over heels. When he picked himself up and looked to see what had tripped him, he could see the material of the girl's dress through the dirt which he had kicked up.

The police were immediately notified and Inspector Fink and Sergeant Schmidt hurried to the scene. The supervisors from the orphanage had quickly herded the children away from the shallow grave and the body had not been uncovered.

So far, there was no certainty that it was Gaby in the grave, but it was a girl, and it would have been strange if it had been someone else.

It was Gaby Goerke as the Menden coroner, Doctor Martin Hofmann, quickly determined once he had brushed the dirt away from the child's face.

She lay on her back, her hands folded over her breasts, and her legs close together, but with her skirts raised so that she was naked from the navel down. She was wearing her knee-length stockings and shoes, but her underpants were missing. They were later found beneath the body when it was lifted out of the grave.

'The cause of death? The cause of death?' exclaimed the inspector in an untypical state of excitement. 'What was the cause of death?'

'Give me a minute,' said the coroner. He was an elderly man with a white moustache and little hair and, although he was very thorough, he was not very fast.

'All I want to know is was she strangled?' said the inspector. 'Was it the strangler?'

'It could be,' said the doctor cautiously. 'There's no blood or any wounds on the body that I can see. Of course, she may have received a blow over the head which is concealed by the hair or . . .'

'How soon can I have a preliminary autopsy report?' said the inspector.

'Not before you get the body over to the morgue,' said the coroner in mild reproof. 'I'll begin immediately you can let me have her.'

The inspector could, however, not let the body be sent to the morgue immediately as he was anxious that the technicians from the small police laboratory go over the area thoroughly before it was moved. He did not know what they might find, but, if there was anything, he wanted to be sure they found it.

His caution was rewarded. The technicians found a button. As it was buried beneath the earth with the corpse, and as it did not belong to any article of her clothing, it was possible that it belonged to the murderer. It was a shiny, black button, and the technicians thought that it might have come from a man's trousers; not the fly, but a button closing a hip pocket or something of that nature.

The button was slipped into a small plastic sack and taken to police headquarters where, to the surprise and delight of everyone concerned, it was found to have part of a fingerprint on it; or rather, said the technicians, a thumb print. The button had apparently been one to a hip pocket and the owner of the trousers had rested his thumb on it while unbuttoning the pocket. There was not enough of it to make possible a positive identification, but it could serve as a useful indication in the event of an arrest.

An arrest was made even before Doctor Hofmann had completed the autopsy. The children from the orphanage had been right. There had been a man running through the woods that afternoon. He *was* shaggy, and he had been seen and recognized by other witnesses.

His name was Ferdinand Sachs and he was considered by the Menden police to be Menden's most dangerous sex criminal, the Strangler not counted.

Sachs was twenty-four years old and had a record of a long string of offences against female children and very young girls. As a suspect he was far from ideal, for he was not known to have ever attacked a victim as old as Gaby Goerke to say nothing of the still older girls in the series.

On the other hand, Sachs was a trifle over six feet tall, wore his hair in a shaggy, uncombed mop reaching nearly to his shoulders, and he had been in the woods at the time that Gaby Goerke was murdered.

This time was, according to the coroner, a little after six in the evening of 8 July. The girl had not been strangled, but smothered, the nose and mouth having been held shut until she died of lack of air. It had been a rather slow, painful death, and it was precisely the sort of death which would result from a continued application of the strangler's grip.

On the subject of sexual molestation the coroner was less definite. There were, he said, certain indications that penetration might have taken place, and the fact that the

71

body had been found with the genitals exposed tended to confirm that there had been some sort of sexual activity. There were, however, no traces of semen in the vagina.

Finally, the autopsy report concluded with the remark that there was no indication of a struggle, and Gaby had apparently not made the slightest effort to defend herself. The coroner found this strange.

So, too, did the inspector. He was wondering whether he was looking for one man or two. Was the murderer of Gaby Goerke the same man who had attacked Gerda Schaefer, Ilse Diederich, Liselotte Goebels and Maryse Lang? Or was it someone who had taken advantage of the publicity to fake a crime in the series?

Ferdinand Sachs swore by everything holy that he had had nothing to do with the murder of Gaby Goerke. He was, he said, incapable of sexual arousal by a girl who was already past puberty. The only thing that excited him was a female child under the age of ten and, even with her, he was capable of nothing more than masturbation.

The inspector would naturally have paid no attention to such a declaration had it not been for the fact that it was supported in the records by the statements of the psychologists and psychiatrists who had examined and treated Sachs at the various times of his arrests. According to what they had said, he was no more capable of sex with a fifteen-year-old girl than he would have been with a fifteen-year-old hippopotamus.

However, it appeared that the murderer of Gaby Goerke had not had sex with her and, if he had not, why had he killed her?

There seemed only one possible answer. If Gaby Goerke had been killed by the Menden strangler and had not been raped by him, the reason might be that she had known his identity. Perhaps she had surprised him attacking another girl in the forest and he had eliminated her because she was a witness who could identify him.

But in that case, what of the victim? Had he eliminated her too?

He could not have because there were no suitable females

missing for that date in Menden. If Gaby had known who he was, she had known it through some other means.

The inspector ordered a careful tracing of every male with whom Gaby was known to have come into contact. What he wanted was a list of all those who stood close to six feet tall, were young and sported a soup-bowl haircut. When the list was completed to the satisfaction of Sergeant Schmidt and handed in, there was only one name on it.

The inspector nearly threw the sergeant out of the office. The name was Ralf Goerke.

The sergeant was, however, quite serious. He had checked very carefully and there was no one else answering to that description whom Gaby had known.

Charging a hard-working young man who had only recently married with the sex murder of his own sister was not something that the inspector was prepared to undertake without material evidence, and discreet efforts were made to obtain a set of Goerke's fingerprints, not an easy matter as he had no criminal record.

This was, however, eventually accomplished, and the police identification experts said that the partial print on the button taken from Gaby's grave was identical to that of Ralf's right thumb.

It was not as much evidence as the inspector would have liked to have, but he suspected that it was all that he was likely to get, and two days after Gaby's funeral her brother Ralf was arrested and charged with the murder.

He began by denying it, but a search of his apartment produced a pair of trousers with a button from the hip pocket missing. Other buttons not missing matched the one in the possession of the police and, confronted with this evidence, Ralf confessed not only to the murder of his sister but to being the Menden Strangler as well.

He was not very clear as to why he had begun raping young girls when he had an equally young, attractive and affectionate wife at home, but he explained Gaby's murder by saying that she had recognized him from the descriptions given by the victims in the press and had tried to persuade him to stop. Fearful that she might expose him, he had strangled her to death. He denied any sexual motive to the crime, and even denied having removed his sister's underpants.

Held under observation for over a year Ralf Goerke was eventually found competent to stand trial, and in September of 1982 was sentenced to ten years' imprisonment. This might seem mild to some, but it was the maximum possible under German juvenile law. Ralf was, after all, only eighteen.

Inspector Fink is keeping his file handy. A juvenile sentenced to ten years in Germany rarely serves as much as half of that so Ralf can expect to be returned to society before he has achieved his twenty-fifth birthday. His wife, dismayed by his extra-marital activities, has divorced him and, after five or six years in prison, Ralf may feel that he is in need of sexual relief.

If so, he knows how to get it.

6

NO RECORD, BUT A GOOD TRY

As series criminals go, Ralf Goerke was not very impressive. Although he may well have attacked more girls than the number with which he was charged, his only real claim to originality lay in the murder and possible sexual molestation of his sister.

Of course, Ralf is still young and, as he will soon be out of prison, there is no telling what prodigies he may perform in the future.

One thing is certain. He forms a part of an old tradition extending back to the initiation of criminal record keeping in Germany. The Germans are a serious, extremely thorough people and some of the longest, most gruesome series of crimes have taken place and are still taking place there. Although the police are also serious, thorough people, not all of these crimes are solved.

In fact, it is not always known that a crime has been committed. Like any modern state, Germany loses track of a great many persons every year. Many of these are young people. The ties of the family having been loosened and the authority of the parents usurped by the civil servants of the state; even children of pre-pubertal age go off to live in communes, join the drug scene, take up prostitution or engage in other activities typical of liberated, unsupervised youth. As they may suspect that their parents will not approve of this concept of freedom, they not infrequently fail to tell them where they are.

Sometimes, they cannot. They are delighting unwillingly the customers of some Middle Eastern or North African brothel in return for room and board or they are dead.

In a society containing substantial numbers of disturbed

persons at liberty, girls and young women wandering about the streets alone are an easy prey and, with apologies to the believers in equality between the sexes, there are few females capable of withstanding the unexpected attack of an insane, adult male, possibly armed, and with every intention of obtaining sexual gratification by any means, murder included.

Even for a full-grown woman, there is little hope of escape or successful defence. How much less then for a child: a small delicately built, ten-year-old girl?

The four-pound hammer caught ten-year-old Ulrike Hellmann only a glancing blow on the back of the head, but the pretty little girl went sprawling, the blood from her split scalp welling into the thick, blonde hair with the cute fringe across the forehead.

Like a spider pouncing on a fly, the bearded man was upon her, rolling her on to her back, jerking her short skirt up around her waist and ripping away her panties. Kneeling, he fumbled with his own clothing.

It was 15 May 1981, a glorious, spring day, and Ulrike had been walking home from school along a little trafficked secondary road outside the city of Mainz, West Germany. The man in the red R4 Renault had passed her, slowed, stopped the car and, jumping out, had come bounding back toward her with the hammer in his hand.

Ulrike had turned and ran, but it had been too late. She had been overtaken and knocked down.

But not out. She was still conscious and she began to fight.

Like most young girls in West Germany, Ulrike had been taught not to resist a rapist. The theory was that it was better to be raped and alive than raped and dead. However, theories were one thing and practice was something else. Panic-stricken, convinced that the man was going to kill her, Ulrike Hellmann fought not so much for her virginity as for her life.

There were, at least, a dozen other girls and women who could have told her that she was quite right. The ones who were still alive, of course. Nine of them were not. Whether those who had died had resisted or not no one could say with certainty, but the three who had survived had. Ulrike was the unlucky thirteenth.

The series was believed to have begun on 17 April 1975, at a place less than thirty miles to the south of where Ulrike Hellmann was flopping like a hooked fish under the body of the rapist. The time had been approximately nine o'clock in the evening and Mrs Lilian Dresch, an attractive dark-haired housewife of twenty-eight, had been waiting at a deserted bus stop in Mannheim-Neckarau, a small, residential community.

A rather slight, unkempt-looking man with a full, black beard and moustache had parked his Volkswagen near the bus stop and got out.

Suspecting nothing, Mrs Dresch had not turned around as he walked behind her.

Suddenly an arm was thrown around her chest, a hand crushed her right breast and the man's other hand, coming over her right shoulder drove the blade of a long, sharp knife into her throat.

By some miracle, the point of the knife struck exactly the hard knot of the larynx and failed to penetrate.

Lilian Dresch let out a piercing scream, kicked backward and managed to tear herself loose. For a few seconds the bearded man and his screaming victim stood facing each other. Then, apparently deciding that the screams were going to attract attention, he turned and ran back to the Volkswagen. By the time that people from the neighbouring houses had arrived he was gone.

Lilian Dresch was taken to the hospital and treated for a minor throat wound. She had escaped, but it would be several years before she could bring herself to wait alone at a bus stop again.

The next victim in this series, although no one at that time knew that it was a series, was less fortunate.

On the evening of 9 June 1975, Monika Sorn, a pretty seventeen-year-old secondary-school student, failed to return to her parents' home in the village of Hemsbach, roughly a dozen miles from Mannheim-Neckarau. As the unexplained absence of a pretty, young girl with no tendency to run wild was logically cause for alarm, her parents immediately notified the police.

Search parties were organized, and Monika's body was

found shortly before midnight of the same day. It was lying in a field near one of the roads leading to the village, the skull crushed by a heavy, blood-smeared stone which lay nearby. Nearly all of her clothing had been torn away, and the autopsy would show that she had been raped but, presumably while unconscious or after death. The sperm recovered from her vagina showed that her rapist belonged to blood group AB, subgroup two. Otherwise, there were no clues as to his identity. The stone was too rough to retain fingerprints.

The usual check of known sex offenders in the area was made, but without results. There were plenty of sex offenders in the area because the courts normally permitted their release after short periods of psychiatric treatment which it was believed had cured them of their abnormal tendencies and converted them into useful members of society. In some cases, the cures had to be repeated and even repeated again, but the pertinent authorities did not become discouraged. With time, modern psychology would succeed even in the most stubborn cases.

As a result of this policy the police were forced to maintain files on a great many sex offenders and it was often fairly easy to determine who had raped whom by reference to the *modus operandi*. Sex psychopaths are creatures of habit and certain elements of their crimes tend to remain constant.

The only conclusion that the police could draw in the case of the murder of Monika Sorn was that, if this was a sex psychopath, it was a new one who was just starting out in the business. There was no recent record in the police files of a local murderer-rapist who beat in his victim's skull with a rock and then raped her while she was dying or already dead.

Although the next murder took place only a little more than three months later, it was not immediately connected to the murder of Monika Sorn because the scene was the village of Elmendingen near Bruchsal, which is approximately as far south of Mannheim as Mainz is to the north.

On 13 September 1975, eleven-year-old Liane Woessner, a vivacious, dark-haired girl, somewhat prematurely developed for her age, set off on her bicycle to visit her aunt in Bruchsal.

When her aunt, who was expecting her, became concerned by the fact that she had not arrived and called her parents over the telephone, it was discovered that she was missing and the police were notified.

The Bruchsal police found Liane Woessner rather quickly. She had only been dead for a few hours. Like Monika Sorn, she lay in a field near a secondary road leading from Elmendingen to Bruchsal and, like Monika Sorn, her skull had been smashed. Not with a stone this time, however, but with what the autopsy report described as a heavy, blunt object; probably a hammer or the back of a hatchet.

However prematurely developed she might have been, Liane had been a virgin and the rapist had had much difficulty in penetrating her, cutting himself in the process and leaving traces of his own blood on her thighs and sex organs. From this and from the semen recovered from her vagina, it was possible to determine that his blood group was AB, subgroup two. It was not an important clue. Many persons have this same blood group.

None the less, it was the only clue that the police recovered. Liane's bicycle was found in the ditch and her murderer had presumably thrown it there, but he had not left any fingerprints on it.

Perhaps because it was his first year, 1975 was an exceptionally busy time for the man who would eventually become known as the Hammer Murderer. His success rate was, however, only fifty per cent as he had not yet developed the deadly efficiency which would characterize his later activities.

The final crime by the Hammer Murderer for 1975 took place three days before Christmas in the charming little town of Weinheim, scarcely more than a village but boasting no less than three large and imposing castles in comparatively good repair, and less than ten miles from Mannheim with which it is connected by an electric inter-urban street-car service.

On the afternoon of the day, seventeen-year-old Susanne Bach, an attractive, dark-haired salesgirl in one of the local stores, was passing through a strip of city park when a man with a beard came up behind her and without warning struck her savagely twice on the head with a heavy hammer.

Susanne was knocked unconscious and fell forward on her face, but there were other pedestrians in the immediate vicinity and the Hammer Murderer ran off without doing anything else.

Susanne was taken to the hospital where she was treated for concussion. Her skull was, fortunately, not fractured, and she recovered with no ill effects other than a compulsive tendency to look over her shoulder whenever she was passing through a public park.

The Hammer Murderer had concluded his first year with two successful rapes and murders and two failures on both counts. It was not a bad beginning, but he may have been discouraged by the failures because it was not until autumn of the following year that another crime occurred which would eventually be attributed to him.

However, a considerable amount of time would pass before anyone realized that a murder had taken place.

Eighteen-year-old Monika Pfeifer was reported missing on 11 October 1976 by her parents, but the police in her hometown of Mainz did not suspect homicide. Rather, they thought her a possible victim of white slavers.

The white slave dealers are quite active in Central Europe and, particularly, West Germany which has a high percentage of attractive girls. Monika was more than attractive. She was beautiful with a stunning figure and long, naturally blonde hair which hung nearly to her waist, precisely the type that would fetch a top price in any North African or Middle Eastern harem or brothel.

The police, therefore, concentrated their investigation on the activities of white slavers in the area, and eventually apprehended several who were given short jail sentences and deported. Although they admitted to having traded mostly in blonde girls, none of them could recall the name Pfeifer, but this was not thought strange as they had not been interested in the girls' names in any case. Monika remained missing without trace.

Until 6 January 1977, at least. On the afternoon of that date, she was literally fished out of the River Rhine.

Although the famous Rhine now is and has been for some time little more than an open industrial sewer, optimistic Germans still attempt to fish its murky depths. One of these optimists sitting on the muddy banks of the river to the west of Mainz thought that he had hooked the biggest catfish in Europe, but it was Monika. The fish hooks had become tangled in her hair, which was about all there was to become tangled in as her body was completely naked.

Considering that she had spent the entire winter in the river, the body was in remarkably good condition and her parents had no difficulty in identifying her. The autopsy showed that her skull had been crushed with a heavy object, presumably a hammer, at about the same time that she had disappeared, and there was reason to believe that she had been raped. Although unusual for a beautiful, eighteen-year-old West German girl, Monika had been a virgin and her hymen had been ruptured either before or after death.

Coincidentally, while this autopsy was being carried out on 7 January, one day after the discovery of the body, a twenty-two-year old university student in Mainz was having a frightening experience.

It was approximately four o'clock on that afternoon and Barbara Kiel, dark, pretty and twenty-two years of age, had left the university, crossed the university parking lot and was walking down a narrow, deserted road with a stone wall along one side.

Presently, a Volkswagen came up behind her and deliberately attempted to crush her against the stone wall.

The man behind the windscreen and the sole occupant of the car had a full, black beard and moustache and looked, she thought, rather young. She did not, however, have much time to look at him as the bumper of the car broke both her legs and knocked her to the ground.

A girl with considerable presence of mind, Barbara Kiel huddled up to the base of the wall as close as she could. This prevented the driver from running over her and, after a few frustrated attempts, he gave up and drove away.

Barbara Kiel was eventually found by passers-by and taken to the hospital where she recovered from her injuries. Although she did not know it, she enjoyed an enviable distinction. She was the last-known victim that the Hammer Murderer failed to kill.

He did not fail on 28 March 1977, when he attacked one of Barbara's fellow students at the University of Mainz, twenty-three-year-old Sylvia Lauterbach, a lovely, dark-haired girl who had been walking along a path through the fields in the direction of the village of Bretzenheim where she planned to visit a friend.

Her corpse was found the following morning a dozen yards from the field path. She had been stripped naked with the exception of her stockings and shoes, raped, and her head had been crushed by multiple blows of what was believed to be a heavy hammer.

There was less questions this time that the murder weapon had been a hammer, for it had been driven far enough into the girl's head to leave a print of its shape. The police laboratory in Mainz estimated it to be a four-pound hammer of a type used in heavy metalwork and masonry. Four short dark hairs were found under Sylvia's fingernails, and the laboratory said that these came from a man's beard. Otherwise, they found nothing.

Like all of the preceding cases, the murder of Sylvia Lauterbach remained unsolved for lack of possible leads to investigate. Her circle of social and other contacts was routinely investigated, but produced no plausible suspect.

The police had not thought it would. Most murders are committed by persons known to the victim and so are most rapes, but, if the two are combined, it is more frequently a stranger who has chosen the victim because of personal attraction or convenience.

Moreover, when such a sexually motivated murder takes place it is rarely an isolated incident. The abnormality which led to one rape and murder will lead to others, and many elements of each succeeding case will remain identical as they are essential to the satisfaction of the murderer's emotional needs.

It was, therefore, the Mainz police Criminal Investigations

Department which first realized that a series was underway and took steps to assemble the files on unsolved sex murders or attempted murders in the southern half of Germany.

'Between the beginning of October last year and the end of March this year, we have had three cases of attacks on young women in the Mainz area,' said Inspector Walter Herschel, chief of the Mainz homicide squad, speaking to his plump, blond, and rather expressionless assistant, Detective-Sergeant Mark Schultz. 'The Kiel case is a little different than the other two, but it's the same sort of vicious attack. I think it's clear that what we have here is a series. Tell the records section I want a computer printout on all similar *modus operandi* in the south of the country for the past three years.'

A few years earlier, this would have represented a monumental task for the records section, but, for the computer, it was only a matter of hours before it came up with the files of Monika Sorn, Liane Woessner, Susanne Bach and, because of the Volkswagen and beard in the Barbara Kiel case, Lilian Dresch.

'Uh-huh. Just what I thought,' said the inspector, adjusting his thick, heavy body in the chair and squinting with small, sharp, deep-set eyes at the computer printout. 'It's a series. Is this all?'

'All the unsolveds,' said the sergeant. 'Records has the computer still searching for parallel cases where the identity of the murderer or attempted murderer is known. They needn't have all been unsolved.'

'Let's hope they haven't,' said the Inspector. 'Otherwise, all we can do is wait for him to kill the next one.'

It was not a long wait. The computer was unsuccessful in turning up a valid suspect and on 29 April 1977, twenty-one-year-old Marie-Therese Majer was raped and murdered. She had been walking along a country road near Schriesheim, a village outside the town of Heidelberg and almost equidistant from Weinheim and Mannheim. Like her fellow victims, she had been stripped naked, forcibly raped, and her skull had been smashed in with a heavy hammer, although not in that order.

83

It was the Hammer Murderer's invariable custom to begin by smashing in his victim's skull. Only when the girl was unconscious or dead did he proceed to removing her clothing and raping her. Whether his earlier attempts had shown that girls were more easily stripped and raped if they were unconscious or dead or whether he was incapable of sex with a living, conscious victim was not known.

The inspector pounced on the Marie-Therese Majer case, which he saw as an opportunity to end the bloody career of the Hammer Murderer before he claimed still more victims. A huge detachment of plain-clothes officers under the command of Sergeant Schultz was rushed to Schriesheim with orders to leave no stone unturned in the effort to uncover any possible clue to the identity of the murderer and reinforcements arrived from Heidelberg, Mannheim and Weinheim.

The operation was a total failure. As usual, the only traces of his presence which the Hammer Murderer had left behind were the marks of the deadly hammer on the head of the victim and his semen in her vagina. It showed that he had blood group AB, subgroup two, but the police already knew that.

Copies of all the records of the known or suspected cases, the autopsy reports where pertinent, statements of survivors, and the results of the investigations undertaken in each case had now been assembled in Inspector Herschel's office where they were being studied to see whether something which had failed to provide a clue in one case might not serve to provide a clue in another. So far, all that had been determined was that there was a near certainty that all of the cases were the work of one man, that he was young, wore a dark beard and moustache, was rather slightly built and drove a Volkswagen, either dark grey or blue. He never said a word or made a sound, but struck immediately and without warning.

Once again, the efforts of the investigators failed to provide a lead which could be followed up, and the inspector had no recourse but to sit back and wait for the next case. This time it was going to be a long wait.

On 21 April 1979, just eight days short of two years after the death of Marie-Therese Majer, fifteen-year-old Gudrun

84

Thomé, a secondary-school pupil who lived with her parents in the village of Rot near Heidelberg, disappeared without a trace. As Gudrun was very pretty and far from unapproachable, the local police suspected white slavers or an affair, possibly with an older man, but when the report of the disappearance arrived at the office of Inspector Herschel who now routinely received all reports of murdered or missing females, his first thought was of the dormant Hammer Murderer and he sent Sergeant Schultz down to Heidelberg to work in association with the Heidelberg criminal police.

A massive search of the area was undertaken with particular attention paid to the fields alongside the less heavily trafficked roads. Gudrun was found lying in one of them less than a mile from her home village.

The girl had fought hard for her life. There were traces of skin and beard hairs under her fingernails, and her left index finger was broken. She was badly bruised about the chest and shoulders and, for the first time, one of the Hammer Murderer's victims showed the typical black bruise marks on the insides of the thighs where she had clamped her legs over the rapist's hip bones in a vain attempt to prevent penetration. The Hammer Murderer could, it seemed, have sex with a living, conscious victim.

Gudrun had been alive and conscious when she was raped, a far from pleasant experience, because although she had not been a virgin, the rapist had been remarkably brutal. Her suffering had, however, apparently not lasted long as she had been quickly killed with blows to the head from the now hideously familiar hammer. As usual, the murderer had left no clue to his identity other than a few hairs from his beard and his semen in the vagina of the victim. It was that of a man with blood group AB, subgroup two.

Nine days later, a second, almost identical report landed on Inspector Herschel's desk. This time the victim was sixteen-year-old Ellen Abel, who came from the city of Saarbruecken nearly a hundred miles to the west of Mannheim.

Ellen had set out to hitchhike to a local discotheque on that evening and, as her parents had not expected her to come home very early, it was the following day before they became alarmed and called the police.

Like Gudrun, Ellen was found lying in a field near a secondary road, her clothing torn from her body, her legs still spread wide in the classic sprawl of the rape victim, and her head crushed with blows from the hammer. Unlike Gudrun, she had been dead at the time that she was raped. There were no bruise marks on the insides of the thighs.

The series had resumed with a vengeance and Inspector Herschel, frustrated and desperate over the continuing deluge of murders of girls and young women which he found himself powerless to prevent, braced for a bad year, but, following the murder of Ellen Abel, the attacks came to an abrupt halt. No new reports were received.

'Maybe he's dead,' said the inspector, having a quiet, semi-official lunch with his assistant on New Year's Day of 1980 in an inexpensive tavern not far from police headquarters. 'It's been eight months now. Maybe he's been run over by a truck.'

'It was a lot longer stretch between Majer and Thomé,' said the sergeant with callous disregard for his superior's feelings. 'I think he's just gone somewhere else. Saarbruecken was a good deal further away than any of the others. I think he's moved out of the area.'

'I hope he's moved out of this world,' said the inspector.

Neither the sergeant's theories nor the inspector's hopes were to be confirmed. By 4 June 1980 the Hammer Murderer was back, crushing the skull of twenty-year-old Marie-Elsa Scholte in a field near the town of Ludwigshafen on the west bank of the River Rhine across from Mannheim. After having crushed her skull with his hammer, he rather carefully removed her clothing and raped her. There were some indications at the autopsy that he had undertaken certain manipulations of the corpse, apparently for the purpose of stimulating himself.

'He's becoming jaded,' said the inspector. 'It's no longer enough for him to simply murder and rape the girl, he has to have additional stimulation. The next thing he'll begin torturing them before he kills them. My God! Where will he strike next?'

'Well, wherever it is, it won't be Ludwigshafen,' said the sergeant confidently. The Hammer Murderer had never struck twice consecutively at the same location.

On 23 February 1981, less than a year later, the Hammer Murderer killed sixteen-year-old Gabriella Bohn. In Ludwigshafen.

The girl had been, like so many of the other victims, a high-school student, pretty, dark-haired and a virgin. She had been raped after death and she had not put up any resistance, but she had suspected what was coming and had attempted to flee. The marks of her running feet and those of her deadly pursuer's were clear in the earth. They ended in a great splotch of blood where the back of the girl's head had split open under the impact of the hammer blow.

The murderer had then dragged her on another half-dozen yards before removing her clothing and satisfying his sexual needs.

The police learned something new about the hammer murderer. He wore size eight and a half, B-width shoes.

The inspector was surprised and grateful to learn even that much. Up to now the Hammer Murderer had been astonishingly lucky. Not once in the long series of his crimes had he suffered the misfortune of being interrupted by passers-by: a truly remarkable circumstance in heavily populated West Germany where there is nearly always some traffic even on the most isolated roads.

'Sooner or later though, his luck has got to change,' said the inspector grimly. 'Sooner or later, someone is going to come by when he's actually attacking the girl.'

By sheer coincidence, on that day of 15 May 1981, and at almost the precise time that the inspector was voicing his opinion concerning the luck of the Hammer Murderer, less than three miles away little Ulrike Hellmann was fighting like a baby tiger for her life. Not a particularly large or strong girl, she would have already been dead had the Hammer Murderer not decided that raping her alive would prove more exciting.

He had, therefore, forced the struggling girl's legs apart, and was engaged in the difficult process of achieving penetration of such a young girl when thirty-four-year-old Karl Lenk came riding down the road on his bicycle. He saw the parked Renault R4 and the couple lying on the ground and, for a moment, he thought that they were simply making love.

Then Ulrike saw him and began to scream at the top of her voice. Startled, Lenk took a closer look, saw that the naked girl lying under the bearded man was no more than a child and leaped off his bicycle to run shouting in the direction of the rapist.

The Hammer Murderer scrambled to his feet, caught up the hammer which lay on the ground nearby and, running to the Renault, climbed in and roared away.

Lenk ran forward and knelt beside the shaking, naked, but uninjured girl. 'AL-204, AL-204,' whispered Ulrike with trembling lips.

'That's right,' said Karl Lenk who had also looked. 'That's his licence number. AL-204.'

The Hammer Murderer's luck had finally changed.

Not longer thereafter, Sergeant Schultz, flanked by two detectives with their machine pistols in their hands, walked past a red Renault R4 parked at the edge of a little meadow outside the town of Alzey, twenty miles to the south of Mainz, to where a young, bearded man was lying on the grass reading a book.

'Can I help you?' said the young man pleasantly, looking up from his book.

'I think so,' said Sergeant Schultz. 'I hereby arrest you on charges of the attempted rape and murder of Ulrike Hellman on 15 May 1981. You are cautioned that any statement you make will be taken down in writing and may be used against you. Do you have anything to say?'

Twenty-seven-year-old Bernd Bopp, a teacher at the secondary school in Alzey, had nothing to say, but a search of his car turned up the famous four-pound hammer in the trunk. The police laboratory would later find traces of at least four different blood groups on it.

Taken to police headquarters and formally identified by

both Ulrike Hellmann and Karl Lenk, Bopp became cooperative and confessed to the unsuccessful attacks on Lilian Dresch, Susanne Bach, Barbara Kiel and the murder of Sylvia Lauterbach. He did not deny the other murders, but said that, although he was certain that he had killed a large number of girls, he could not remember the precise places or circumstances of the crimes. He had, in any case, never known the names of any of his victims until they were published in the newspapers.

As is usual in such cases, Bopp was sent for psychiatric observation and evaluation while awaiting his trial. According to the psychologists, the motive for his crimes was unrequitted love. He had been hopelessly in love with Mechthild Karl, the twenty-three-year-old daughter of his German teacher at the time that he had been in school, but had never worked up the nerve to ask her to have sex with him. Instead, he had read German classical authors with her. Mechthild had found this boring and had transferred her interest to other, less literary-inclined suitors. Bopp had responded by beginning to rape and murder women and girls. Most of them had borne a certain resemblance to Mechthild.

At his trial, Bernd Bopp was unable to offer even as much explanation for his crimes as had the psychologists, but he did assure the court that, if he were released from prison, even after twenty years, he felt certain he would resume them. He had, he said, made certain preparations.

And indeed he had. During the course of the search of Bopp's apartment, a neat notebook entitled 'Diary of Death' had been found. It contained the names and addresses of 139 girls between the ages of eleven and twenty which Bopp had assembled, mainly from magazines carrying classified advertisements for friendship contacts and pen pals.

On 8 October 1981 Bernd Bopp was sentenced to life imprisonment.

The average time served on a life sentence in Germany is seven years.

The police do not like to think about what may happen if Bernd Bopp gets out of prison in seven years.

7

THE DEVIL IN MR JONES

Things have changed a good deal in Germany since the end of the war, and it would appear that they have in England too. Instead of the once popular 'muddling through', the British murderer now often goes in for careful planning, schedules, complex alibis and the confounding of police nostrils through the generous use of red herrings, where still commercially available.

However, England does not lack men who are capable and prepared to meet these challenges and, sometimes, when they do, the results are unexpected and spectacular.

They were certainly unexpected for thirty-four-year-old Mary Jones when, on the afternoon of 15 November 1978, a grey and chilly day, she found herself lying curled up in a large, wicker trunk, her hands bound tightly with stout cord, and her skirt pushed up to expose the bare thighs above her stocking tops and, actually, a good deal more as she had only a short time previously removed her underwear.

It was only when the heavy stones were being tucked into the corners of the trunk around her body that she began to have an inkling of what was in store for her.

By then it was too late to do anything more than appeal with her eyes. She could not move. She could not scream for the handkerchief bound over her mouth suppressed everything except smothered moans and mumbling and, in any case, there was no one to hear.

Even then, she still had not grasped the full horror of the situation. It was a silly joke. It had to be. They had just finished making love. You couldn't make love to someone and then drown them like a cat. It had been such wonderful love-making too. It was years since she had experienced so much pleasure from the sex act.

But she was agonizingly conscious of the nearby river and the strange, bearded face bending over her was without trace of mercy. A wave of pure terror swept through her mind with such force that she nearly fainted. She knew that she was going to die, and she knew what that death would be. It would be hideous. It would be soon.

The cold light of the November afternoon was abruptly blotted out as the wicker lid of the trunk clapped shut and the wooden pins which held it slid into place.

There was jolting and a sensation of movement as the trunk was lifted and dragged over the muddy gravel of the bank of the little river a few miles from the outskirts of the city of Manchester.

Although the top of the trunk was closed and fastened, it was not completely dark inside. Light was coming through a million tiny openings in the wickerwork. It was not only light which could pass through those little holes. So, too, would water.

She heard the man grunt as he gave a final effort and sent the trunk tumbling over the edge of the nearly perpendicular bank.

There was a terrible splash and the river water rushed in through all the little holes in the wickerwork. It was muddy and icy cold and not very deep. If she could have stood up, her head would have been above the surface of the water.

But she could not stand up because she was in the closed trunk, and she could not get out because her hands were tied and the weight of the stones had carried the trunk straight to the bottom.

Under the unreasoning impulse for self-preservation which refuses to cease hoping long after there is no hope, she extended her own suffering by holding her breath.

It could not, of course, last very long and, even as the current began bumping the trunk along the bottom downstream, her tortured lungs gave way and the cold, muddy water rushed into her mouth and nostrils, constricting her throat so that neither water nor air could enter. There was pain, fear, a feeling of suffocation and then nothingness.

That Wednesday evening, when Mary Jones did not return

to her cosy cottage on the outskirts of Liverpool, some thirty miles to the west of Manchester, her husband, a clean-shaven, handsome man who did not look his thirty-five years, spent the evening telephoning her friends and relatives. No one knew where she was and, on the following morning, Henry Jones called the Liverpool police. His wife, he said, was missing.

A detective from the Department of Missing Persons came out and took a statement from Jones. There was not very much to report. Mary and Henry had met at the end of 1968, shortly after Henry had been made office manager of the export-import firm for which he worked, and they had married in May of 1969. Prior to the marriage, Mary had been a secretary in another export-import firm, but she had stopped working once she was married.

The cottage in which they lived was actually Mary's, as she had inherited it from her first husband who had died a number of years earlier. According to Jones, the couple had neither financial nor domestic problems and he knew of no reason why his wife might have disappeared.

The detective, who did nothing else but work on such cases, asked rather bluntly whether Mrs Jones had had any male friends. Jones turned brick-red with irritation and embarrassment, replied stiffly that it was out of the question and then, after a moment's hesitation, said rather shamefacedly that in looking through his wife's address book for possible people to call concerning her whereabouts, he had come across the name of Tony Saunders. He did not believe for a moment that his wife had been engaged in an extra-marital affair, but he did not know any Tony Saunders and Mary had never mentioned the name to him.

The detective asked to see the address book and was given it. The name was written in long hand on the page reserved for names beginning with S, but there was neither address nor telephone number.

The detective inquired about Henry Jones's working hours and then took his departure. He did not, however, leave the area, but called on several of the neighbours. He was interested in learning if Mrs Jones had been, perhaps, receiving a male visitor in the afternoon while her husband was at work.

Almost by chance because he had no real reason to do so, he mentioned the name of Saunders and, to his surprise, one of the ladies immediately recognized the name.

A young man, she said, wearing a neatly trimmed beard and glasses had called at her house the preceding week. He had introduced himself as Tony Saunders from Brown & Company, and he had, obviously, wanted to sell her something. What it was she did not know, because she had said that she was not interested before finding out what it was and had closed the door in his face.

The detective went back to some of the other houses that he had already called on and found that Saunders had been at two of them. At one he had been turned away, but at the other he had received more of a welcome. He had not, however, made a sale as the housewife said that she could not make out very clearly what he was selling. She had found him quite personable and had given him a cup of tea.

The detective went back to headquarters and made up a report of the missing-person case of Mary Jones in which he said that there was some reason to believe that the woman had gone off with a door-to-door salesman named Tony Saunders.

Although Henry Jones had said that their married life was completely satisfactory, Mary might have had different ideas. They had been married for ten years, they had no children and women sometimes became more bored with their lives than their husbands realized.

Mr Jones called several times during the following days to ask what progress was being made in locating his wife and was assured that they were working on it. As a matter of fact, they were. One of the very junior officers in the Missing Persons Department had been sent around to check all of the firms named Brown & Company, of which there were several, to see whether any of them employed a salesman named Tony Saunders. The police could not, of course, bring Mrs Jones back to her husband against her will, but they could at least reassure him that she had come to no harm and was in good hands so to speak.

By the following Monday, 20 November, the detective was still going around to the companies with no success to report. However on that morning, a twenty-eight-year-old labourer, attached to the Department of Roads and Bridges, discovered the wicker trunk grounded on a gravel bar some four miles downstream from the point where it had entered the river.

The worker was wearing a raincoat and rubber boots because the weather had taken a turn for the worse and a mixture of rain and sleet had been falling since early that morning. He was, therefore, well equipped to wade into the stream and investigate what might be inside the trunk and he did so.

Not normally a very excitable young man, he was so startled by his discovery that he staggered backwards, stepped into a hole and was swept downstream himself for some distance.

Regaining his feet, he scrambled out of the river and ran as hard as he could go, dripping wet, to the nearest village where he telephoned the police.

A detachment was immediately sent out from Manchester, and the trunk was lifted out of the river and brought to the Manchester police morgue. There it was quickly determined that the dead woman inside was Mrs Mary Jones, the murderer having considerately dropped her handbag containing her driver's licence and other papers into the trunk with her. As her address was also on the driver's licence, it was only a matter of a few minutes before the Missing Persons Department in Liverpool knew that one of their cases had been solved.

Solved for the Missing Persons Department, at least, but not for the Liverpool homicide squad who were faced with the fact that Mary Jones had obviously been murdered; drowned like a cat in the wicker trunk with a number of heavy stones tossed in to weight it down. Her body was therefore transferred to the Liverpool police morgue, and after being positively identified by her husband, the investigation started.

Like many homicide investigations, it began with the autopsy. This carried out by an assistant medical examiner from the Liverpool Coroner's Office, a comparatively young man with a round, serious face and neatly parted dark blond hair.

According to his report, the woman had been dead for approximately five days and in the water for the same length of time. The water being cold, the corpse was well preserved.

The immediate cause of death had been drowning, and Mrs Jones had known that she was going to drown and had been conscious at the time because she had ruptured a number of minor blood vessels in attempting to hold her breath.

There were no indications of violence on the body, although the cords binding the wrists had cut deeply into the flesh as a result of her struggles to free herself. There were a few minor scrapes on the knees, hips and buttocks, which were probably the result of her desperate movements within the trunk as she was drowning.

The examination of the genitals indicated that Mrs Jones had engaged in sexual intercourse, with a man whose blood group was O, very shortly before her death. Ejaculation had taken place at maximum penetration, and Mrs Jones's participation in the sex act had been enthusiastic for her vagina had been flooded with her own lubricating secretions.

The doctor noted that neither the bindings on the hands nor the gag had been applied in a deliberately painful manner, and that all of the cuts on the wrists appeared to be due to her own struggles and, from this, he concluded that Mrs Jones had submitted voluntarily to being bound and gagged. It had been, he suggested, a part of the sexual activities. The murderer had bound and gagged his victim in what she had believed was no more than a form of sex play, had engaged in intercourse with her, and had then drowned the helpless woman like some unwanted animal thrown into a pond in a sack with a stone in it.

The detective-inspector who had taken charge of the case immediately called for a search of the records. A man who would commit such a cruel and cold-blooded murder would, in his opinion, have to be as mad as a hatter, and compulsive killers of that type normally held to the same *modus operandi* in all of their crimes.

His assistant, a rather slight, sandy-haired, sergeant of

detectives, with the quick movements and something of the appearance of a fox, had the records checked and reported that there was no record of any such crime ever having taken place in England since the time that the police had begun keeping records.

This answer did not please the inspector at all. It presumably meant that some madman was only now just beginning his career. There was no telling how many other women he might murder before he was apprehended.

Although the medical experts agreed that the crime was probably the work of a seriously unbalanced person because it was hard to conceive of a man in his right mind callously drowning a young and attractive woman with whom he had just had intercourse, it was also possible that this was exactly what the murderer had wanted the police to think.

And because this possibility had to be considered, the inspector requested the Department of Missing Persons to send over a report on their investigations into the affair. He had spoken with Henry Jones personally at the time that the identification of the body was made, and he was aware that Jones had turned in a missing-person report on the day following his wife's disappearance.

The file was brought promptly to the inspector's office, and within a half-hour most of the Liverpool police were engaged in an active hunt for Tony Saunders.

The ones who were not were out canvassing the houses around the cottage where the Joneses lived to obtain as many witness sightings and descriptions of the mysterious salesman as they could assemble.

This operation was not particularly fruitful, and only one other house was found where Saunders had called. All of the descriptions, however, tallied closely. Saunders was a tall, well-built young man with a full beard and moustache and black, horn-rimmed glasses. He was neatly, but a little flashily dressed in a slightly loud checked suit with a regimental tie of some kind, and he was well spoken, although his voice was rather low and hoarse as if he had a sore throat.

Mrs Jones's address book had also been obtained from her husband and brought to police headquarters where it had been carefully studied. Significantly, the name Tony Saunders was the only one in the book which did not carry an address or a telephone number. It was possible that Mrs Jones had never known where her murderer lived.

It was also possible that she had not known his real name. It seemed scarcely probable that the man would have gone around from door-to-door, posing as a salesman, and giving his right name. Unless, of course, he really was a salesman, but that the inspector did not think. At none of the houses where he had called, not even the one where he had been invited in for a cup of tea, had he really tried seriously to make a sale or even revealed what he was selling. The salesman act was, in all probability, no more than a cover-up.

None the less, the inspector, a square-faced, square-bodied man with a somewhat florid complexion and a prominent jaw, was inclined to be optimistic. If the killer had been going from door to door in the area around the Jones's house, he had very probably been doing the same thing elsewhere and, if he had seen enough people, there was always a good chance that he had let slip something which would make it possible for the police to trace his identity.

An appeal was, therefore, run in the newspapers requesting housewives who had received calls from a door-to-door salesman named Tony Saunders to report to the police. The inspector was anticipating dozens of calls.

There was not a single one.

Puzzled, the inspector sent his men out to make spot checks in the various residential neighbourhoods. As it was possible that Saunders had used a different name in other places, they were equipped with what the witnesses said were excellent police sketches of the suspect made from the descriptions of the housewives on whom he had called.

One door-to-door salesman with a full beard and glasses was located. He was twenty-eight-year-old Thomas Henley and he had a police record, having served eight months of a fourteen-month sentence for assaulting a teenage girl in a park six years earlier. It had never been entirely clear what Henley had had in mind when he assaulted the girl and he, himself, was not very helpful, saying merely that the girl had laughed at him. He had ripped off most of her clothing, but had not made any actual attempt to rape her.

Taken into custody and placed under interrogation, he consistently denied any connection with the murder and insisted that he had never been in the Lodge Road area, the district where the Jones's house was located, in his life.

Placed in a line-up of men of similar appearance with beards and glasses, he was picked out by two of the housewives on whom the mysterious Tony Saunders had called, but the other witnesses failed to identify him and picked other men in the line-up who were, of course, innocent.

The results were inconclusive, but the interrogation of Thomas Henley continued and so, too, did the search for Tony Saunders. It was possible that Henley was Tony Saunders, but so far there was no real evidence of it.

In the meantime, other routine lines of investigation were being undertaken. Efforts were made to locate the point at which the body had entered the water in the trunk and Mrs Jones's relatives and close female friends were being questioned to see if she had ever mentioned involvement with a man other than her husband.

Actually, both of these not very promising leads produced more useful information than what had been considered the very solid clue of Tony Saunders's name in Mary Jones's address book and his calls on other housewives.

Tests made with the wicker trunk containing a sandbag of the same weight as Mrs Jones were so successful that the police were able to pinpoint within a half mile the point along the river where the trunk had entered the water, and a subsequent search soon located the scene of the crime. A few short pieces of the same cord with which Mrs Jones's hands had been tied were found, and there were marks in the mud and gravel where the trunk had been pushed and dragged to the bank of the river. In a clump of brush behind a large tree, a pair of knickers which Henry Jones identified as being similar to those owned by his wife, were found. They were not torn or stretched, but had been deliberately removed, possibly by Mrs Jones herself.

However, that was all. There were traces of tire marks

where a car had pulled off the road near the scene of the crime, but the rain had washed them out to the point where they were of little value for purposes of identification and, in any case, there was no evidence that they were connected with the murder.

The scene of the crime had been successfully located, but had not provided the investigators with anything valuable. Mrs Jones's conversations and confidences with her friends were to prove rather more useful.

Surprisingly, the information obtained here tended to lead the investigation off in a totally different direction. As early as 1975 Mrs Jones had begun to dye her hair, make more extensive use of cosmetics and dress more attractively. She had told her friends or, at least, some of them, that she was doing this because her husband was having an affair with a younger woman and she hoped to win him back. He had, it seemed, asked for a divorce, but she had refused.

To the relief of the police, this put the case in a more familiar frame. A man in his middle thirties, married ten years and probably a bit jaded with married life, becoming involved with a younger woman, asking for a divorce and being refused was classic. Such situations frequently ended in murder, particularly if the husband enjoyed a good position and could not afford a scandal.

If this information were true, then the inspector thought that his case was more or less solved. He knew who the murderer was. It was Henry Jones. However, whether he would be able to assemble sufficient evidence to bring him to justice was another matter. Jones had apparently gone about the murder in a vexingly devious manner. He had not done it himself, but had hired the mysterious Tony Saunders to do his dirty work for him.

The first thing, however, was to determine whether Jones had actually been having an affair or whether it was merely a figment of his wife's imagination. If what she said was true, then the affair would have begun when Jones came into contact with some young woman during the summer of 1975.

Although the investigations had to be carried out as discreetly as possible because there was no way of knowing whether innocent persons might be involved, it very quickly produced evidence that Henry Jones had, indeed, been having a very passionate affair and with, for him, an extremely important person.

Her name was Mildred Masters, and she was none other than the only child of the owner of the company for which Jones worked.

The implications were obvious. Jones was in a position to become, not an employee, but an owner of the company and to receive, thrown into the bargain, a lovely, twenty-two-year-old substitute for his now slightly faded wife of ten years. It would take a firm character to resist such temptation and Jones apparently did not have one.

He had asked for a divorce and had been refused. Mary Jones must have appeared to him as the sole, unreasonable obstacle to his happiness. From that conclusion it was only a step to the decision to get rid of her and he had done so, hiring the elusive Tony Saunders to seduce Mary and then murder her.

Certain as he was over what had happened, the inspector could not see how he was going to prove it. Saunders, whose name was almost certainly not Saunders, would have taken the payment for his deed and departed long since. He could well have left England by now, but it would not even have been necessary. Without knowing his name or any details concerning his person, there was no way in the world that he could be traced. There are a great many young men with beards and glasses in England.

The only possibility was if witnesses could be found who had seen Saunders and Jones together. There would have had to be some contact between the two men to arrange the details of the murder and hand over the money if nothing else.

Thomas Henley was still in custody and there was, of course, the possibility that he was Jones's hired killer. He continued, however, to deny all connection with the case and the questioning had not produced any flaws in his statements. Eventually the inspector would be forced to release him. There was no physical evidence to connect him with either Henry or Mary Jones.

It was decided, therefore, to concentrate the investigation on Jones's contacts and movements within the two or three months preceding the murder in the hope of coming across a young man with a beard who wore glasses and, possibly, sometimes called himself Tony Saunders.

While efforts in this direction were still proceeding, but without, as yet, any results, an investigator came up with the first piece of evidence tending to establish proof of Jones's guilt, although, perhaps, insufficient to obtain an indictment.

Going through Mary Jones's address book for the dozenth time, it occurred to him that the entry of the name Tony Saunders was not quite the same as the other long-hand entries. The lines of the script were not straight, smooth slashes of the pen, but slightly rough and irregular.

Taking the book to the police laboratory, he showed it to one of the handwriting experts and asked if the handwriting for the entry Tony Saunders was identical to that of the handwriting for the other entries.

The expert barely glanced at the book and immediately said that it was not the same. The name Tony Saunders had been written in imitation of the other entries in the book, but it was not identical.

It was not very difficult to obtain samples of Henry Jones's writing and, although the experts could not be completely certain, they were of the opinion that it was Jones who had written the name of Tony Saunders into his wife's address book.

There was now little question in anyone's mind but that Henry Jones was the murderer of his wife. There was also, however, little question in anyone's mind but that he was probably going to get away with it. His contacts with Tony Saunders had been so well covered that it was impossible to trace them.

The inspector, who had been holding back a number of details concerning the case from the press, gave up, suspended the operation, and made public what was known of the matter, including the actual scene of the crime which had never before been revealed.

The round-up story on the case appeared in the Manchester newspapers and almost immediately a sixty-eight-year-old man telephoned the police. He had, he said, information which he thought might be of interest to them.

It was indeed. The man had been passing near the scene of the crime on the afternoon of 15 November and had seen a small delivery truck parked near the river. He had not seen any persons, but he had thought that it was strange that a delivery truck for an export-import company should be parked in such a place and at such a time. He had remembered the name of the company printed on the side of the truck. It was the company for which Henry Jones worked!

The inspector did not know whether even this was going to be enough or not, but it certainly called for further action, and Henry Jones was taken into custody while a group of experts from the police laboratory, armed with a search warrant, went over his house in the hopes of finding something that might be connected to the crime.

They did not and they did not find any trace of the crime in the pick-up truck which Jones normally drove.

Making their report to the inspector in his office, the technicians said that the only thing that they had found that was in any way unusual was a number of theatrical costumes apparently belonging to Jones.

The inspector replied absently that they already knew that Jones was interested in amateur theatricals and had been taking parts in plays since he was a child. He apparently enjoyed running around with false whiskers and a wig.

Suddenly, the inspector stopped speaking and for several minutes there was a dead silence in the office.

Then, someone said something about it being impossible, but it was not impossible and it occurred to them all at one and the same time.

They had found Tony Saunders.

Jones began by denying that he had disguised himself with a beard, glasses and unusual clothing to go around and present himself to the neighbours as Tony Saunders from Brown & Company, thus setting up a fictitious murderer for his wife. In the end, however, he broke down and confessed.

He had, he said, been in an impossible position. He was in love with Mildred and his entire future depended upon being able to marry her. Mary would, however, not consider a divorce. There was no other solution; he had to get rid of her.

He had always been fond of amateur theatricals and dressing up so that the idea of establishing a false identity for murder came to him naturally. Early in October he had bought the glasses, a false beard and moustache and the suit without telling Mary anything about it. He had then come to ring his own doorbell and play the part of a door-to-door salesman. If Mary failed to recognize him, no one else would either, he thought.

Mary did not recognize him and was astonished when he pulled off his beard to reveal his true identity. Both he and she had found the situation stimulating and they had made love passionately.

Over the next month, further passionate love-making had taken place, always with Henry in disguise, and he had, without her knowledge, began making calls on the neighbours so as to establish the false identity. He had even told Mary to call him Tony Saunders and she had done so.

On the day of the murder he had slipped away from his work in the company van and had gone home after donning his disguise. Mary had been delighted to see her lover, Tony Saunders, and he had proposed making love in the open as an added element of excitement.

Mary had enthusiastically agreed, and they had driven to the river with the wicker trunk in the back of the van. Mary had not even noticed it.

Nor had she thought it strange that he bound and gagged her prior to intercourse. They had often practised bondage and simulated sadism in their previous relations.

Mary had found the location outdoors, the tying and gagging and the disguised appearance of her husband highly stimulating, and she had had multiple orgasms.

Then it was time to die.

On 26 October 1979 it was time for sentencing. Good actor but bad husband Henry Jones was sent to prison for life.

8

JAILED TEN YEARS FOR
EXCEEDING
THE SPEED LIMIT!

Henry Jones was, perhaps, unfortunate in being British. In some other countries justice would have been less stern. It would have been reasoned that Henry was in a position of stress, that he was not in complete possession of his faculties, possibly that he had had an unhappy childhood and that his siblings had received sweets from the mother when he had received none. In the end, he would have been given ten years and a scolding, meaning that he would be out and ready to remarry in five, a happy prospect for the true crime writer, if not necessarily for the future spouse and/or spouses.

However, this rigour in sentencing does not extend to all parts of the Commonwealth and less than a year following Henry Jones's lethal game of charades, another husband was to find a more understanding jury.

Of course, he was not a simple office manager. He was very wealthy.

As a general rule, very wealthy persons tend to occupy luxury mansions with extensive grounds and, as their wives can rarely be persuaded to do the cooking, the house work and take care of the garden single-handed, they employ large staffs of servants for these purposes.

This was the case with Mr Nigel Kearns, a thirty-four-year-old foreign-exchange dealer who had dealt so nimbly that he was generally conceded to be the richest man in all Adelaide, no mean distinction in a city now nearing a population of a million residents.

If Nigel Kearns was successful financially, he was even more so socially and matrimonially, being one of the brighter stars in the Adelaide social firmament and his wife none other than the dazzlingly beautiful Pamela who had been elected Miss Australia at the age of thirteen, had repeated the feat at age nineteen and had stupefied the competition with a third success at the ripe old age of twenty-one. After this, there was obviously no one she could marry in Adelaide other than Nigel, and there was no one in Australia that he could marry other than her.

The ceremony had, consequently, been carried out in the presence of every soul in Adelaide who was of the slightest social importance and the Kearns had withdrawn to their luxury mansion to live happily ever after.

As would, presumably, their many servants, one of whom was, on this morning of Sunday, 15 January 1980, struggling to get out of bed.

Actually, this should not have been very difficult. Miss Nellie Cooper, a housemaid by profession if not inclination, was just barely nineteen years old, pretty and rather athletic. Left to her own devices, she would have risen early that Sunday to go off to the beach for some swimming, but, as it happened, this was her duty Sunday and she would have to remain at the house. Hence the reluctance in rising.

Washing and getting into her clothes, Nellie reflected that, all in all, it could be a great deal worse. With three house-maids on the staff, you got, at least, two Sundays out of three free and you were better off than the two gardeners who had to work every other weekend. The cook, of course, took his one day off a week with no replacement at all, but cooks were hard to find. If a person had to make a living as a housemaid, then it was best as a housemaid for a rich family and this was the richest family around.

The servants' quarters were on the top floor of the three-storey building, and Nellie made her way down the backstair to the kitchen where she prepared herself a cup of coffee and some toast. There was no great hurry. It was unlikely that Mrs Kearns would ring for her much before ten o'clock. She was not an early riser and certainly not on a Sunday morning.

As for Mr Kearns, he was visiting his brother who was not poor either and who lived on a country estate sixty miles away. He would not be back before Monday or Tuesday at the latest.

Nellie Cooper drank her coffee and ate her toast. She then had a second cup of coffee, tidied up the kitchen a little, and eventually went out to wander through the magnificently furnished rooms of the great house. They represented for her an intimidating amount of work, but they were very splendid to look at.

By ten o'clock Mrs Kearns had still not rung for her breakfast and Nellie, bored and impatient for the day to pass, came to the conclusion that she would go up and see if Mrs Kearns was in her bedroom at all. Now that she thought of it, it was more than likely that she was not. Nellie knew a good deal about her mistress's sleeping arrangements, and that was not all that Nellie Cooper knew about Pamela Kearns. With so many servants in the house there was a good deal of gossip, and it was common knowledge that while Mr Kearns was exhausting himself in racking up still more millions to the point where he came home late in the evening and fell exhausted and limp into bed, Mrs Kearns was making the rounds of the beaches and the more expensive cafés where she acquired a large number of new friends, all young and all male. Very male.

Trudging up the stairs to the bedroom on the second floor, Nellie Cooper reflected that she need not have got out of bed so early at all. With Mr Kearns visiting his brother sixty miles away and not due to return until Monday or Tuesday evening, Mrs Kearns would almost certainly have taken the opportunity to spend an undisturbed night with one of those young, handsome and extremely virile chance acquaintances.

However, to be on the safe side, Nellie very quietly eased open the door of Mrs Kearns's bedroom and peeked inside, confidently expecting to see an empty, neatly made bed.

What she actually saw gave her such a start that she lost her balance and half fell through the door, bumping her forehead painfully against the door handle.

The bed was not neatly made, but a mess with sheets and

blankets thrown back over the foot and half on to the floor. Lying on it was a totally naked woman whom Nellie assumed was Mrs Kearns. She was lying on her back, but Nellie could not see her face because lying on top of her was an equally naked man. Nellie had no idea who he might be, but she was certain that it was not Mr Kearns. This man was heavier, less muscular, and his hair was almost black whereas Nigel Kearns's hair was medium brown.

Half falling into the room, Nellie had made considerable noise and she was astounded to see that the figures on the bed had failed to react in any way. Were they so exhausted by their activities that even such sounds would not wake them? And how could they sleep in that position in the first place.

Suddenly, Nellie Cooper felt very uneasy and even frightened. There was something wrong here, terribly wrong. She felt she had to do something, but she did not know what to do. How could she go up to the bed and rouse her mistress when there was a man sleeping on top of her? Something like that could cost her her job.

On the other hand, it did not seem right to simply go away and ignore the whole thing. The people couldn't be sleeping like that. They were sick or unconscious or drunk, or maybe they had taken drugs. In any case, she had to do something.

Tense and beginning to tremble a little, she approached the bed and stretched out a hesitant hand in the direction of Pamela Kearns's shoulder. From this angle she could see that it was Mrs Kearns, but her fingers never reached the bare shoulder because what she also saw was the small, brown hole, ringed by a bluish-black welt, in the flesh just above the right eyebrow. A narrow thread of blood had run from the hole, around the corner of the eye, and down over the cheek to form a dark spot on the white pillow case.

Pamela Kearns's lovely features were calm and composed and her eyes were shut, but Nellie Cooper was not deceived. Her employer was not sleeping. She was dead.

In the shock and confusion of the discovery, Nellie jumped to the conclusion that it was the man lying on top of her who had killed her and she stumbled backward and bolted out of the room. Frightened nearly out of her wits, she raced up the stairs to her own room, locked the door and began frenziedly pushing furniture against it. It was some little time before she had calmed sufficiently to realize the senselessness of her actions and began to think rationally.

Cautiously pulling the furniture away from the door, she quietly unlocked it. Although she had recovered from her initial reaction of hysterical panic and now realized that the man lying on top of Mrs Kearns must be dead as well, she was terrified that the murderer might still be in the house. She was assuming that he would be a burglar or thief of some kind. There was always the danger of this in such large, luxury mansions.

Creeping silently out of her room, she tiptoed down the corridor to the door of the room occupied by the gardener who should be on duty that weekend where, unwilling to knock or call out for fear of attracting the attention of the murderer, she tried the door handle and found that the door was unlocked.

The gardener was, however, not inside which was as it should be. At that hour of the morning he would be long since at work in the garden outside. She was going to have to go downstairs and through the big, empty house alone.

Removing her shoes so as to make no noise going down the stairs, she vacillated indecisively as to what she should do. Should she risk telephoning the police from one of the house telephones and, perhaps, be surprised by the murderer in the middle of the call? Or should she simply slip outside and run through the garden until she found the gardener?

This was obviously the safest choice, but what then? Patrick, which was the gardener's name, would, undoubtedly, rush inside to see what was wrong and the burglar might very well kill him too. The fact was, Nellie was rather favourably inclined toward this handsome, unmarried gardener, only three years older than herself, although there had been so far no declarations of intent by either party.

All in all, it might be better not to inform the gardener and, recalling that there was a telephone in the pantry used by the cook for ordering groceries and other household supplies and that the pantry had a stout door which could be locked, she went to it and locked herself in.

She was seized again by panic for an instant or two when it occurred to her that the burglar might have cut the telephone wires and that she would not be able to call out, but the reassuring dial tone came on immediately. Minutes later, Nellie Cooper was speaking with the duty officer on the communications desk at police headquarters in downtown Adelaide.

Speaking as clearly and calmly as she could manage, Nellie gave what she believed to be an accurate account of the circumstances. She was the housemaid at the home of Mr and Mrs Nigel Kearns. A burglar had broken into the house and had murdered Mrs Kearns and another person. She was locked in the pantry. Would the police please come as quickly as possible?

The communications officer replied that they would be there before she could hang up the telephone and, although this was not literally true, a patrolcar did arrive at the house within a matter of minutes. The two officers in it came first to the pantry to make certain that Nellie was all right, but they had to show her their badges through the keyhole before she would open the door. Nellie was a badly frightened girl, and she was not taking any chances now that deliverance was so close at hand.

The question of identification being solved, Nellie led the officers to the bedroom where her employer and the un-identified man lay. Their conclusion was the same as hers had been, namely that Mrs Kearns had been shot through the head. So too, it seemed, had the man. The murders had apparently taken place while the couple were actually en-gaged in intercourse.

As neither officer thought of asking Nellie who the man was, they assumed that he was Nigel Kearns and, although the theory of a burglar did not seem as likely to the police officers as it had to the housemaid, they agreed with her that the murderer might still be in the house.

There was a telephone in the bedroom and one of the officers immediately called police headquarters, confirming

Nellie's report of a double homicide and asking for a cordon around the house to prevent the escape of the murderer if he was still there. Minutes later, there was patrolcars racing in from every direction, but without sirens or warning lights. The cordon around the Kearns mansion went into place silently, efficiently and very quickly. The communications desk duty officer knew very well who Nigel Kearns was.

So too did the inspector of detectives who, with his assistant, a detective-sergeant, was on duty in the offices of the Criminal Investigations Department on that Sunday. Picking up the keys to one of the departments cars from the squad room, they raced to the scene with the siren wide open. Behind them, two specialists in heavy body armour, a squad of detection experts from the police laboratory and an expert in forensic medicine, were piling into a police van which would follow. If Nigel Kearns and his wife had been murdered under the circumstances as they had been described to police headquarters, this was one of the most important cases of homicide in Adelaide and no effort was being spared.

At the house the inspector, a short, brisk man with intimidatingly cold, grey-blue eyes and a sandy moustache running like a straight bar across his upper lip, found the police cordon so tight that not even a mouse could have squeezed through and the house itself full of police officers. They had just completed searching the building from attic to basement and had found no trace of the burglar.

No sooner had the inspector entered the bedroom than he began to suspect why. 'My God!' he said in a low voice, placing his lips as close to the sergeant's ear as he could manage, 'That's not Nigel Kearns.'

The sergeant, a very large, young man with a round, good-natured face and rather unruly, short, blond hair, had bent down to listen to what his chief was saying and he straightened up abruptly, walked to the edge of the bed and bent nearly double in order to get a look at the dead man's face.

'You're right,' he said. 'It's not Kearns. I've seen his

picture in the newspapers. That's Mrs Kearns though. There's nobody in Australia who wouldn't recognize her.'

'You realize what this means, of course?' said the inspector.

The sergeant nodded dumbly. Like the inspector, he had immediately grasped that the murderer of Pamela Kearns and this as yet unidentified man was very probably Nigel Kearns himself.

'We're going to have to go about this discreetly,' said the inspector. 'Kearns is an intelligent man and he'll have the best lawyers that money can buy. Unless I'm greatly mistaken, we're not going to find very many clues to the identity of the murderer here.'

The inspector was not mistaken. Someone had obviously entered the bedroom while the dead couple were engaged in intercourse and, having shot them, had left, closing the door behind him. There were no fingerprints on the door handle, but the laboratory technicians were able to observe certain smears on the polished brass which could have been made by someone wearing gloves. Aside from this, there was not the slightest indication of the murderer's presence in the bedroom at all.

Or, perhaps, there was. Nigel Kearns's fingerprints would eventually be recovered from many places in the room, but why should a man's fingerprints not be in his own wife's bedroom. It would have been strange had they not been there.

While the laboratory specialists began their examination of the room and the doctor began his examination of the bodies, the inspector and the sergeant took the statements of Nellie Cooper and the gardener, the only servants on duty who were known to have spent the night in the house.

Nellie's statement was very long as she went into excruciating detail concerning her discovery of the body. It was the most impressive event of her life up to now and she remembered practically every second of it.

Patrick's statement was very short. He had got up at the usual time and had gone to work in the garden as he was supposed to. He had not known that anyone had been murdered in the house. He was not, he added rather shortly, in the habit of looking into his mistress's bedroom before taking up his duties for the day.

Neither Nellie nor Patrick had heard the sounds of shots or anything else during the night, although both had been in their rooms on the top floor. However, test firing carried out by the detection experts showed that the sound of a .38 calibre pistol shot fired in the bedroom downstairs could barely be heard in the servants' quarters and was definitely not loud enough to awake anyone sleeping soundly.

It had been a .38 calibre pistol or so thought the doctor, although he said that final confirmation would have to wait until he had performed the autopsy and removed the slugs from the victims' brains where they were still lodged. A tall, thin, wiry man with a black moustache and a grave, rather ponderous manner of speaking, he reported that the man had died at almost the precise instant of arriving at his sexual climax. As it seemed unlikely that this would be a coincidence, he suggested that the murderer had been waiting outside the door, listening to and, perhaps observing the couple engaged in intercourse inside and had chosen the moment of orgasm for the murder, possibly because the victims' attention would then be concentrated on what they were doing and it would be possible to approach the bed unnoticed, even though the lights were on. Mrs Kearns, he said, appeared to have had several orgasms but whether the last had been at the moment of death or not, he could not say. Whatever the case, the couple had been at maximum penetration at the time.

Like the inspector, the doctor had immediately seen that the man was not Nigel Kearns and he asked if the inspector had any idea who he was.

The inspector knew exactly who he was. His driver's licence and other identification papers had been found in his wallet in the clothing hung neatly over a chair in the bedroom. He was twenty-nine-year-old Kenneth Craig, an unmarried middle-level management employee of an insurance company. One of the inspectors' men was now on his way to Craig's parents to report his death, arrange for the official identification at the police morgue and attempt to find out what they had known of Craig's relationship to Pamela Kearns, if anything.

Another three detectives were with the sergeant in a police car headed for the country estate of thirty-nine-year-old Ronald Kearns, Nigel Kearns's brother. Nellie Cooper had said that that was where her employer was spending the weekend and the sergeant had orders to take him into custody simply on the basis of the circumstances. There was sufficient evidence of motive and opportunity to bring charges of homicide against him.

Orders were orders and the sergeant did bring Nigel Kearns back to Adelaide with him, but he was careful to avoid informing him that he was under arrest and he was very polite and considerate in his manner.

The fact was both Ronald Kearns and his thirty-six-year-old wife Sheila had immediately confirmed that Nigel had spent Saturday night with them, and that it was not possible that he could have left during the night because the only car that was not locked up in the garages was one belonging to Sheila and it was parked directly under her bedroom window. It was a sports car which made a good deal of noise and it would have been impossible to start it without waking her.

This was bad enough, but there was worse to come.

Having completed the autopsies and having recovered two .38 calibre bullets which had been fired from a gun for which the ballistics department could find no record, the doctor reported that Kenneth Craig and Pamela Kearns had died almost simultaneously sometime between one-fifteen and one-thirty in the morning of Sunday, 15 January. Ronald and Sheila Kearns had said in separate statements that they and Nigel had only gone to bed at around midnight. For Nigel to have left the estate early enough to cover the distance to Adelaide and murder his wife and her lover by one-thirty in the morning, he would have had to drive extremely fast or leave while his brother and his sister-in-law were still awake. They were prepared to swear that he had not.

'Could they be protecting him?' said the sergeant.

'I doubt it,' said the inspector. 'They made their statements independently and they checked. If they were false, that would mean that they had worked the whole thing out in advance and I don't believe that they would do that. These are wealthy, highly respectable people and I doubt that they would condone murder even if the murderer was Kearns's brother. Besides, I've listened to enough statements in my life that I think I know when someone is telling the truth. Neither Kearns nor his wife think that Nigel did this. They probably think that he had good reason to and they're both relieved to know that he didn't.'

'That was the impression that I got too,' said the sergeant slowly. 'They were both relieved.'

In the meantime, the investigation into Pamela Kearns's more intimate social contacts had been pursued far enough by now to establish that, had Nigel Kearns been inclined to murder his wife for her sexual infidelities, he had had ample motive for close to five years.

Nigel and Pamela's marriage had been something of a fairy-tale romance. Chosen in free competition as the most beautiful woman in Australia, Pamela was at the height of her career when in March of 1970 she met Nigel Kearns who was already well on his way to his second million dollars and the eventual title of richest man in Adelaide through his dealings in foreign exchange.

In a way, they were an ideally matched pair. Pamela, who despite her appearance was a somewhat calculating maiden, had apparently had little contact with the opposite sex and had stated publicly on more than one occasion that she had no intention of becoming romantically involved with anyone other than a very wealthy man, and then only if officially engaged to be married. Nigel, no more given to impulsive emotions than his wife, had been busy making money and had little interest in such time-consuming and unprofitable activities as love and sex.

His interest in Pamela had been, it seemed, mainly because she was a celebrity and thus represented another trophy to be added to his successes. Characteristically, he had not wasted much time on courtship and preliminaries. Nigel and Pamela met in March; they were formally engaged in May; in July they were married. It was the most important social event of the year in Adelaide.

Following the wedding, there had been the obligatory world-tour honeymoon and, this taken care of, Nigel had bought the mansion in the most exclusive suburb of Adelaide, had staffed it with servants, had provided his wife with an unlimited supply of money and had gone back to making more of the same. He was, it was said, devoted to his beautiful wife, and there was nothing that she might desire which she could not have.

Except Nigel. Nigel liked Pamela, but he loved money, or rather, not the money itself, but the process of making it. The money actually did Nigel very little good. He never had any free time to spend it.

Nor did he have any time for romance. When he returned home after a long day of frenzied foreign-exchange dealings, he was so exhausted that he fell into bed immediately after dinner and slept straight through the night.

Pamela might have been cold in financial matters, but she was far from cold otherwise. Within five years, the magic had gone out of the marriage and she acquired what Inspector Barker thought was probably her first lover. In any case, he was unable to find anyone who reported contact with her at an earlier date.

This first lover was typical of all her subsequent adventures except the last. A handsome, blond beachboy, he had been twenty-five years old at the time. He had met Pamela at the beach where she spent a great deal of her time, and she had been in such a state of deprivation that they had actually had intercourse while in the water under something less than ideal conditions of privacy. He had not known then who she was, but finding out later, had been so impressed by his own conquest that he had never forgotten the incident.

Pamela had forgotten him quickly enough and had moved on to others. The inspector was able to find dozens of them, generally picked up at the beach or in the better-class cafés and bars. They were mostly young men of good families, some of whom worked and some of whom did not need to. If they worked, it was in management positions. Pamela had not been fond of the unwashed masses.

Kenneth Craig appeared to not have differed much from his predecessors, although her affair with him had lasted slightly longer than the average. It was believed that she had met him sometime in August of the preceding year which would mean that they had been lovers for a little over four months.

Craig had seemingly taken the affair more seriously than most. He was, however, not the only one. Two of Pamela's previous lovers, twenty-eight-year-old Bill Rood and twenty-six-year-old Tom Drysdale, had nearly beaten each other to death over her. Both were rich, both had wanted her to divorce Kearns and marry them, and each had accused the other of alienating her affections.

Looked at from the objective point of view of the police investigators, it appeared that there had been little affection to alienate. The inspector's men were not even able to determine whether Rood had displaced Drysdale or vice versa, and there was some reason to believe that she had been carrying on affairs with both of them simultaneously. Pamela had been a girl with healthy appetites and the formidable staying power of the female.

Which was, perhaps, the explanation for her unusually long-term association with Kenneth Craig who was, in certain circles, mildly famous for his prowess in bed or any other convenient place.

The inspector did not, however, realize just how impressed Pamela had been by Craig until he interrogated thirty-year-old Martha Decker, Pamela's closest girlfriend and her only confidante.

Up to this point, the inspector had been inclined to regard either Bill Rood or Tom Drysdale as the most likely suspects. Both had been interrogated, but neither had been charged as there was no evidence against them. Their value as suspects was, moreover, considerably reduced by the fact that both had had an equal motive. This precluded charging either the one or the other, as the one charged could point out that there was no more reason to suspect him than the other lover. On the other hand, the police could not bring charges against both because it was clear that the murders had been carried out by one man only.

As a result, the inspector had begun to think that he was not going to solve his case, but what Martha Decker had to say put a different complexion on things. According to her statement, Pamela had been, perhaps for the first time in her life, emotionally involved in her affair with Craig. She had wanted to marry him, but she was unwilling to relinquish Kearns's money. What she wanted was for Kearns to bring a divorce action against her so that she could obtain a generous settlement. She had, therefore, been almost flagrant in the affair with Craig and this explained why she had entertained him in her own home, something that she had never done with any of her other lovers. Nigel, said Martha Decker, had known about the affair since November of the preceding year.

This information put Nigel Kearns back at the head of the list of suspects, but it did not help the inspector solve his case. Kearns's alibi was absolutely watertight.

Up until Monday, 21 January 1980. On that date Mrs Sheila Kearns received a ticket for speeding. She had been photographed by a radar control doing close to eighty miles an hour in a thirty-mile-an-hour zone outside Adelaide.

Mrs Kearns was furious. Coming personally to the traffic department at police headquarters, she pounded on the desk and shouted that their radar equipment was defective. According to the charge, the offence had taken place at thirty-five minutes past midnight on 15 January. At that time she had been sound asleep in bed on the Kearns estate sixty miles away.

The equipment was not, however, defective and, if it did not show the driver, the camera had recorded very clearly the licence number of the speeding car. Sheila Kearns was going to have to pay her traffic ticket.

Bewildered, but unable to refute the evidence of the photograph, Sheila Kearns had no alternative but to pay and, had the murder of Pamela Kearns not been so recent and fresh in the minds of the police, the matter might have rested there. As it was, the officers of the traffic department found the incident strange and sent a report on it to the Criminal Investigations Department.

The inspector took one look at the report and knew that his case was solved. Somehow Nigel Kearns had managed to make use of his sister-in-law's car, had driven to Adelaide at breakneck speed, had murdered his wife and her lover, and had returned with what would have been a perfect alibi had it not been for the radar speed trap and the camera.

Confronted with the evidence, Kearns confessed and explained. He had known of his wife's infidelities and her plans to obtain a large settlement from him in return for a divorce. He had decided to murder her and her lover, and had deliberately arranged for the alibi by going to spend the weekend with his brother and sister-in-law. Immediately that they had gone to bed, he had crept out of the house, had taken the sports car out of gear and had pushed it without starting out into the road and to the top of a slope leading away from the house. He had only started it when he was safely out of earshot.

After a very fast trip, he had arrived in good time to stand listening outside the bedroom door while his wife and her lover approached their mutual climax. When he walked quietly into the room, they had been too occupied to notice him. He did not think that either had realized that a third party was present.

On the basis of his own confession, this was a coldly premeditated double homicide, but there were, of course, extenuating circumstances. Nigel Kearns was a wealthy and important man.

That, in itself, might not be regarded as an extenuating circumstance, although it sometimes has been, but the impressive list of men with whom his wife had deceived him was. As his attorney pointed out, it was bad enough that his wife was out picking up lovers while he was at work. Having to finance her future life with a new husband was too much.

The court was inclined to find some merit in this argument on 8 January 1982 sentenced him to the modest term of ten years' imprisonment.

9

NAPOLEON CAME FROM CORSICA AND IT IS EASY TO SEE WHY HE LEFT

With the exception of the carefully devised alibi, the case of the Pamela Kearns murder is classic; banal even. Money and sexual infidelity are at the base of a great many homicides, with sex enjoying a large lead over cash.

Although the media have been proclaiming sexual revolution and liberation for close to twenty years, a great many individuals have failed to get the message. Knowing full well that extra-marital activities of the spouse are nothing more than an expression of self essential to the satisfactory development of the personality, they still reach for knife, gun or blunt object when confronted with the spectacle of the companion, legal or otherwise, locked in passionate embrace with the dustman, the lady next door, the mayor, the au pair, etc., etc.

To the casual observer, it would seem that this sort of thing is handled rather straightforwardly in Anglo-Saxon countries or those predominantly so, but among the Latins, the situation can become confused to the point where it is difficult to keep the participants separated in the mind without a chart of relationships. In a place like Corsica, it sometimes seems that it is impossible to murder anyone without involving most of the population of the island.

This confusion exists only in the minds of non-Corsicans, of course. The local inhabitants know very well what is going on without any chart. They also know what to do about it.

The instant that the sound of the twelve-gauge shotgun

blast bounced off his eardrums, Postman Jacques Busquet half fell, half leapt off his bicycle and rolled into the ditch. A Corsican born and bred, he knew the sound of a shotgun when he heard it and he could estimate very exactly what a gunshot in that quiet residential section of the little town of Rutali known as Pantane meant. It was ten o'clock in the morning of Tuesday, 12 February 1980, and it was not the hunting season.

Normally a gunshot in Corsica, where some of the inhabitants are inclined to be excitable, is followed by answering gunshots, but, on this occasion, there were none. Postman Busquet cautiously lifted his head and peered over the edge of the ditch.

Thirty-eight-year-old Ange Casta at whose house he had delivered the mail less than five minutes before was thrashing around and groaning at the foot of the large chestnut tree which stood at the boundary separating his property from that of the Ettoris', the last house where Busquet had delivered the mail before hearing the gunshot.

Crouching in the ditch, he watched attentively but uncomprehendingly as thirty-six-year-old Angele Ettori emerged from her house and ran to where Casta was lying on the ground. Squatting down beside him, she attempted to lift his head.

She had hardly arrived, when Mathilde Casta, the forty-one-year-old wife of the wounded man, came rushing out of her house and fell upon Angele like an avenging fury. She had a small paring knife in her hand and she was apparently attempting to disembowel the other woman.

Angele fought back. They were both small, slender women, but wiry and astonishingly strong and almost evenly matched. Suddenly both began to scream at the top of their voices.

Postman Busquet climbed out of the ditch, hurriedly collected his mail sack and his bicycle and, mounting the latter, pedalled away as fast as he could go. The screams meant that large numbers of the Ettori and Casta clans would be arriving shortly and he did not want to be present when they got there.

He had not got a hundred yards down the road when the policecar from the gendarmerie station at Murato passed him heading in the direction of Pantane. It was doing close to ninety miles an hour, its sirens screaming like tortured tom cats and gendarmes hanging all over it. They were armed to the teeth. In Corsica, a major problem of the police when someone has been shot is to prevent the relatives of the family clans involved from killing each other.

They were none too quick. Corsica, the big French island in the Mediterranean off the coast of Italy and the birthplace of Napoleon, has a great deal of unemployment and many of the men of the Ettori and Casta clans were at home. They came boiling on to the scene, armed with knives, iron bars, shovels, axes or anything else that they had been able to scoop up. Their women came with them, more savage, more bloodthirsty, and deadlier than the males. In some respects, the Corsican woman is very thoroughly liberated.

Fortunately, there was a certain amount of confusion before the battle lines could be drawn and the policecar coming to a halt with a howl of brakes that drowned out the siren, the gendarmes peeled off it like grapes and waded in. Their tactics were simple: arrest everybody in sight.

In the meantime, the rest of the village was on the way. Rutali mayor Francis Maroselli arrived, wheezing like a walrus and bringing with him the local physician, Dr Lucien Monal, with whom he had happened to be speaking in the town hall less than a hundred yards away when the shot rang out. They were followed by the village priest, Father Giuliani, who came carrying the necessary for the last sacrament just in case.

Dr Monal, a very short, very stockily built man with blue-black hair and a small, black moustache, ran forward to where Casta was now lying motionless at the foot of the tree and knelt down beside him. Immediately he began signalling over his shoulder for the priest.

Father Giuliani hurried forward, knelt down and began to intone the rites of the last sacrament. Casta was lying on his back, his mouth and eyes wide open. Blood was gushing from between his lips and his breath came in long, rattling gasps.

Abruptly, the breathing ceased altogether and the powerful, longshoreman's body went as limp as a piece of string.

Father Giuliani crossed himself, concluded the ritual and got a little shakily to his feet. He, too, was a Corsican born and bred, but he was more appalled than attracted by violence.

The doctor automatically started to cross the arms of the dead man over his chest and then caught himself. The chest was a sea of torn flesh and ripped fabric from the shirt he had been wearing, and it was obvious that this was a matter for the investigators of the criminal police. They would want the body as undisturbed as possible.

The gendarmes had, by now, got the situation under control and had taken into custody a baker's dozen of Ettoris and a carefully balanced equal number of Castas, not counting the widow and Angele Ettori, who had been separated by four badly scratched gendarmes.

All the Castas were shouting that it was Angele who had murdered Ange and she and the Ettoris were not denying it, confiding their remarks to picturesque insults and abuse. It seemed, however, that there were no actual witnesses to the shooting.

Assured that open warfare had been averted, the captain in charge of the gendarmerie detachment came over and looked expressionlessly at the corpse for about a minute and then went off to the gendarmerie van to telephone the Criminal Investigations Department in the nearby city of Bastia over the police radio. Any homicide investigation in the northern half of the island would be carried out by the Bastia CID. The gendarmerie was not equipped for it.

Bastia is the largest city on the island, although, with a population of a little over fifty thousand, it barely surpasses in size its rival of Ajaccio on the west coast and further to the south. Despite its small population, its police have a large and efficient criminal investigations department as it has to handle the investigation work for all of the smaller communities surrounding it. There is always plenty to do. Whatever other unemployment there may be on the island of Corsica, there is none with the police.

The distance not being great and it being the middle of the morning of a week day in winter when all of the departments at police headquarters were at full strength, the corpse had scarcely ceased bleeding when Inspector Louis Sardinelli, senior investigator and homicide squad chief, arrived at the scene with his assistant, Detective-Sergeant Jean Ventura. They found most of the population of the village of Rutali present including the husband of Angele Ettori, thirty-eight-year-old Paul Ettori, who had been notified of the events at his job as a garage mechanic in the nearby village of Valrose and had promptly hurried home. He was a small man, brown-skinned and very heavily moustached.

Having taken a look at the corpse, the inspector asked a few questions and then went to the Ettori house where he found a twelve-gauge shotgun lying on the floor in front of the second-storey living-room window. From the window, there was a clear line of fire to the chestnut tree where Casta had been shot down.

The inspector, a compactly built man whose black hair was going a little thin on top, did not touch the gun or anything else, but went back outside and told the sergeant to call Bastia and have a squad from the police laboratory sent out.

'Is it necessary?' said the sergeant. He was a much younger man, round-faced, good-natured looking and disarmingly informal in his manner. 'The woman admits that she shot him.'

'She may change her mind,' said the inspector. 'In any case, the court will expect us to present whatever material evidence there is here. It's what we're paid for.'

The sergeant shrugged and went off to carry out his orders.

The inspector walked over to where Angele Ettori was standing with her husband, her fifteen-year-old son, her eleven-year-old daughter and two gendarmes.

'Did you shoot him?' he asked.

Mrs Ettori nodded silently, casting down her eyes.

'Why?' said the inspector.

'He was after me,' said Mrs Ettori, her voice an almost inaudible whisper. 'I was afraid.'

The inspector looked at the body lying under the chestnut

tree and up at the window of the house. The distance was approximately forty yards.

'You do not need to make a statement,' said the inspector. 'If you wish to speak to an attorney first, you may do so. However, if you want to make a statement, my assistant will take it down as soon as he returns. You understand that it can be used against you later?'

Mrs Ettori said nothing, but Paul Ettori began to yell that there was no need for an attorney or anything else. The man had been persecuting his wife. She had defended herself. It was her right.

At this, all of the Castas began shouting and cursing the entire Ettori family, Angele in particular, the most frequently used expression being 'putana', the local term for 'whore'.

The inspector looked questioningly at Mrs Ettori.

'They think I was having an affair with Ange,' she whispered, looking down at the ground and turning an attractive shade of dusky pink. 'It is not true.'

The inspector sighed. 'We shall see,' he said. 'Here is Sergeant Ventura now. He will take your statement and make a recording of it on this little tape recorder. You understand that you are under no obligation to make any statement at all unless you so wish?'

Angele Ettori did so wish and she made a rather short statement in which she said that Ange Casta had been pursuing her for some time. When she had gone to the post office or to do her shopping he was always there, and he had even come to the mayor's office where she worked as secretary to Mayor Maroselli and had attempted to kiss her against her will. She was a respectable woman and she had refused his advances, but he had become only more insistent. On that morning, he had been in his garden when she came out to collect her mail, and he had called out that he was coming over that afternoon and bringing a friend. They would deal with her, he had said menacingly.

Mrs Ettori said that she had been so frightened by this threat that she had gone to the garage and picked up her husband's shotgun which he had bought for hunting. The shells were kept in the bathroom and she had chosen one at random and had fired out the window in the direction of Casta who was standing under the chestnut tree with the intention of frightening him. When she saw that he had been hit, she had immediately called the gendarmerie at Murato. She had thought that they would bring an ambulance.

It was obvious that, if this statement were to be accepted, the maximum charge would be unintentional homicide, and the inspector formally took Mrs Ettori into custody and sent her to Bastia to be detained until such time as the instructions judge would decide whether she should be released or held until the trial took place.

The names and addresses of all the persons in custody were then verified and they were ordered to disperse. This they did, but began almost immediately a pitched battle less than two hundred yards from the scene which was, however, quickly broken up by the gendarmes who had been anticipating just such a development.

A little later, a squad car with four technicians from the police laboratory in Bastia arrived, examined the gun, reported that there were latent fingerprints on it, and took it back with them. It was the only piece of evidence as there was, of course, nothing of significance to the investigation either near or on the corpse.

This too was taken away to the police morgue in Bastia where a routine autopsy was carried out on it for the purposes of the official report establishing cause and time of death. A small handful of buckshot was recovered from the body, but was of no value to the investigation as, unlike a rifle or pistol, it is not possible to determine from what gun the shot of a shotgun shell has been fired.

Long before these measures had been completed, the inspector had, of course, returned to his office in Bastia. There was nothing for him to do in Rutali. The statements from the very large number of persons there anxious to make them would be taken by the investigations officers from his department. He already knew that no actual witnesses to the shooting had been found and any statements made would be mainly useful in establishing the motive. As Angele Ettori had already confessed, it was not her acts but her reasons for them that were of primary importance for the trial.

The inspector thought that it was murder and not unintentional at all. He knew a good deal about firearms and, in his opinion, it was an exceptional shot who could hit a man square in the chest from a distance of forty yards, even with a shotgun. To make the feat the more difficult, the charge had been buckshot, meaning that there had been a relatively small number of pellets. He, therefore, found Mrs Ettori's statement that this was the first time in her life she had ever fired a gun hard to accept.

So did the Castas. What with court dockets as crowded as they are, justice does not move very swiftly on the island and it was early summer of 1981 before Angele Ettori was finally brought to trial for the shooting of Ange Casta. She had spent less than a week in detention and, having performed a reenactment of the crime for the police, had been released to look after her family. It was not supposed that she would make an attempt to flee the country or take to the mountains. Indeed, she could hardly do so without admitting that she was guilty of murder and that the shooting of Casta had not been the act of self-defence which she maintained it was.

During this time, the village of Rutali and the surrounding district had been divided into what amounted to two warring camps. The Ettoris were very numerous and all of them swore to heaven that Ange Casta had been a lust-maddened satyr who had tracked Angele Ettori like a weasel hunting down a mouse and with much the same intentions. Had she not acted to defend herself, he would undoubtedly have raped her at the very least and his friends would probably have joined him.

To this, the Castas, who were equally if not more numerous than the Ettoris, replied that Angele was a notorious nymphomaniac. She had tried every trick in the book to lure him away from his legitimate wife, pitifully five years older than Angele and already a widow with two children when he had married her in 1964. It was only when, exhausted by her insatiable sexual demands, he had tried to free himself from her lascivious clutches, that she had confronted him with a choice between make love or die. The honest Ange, now repenting the practically forced infidelity to his faithful wife, had courageously chosen death and had been ruthlessly executed.

Neither of these versions was completely without flaws when compared dispassionately with the facts, but the emotions of the parties involved were so intense that the riot squad from the gendarmerie post at Murato had to make no less than five sorties to avoid the situation degenerating into actual armed conflict. There was, to say the least, a lively interest in the proceedings and outcome of the trial.

And not only among the Ettoris and the Castas. When the trial opened in the last week of June 1981, before the Superior Criminal Court in Bastia, the courtroom was packed with practically every able-bodied inhabitant of the Rutali area. Shops and businesses were closed as there were neither customers to buy nor employees to work in them. Even the mail did not get delivered as Postman Jacques Busquet had been summoned as a witness. He was neither for the prosecution nor the defence, but, as the closest thing to an eye witness to the shooting, was called upon to recount what he had seen and heard.

Also called as witnesses, but by the prosecution were Father Giuliani and Mayor Francis Maroselli. According to the pre-trial claims of the Castas, positive proof would be provided that Angele Ettori had practically raped the unwilling Ange Casta and had wilfully, feloniously and with malice aforethought murdered him when he refused to submit to further sexual persecution.

However, the first word in the trial went to the police, and Inspector Sardinelli gave his testimony in a terse, lucid and matter-of-fact manner. It was by no means the first time that he had been called upon to testify in such cases.

Referring to his notebook for dates and times, he outlined the steps taken by the investigation, starting with his arrival at the scene of the crime at seven minutes to eleven on the morning of 12 February 1980. He described the condition of the body and, using a chart, spotted its position in relation to the Ettori and Casta houses and the large chestnut tree on the boundary between them. The distance between the living-room window of the Ettori home where the shot had been fired and the point where Casta had fallen was one hundred and twenty-seven feet.

He passed on to the recovery of the murder weapon by the technicians from the police laboratory who had found the barrel of the gun still smelling of gun powder which indicated that it had been fired recently. It was a comparatively new gun which had been used but little, and Mrs Ettori's finger-prints were on it in the firing position, including one clear print of the right index finger on the trigger itself. The trigger was not cross-hatched as would have been the case in a more expensive weapon, but smooth and it had taken a fingerprint.

There had been an expended shell in the chamber of the gun when it was recovered by the technicians, and a part box of similar shells of the same make was found in the bathroom of the house. The charges in these shells ranged from number four to buckshot.

It had been determined that the expended shell in the breech of the shotgun had been charged with buckshot and a quantity of buckshot roughly equivalent to the charge had been recovered from the body during the course of the autopsy.

According to the findings of the autopsy report, Ange Casta had died of loss of blood occasioned by the puncturing of a large number of blood vessels in the chest and upper abdomen which had resulted in massive haemorrhaging quickly followed by death. It was an indication of his great physical strength and sturdy constitution that he had continued to breath at all after having been shot, but it was thought unlikely that he had been conscious.

The inspector then ran the tape recording of Mrs Ettori's statement taken at the scene of the crime, commented that her subsequent statements had differed from it in no way, and concluded his testimony with the information that a number of pornographic magazines and photographs had been found under the mattress of the bed which Paul and Angele Ettori shared.

At this there were cries from the Casta side of the

courtroom of 'pictures of herself!', and from the Ettori faction of 'dirty swine!', and the judge had to threaten to clear the court in order to re-establish order.

Sergeant Ventura was then called to the stand and described a re-enactment of the shooting which Mrs Ettori had voluntarily carried out. He had been in charge of this operation as the inspector had been occupied elsewhere. Mrs Ettori, he said, had gone through the motions of loading the gun and firing a shot out the window, but without actually putting a shell into the chamber. In his opinion, the re-enactment reflected faithfully what had taken place on the day in question.

The police testimony had been necessarily short as, there being no question as to who had done the shooting and who had been shot, the investigation had been short. Angele Ettori had never denied shooting Ange Casta and she was not going to deny it now.

A small woman, dark and slender, she looked scarcely more than a child sitting demurely in the witness stand from which she was to tell her story and explain her action before returning to the pen reserved for the accused.

In response to the routine background questioning of the judge, she said she had been born in the tiny village of Cuttoli-Corticchiato in the extreme south of Corsica and had been the oldest in a family of eight children. Her father had been an employee of the highway department and the family had moved frequently.

She had met Paul Ettori toward the end of 1964 and had married him on 26 June 1965. Their first child had been born in 1966 and the second in 1970. She described the marriage as a happy one.

Following the birth of the second child, they had found the quarters in the house of her mother, with whom they had been living up until that time, too crowded and had bought the house at Pantane in Rutali into which they had moved in 1972.

In 1977, Ange and Mathilde Casta and one of the children from Mrs Casta's first marriage had moved into the neighbouring house of which the garden adjoined the garden of the

Ettori house. Mrs Casta's oldest daughter was no longer living with them as she was already married.

For the first two years there had been little contact between the Ettoris and the Castas, but in 1979 Ange Casta and Paul Ettori had become friends, playing cards together, lending each other tools and helping each other with the garden work. Very shortly thereafter, Casta had begun making improper advances toward her; advances which she had firmly rejected.

The testimony of the accused was interrupted by howls of rage from the Casta clan and the air turned blue with insults, curses and threats. The impression conveyed was that the Castas did not agree with the statements of the accused.

The presiding judge, accustomed to such scenes, calmly raised his voice to a shrill yell which penetrated the uproar and made clear that, unless there was total silence in the courtroom within ten seconds the bailiffs would begin clearing it.

There was total silence within ten seconds. No one wanted to miss out on the trial. Mrs Ettori continued.

Casta, she said, had begun with romantic suggestions. A mason turned longshoreman, he was on a different work schedule than Paul Ettori who was a garage mechanic and he was often home when Paul was not. On such occasions he would find some excuse to come to the Ettori house, and he had ended by telling her bluntly that she was the reason for his visits and that he would like to make love to her.

According to Mrs Ettori she had indignantly refused, but Casta had become more pressing. Wherever she went, shopping or on any other errands, he invariably turned up, and he had boldly come to the mayor's office where she worked and had attempted to fondle her. She had continued to resist his advances, but she was gradually becoming frightened.

'Why then, Mrs Ettori,' said the presiding judge, 'did you not tell your husband of these unwelcome attentions? As your husband, it was up to him to protect you from such advances by other men.'

'I was afraid that they would fight,' said Angele Ettori.

'Paul is a good man, but he is not very big. Mr Casta was very big, very powerful. He would have hurt Paul.'

The proceedings were once again interrupted by shrieks of rage, this time from the widow of the victim who leaped to her feet and delivered a passionate eulogy of her dead husband, described as more gentle than a mouse, with such speed that she had almost finished by the time the bailiff, in response to the judge's gesture, picked her up by the elbows and walked her out of the courtroom. She immediately stopped yelling and, as the proceedings resumed, crept quietly back in and recovered her place.

Angele Ettori said that matters had gone from bad to worse and that Casta had begun making obscene telephone calls to her both at work and at home in which he described in crude, physical detail precisely what he intended to do to her. She had been afraid to leave the house, and had asked her husband to drive her to her job in the mayor's office even though it was only a short distance away.

The judge then brought the focus of the questioning to the events of the morning of Tuesday, 12 February 1980, and Mrs Ettori repeated her statement of having been accosted by Casta when she went out to get her mail. He had called out, 'I'm coming over this afternoon with a friend and we'll take care of you.' This had frightened her so badly that she had got her husband's shotgun from the garage, had loaded it with a shell from the box in the bathroom and had fired a shot out the window in Casta's direction.

She had, she insisted, not intended to harm him, but merely to frighten him into leaving her alone. She had not deliberately chosen buckshot over the far less dangerous number four shot, but had merely caught up the first shell which came to hand. In any case, she said, she did not know one charge from another. She had never had a gun in her hands before.

It was becoming obvious that the witnesses for the prosecution and, particularly, the widow of the deceased were going to expire of apoplexy unless they came to make their statements very shortly, and the judge sent Angele Ettori back to the accused box and called Mrs Mathilda Casta.

Mrs Casta was also small, dark and very angry. She said that she knew with certainty that Angele Ettori had been having an affair with her husband because she had personally caught them in the very act of intercourse, once in a ditch at the foot of the garden, once in her own bathroom and once in a cellar. She had appealed to the mayor and to Father Giuliani to intervene and had pleaded with her husband to terminate the affair. He had said that he, too, would like to get out of it but that Angele was hard to shake off, and he had shown her a watch which Angele had given him for Christmas in 1979.

Several more Castas were called to the witness stand, including Mrs Casta's oldest daughter, and all confirmed her statements in detail. Father Giuliani and Mayor Maroselli were more cautious. Both confirmed that Mrs Casta had approached them concerning an affair between her husband and Angele Ettori, but they, themselves, had no personal knowledge of the affair other than Mrs Casta's statement. They had not spoken to Mr Casta nor to Mrs Ettori.

Brought back to the witness stand and questioned about the incident of the watch which she had allegedly given to Ange Casta for Christmas, Mrs Ettori said that she had not given him the watch; he had stolen it from her. She had bought the watch as a present for her husband and Casta had seen it lying on the table, had picked it up and put it in his pocket and had said that, unless she yielded to his wishes, he would tell everyone that she had given it to him.

At this point there was such an outcry on the part of the Castas and such a response from the Ettoris that the judge was forced to clear the courtroom, and it was over an hour before the trial could be resumed. In the meantime, a very large contingent of police strove, with only indifferent success, to prevent bloodshed in the street outside.

There was not much left to the trial in any case. Paul Ettori was called and asked about the pornography under the mattress of the bed of which his wife had already denied all knowledge.

Obviously embarrassed, he said it had been given him by a friend and, as he had no interest in it, he had hidden it under the mattress.

This statement produced some derisive and obscene remarks from the Castas which were followed by cheers as the prosecution called for the relatively harsh sentence of fifteen years.

The defence called for acquittal which produced yells of, 'Why not give her the Legion of Honour?'

In the end the court gave Angele Ettori neither fifteen years nor the Legion of Honour, but sentenced her to the modest term of five years' imprisonment.

The Castas rushed the police with intent to lynch, but were repulsed and the prisoner was led off.

'Be interesting to know what really did happen,' remarked the inspector, leaving the courtroom with his assistant. 'Wouldn't it?'

The sergeant nodded, but, privately, he was not in agreement. In Corsica, sometimes the less you know, the better off you are.

10

RELIABLE DOMESTIC HELP IS BECOMING IMPOSSIBLE TO FIND

Who was mad in the case of the murder of Ange Casta? A difficult question to answer, but for those not resident in Corsica, speculation is, at least, not dangerous.

Ange Casta was, in his pursuit of the housewife next door, not mad, but merely trying to relieve glandular pressure, a common enough ambition in men of his age and state of physical well-being.

On the other hand, the intensity of his pursuit would seem to fall within the range of a minor obsession if not a compulsive urge. Few would-be seducers go to the mayor's office to fondle housewives who are at work there.

And, indeed, if Mrs Casta was telling the truth, and there was considerable evidence that she was, then why would Casta need to fondle Mrs Ettori in the mayor's office? He could have done so with greater privacy in the ditch, the bathroom or the cellar where Mrs Casta was supposed to have surprised them doing more than fondle.

Unless all of the statements made at the trial were unvarnished lies, it would appear that Ange Casta was, at the least, eccentric.

No less so, Angele Ettori. Was she having an affair with Casta or not? Mrs Casta said she was. She said she wasn't. The witnesses testified according to family, but none claimed to have actual, first-hand knowledge.

Assuming that she was, what did she expect to gain by cutting down on her lover with her husband's twelve-gauge?

Assuming that she wasn't, ditto.

One thing is certain: she did not actually expect to kill him.

No evidence was found that she had ever had a gun in her hands before, and there was a blue-black bruise the size of a dinner plate on her right shoulder, indicating that she was not aware that a twelve-gauge has a noticeable recoil and that she had not held it properly or tight enough.

Probably the best reaction to the crime was that of Jacques Busquet. Jump into the ditch until the shooting is over.

Whatever the motives of all parties concerned, Angele Ettori was not particularly clever about her crime and she got sent to jail for it. Others were far more ingenious and ended up in the morgue. However, in the case of forty-five-year-old Petrus de Beer, it was stupidity and not madness which occasioned his downfall.

For a man holding such a high position in the civil service, if he had been determined to murder his wife, he should have been able to hit upon something better than strychnine which leaves such easily detectable traces in the body.

Nevertheless, strychnine was what he had used and, according to the analysis of the stomach contents, it had been administered in a cup of herb tea. There had been a generous quantity of it and forty-two-year-old Doreen de Beer had died quickly, although in great agony. Death by strychnine poisoning is not pleasant. The symptoms are a suffocating tightness in the chest, violent spasms and convulsions.

Petrus de Beer had telephoned his family physician on that evening of 15 April 1979 to say that his wife was not feeling well. Could the doctor come at once?

It was a massive understatement and, although the doctor had come immediately to the luxury villa in the exclusive residential section on the outskirts of Cape Town, the legislative capital of South Africa on the southern tip of the continent, by the time he arrived, Mrs de Beer was so obviously beyond help that he did not even call the ambulance.

As the doctor was unable to say with certainty what had caused Mrs de Beer's death, he refused to issue a death certificate and suggested that de Beer call the police immediately. There would have to be an investigation and probably an autopsy. He did not know what had killed

Mrs de Beer, but it did not look like a natural death to him.

De Beer had called the police and the duty homicide squad consisting of Inspector Jan Brinker, Detective-Sergeant Otto Shryker and a police expert in forensic medicine, Dr Martin Hampton, came out immediately.

Dr Hampton carried out a comparatively short examination of the corpse, following which he took the inspector aside and spoke to him in a low voice.

On the basis of his remarks, the inspector took de Beer into custody, cautioned him on his rights and asked if he would care to make a statement.

De Beer said that he would. It was that he was outraged by the behaviour of the police. He had just undergone the ordeal of losing his beloved wife of many years and, rather than receiving the sympathy and support to which he was entitled, he was being treated like a criminal.

The inspector said that he was being treated like a criminal because there was reason to believe that he was one. He then instructed the sergeant to call police headquarters and have a detachment sent out from the police laboratory. He wanted the villa searched from top to bottom.

As it turned out this was not necessary. The search lasted only a short time as the little bottle, still more than half filled with white crystals, was found in de Beer's desk drawer. It had fingerprints all over it and it did not take long to determine that they were de Beer's.

The corpse of the victim was transferred to the police morgue for the formal autopsy, and de Beer was taken to police headquarters and placed under interrogation.

The autopsy produced exactly the results that Dr Hampton had suggested that it would: death by reason of massive ingestion of strychnine. The interrogation produced nothing.

A huge, red-haired man six feet three inches tall, de Beer held a high administrative position in the civil service and he and his wife had been socially prominent. Despite the evidence of the bottle of strychnine with his fingerprints on it, he vigorously denied any responsibility for his wife's death. He had had, he said, no motive. Asked how he then accounted for Doreen's death, he suggested that she had committed suicide.

This theory did not strike the inspector as very probably as it did not explain what the poison was doing hidden in de Beer's desk or how his fingerprints came to be all over the bottle. There were no fingerprints on it belonging to Mrs de Beer or anyone else.

Nonetheless, de Beer's reaction puzzled the inspector. In the first place, as far as could be ascertained, he was telling the truth about having no motive. The death of his wife had brought him no advantage, financial or otherwise, and there were no reports of domestic friction between the couple.

Moreover, de Beer's refusal to confess to the crime in the face of the physical evidence against him was illogical. He was not a stupid man and he had to realize that he could easily be convicted without a confession on the basis of the evidence alone. Why continue to undergo the unpleasantness of interrogation when a confession would not harm his position and might actually improve it when he was brought to trial for the murder?

There was something else, too. De Beer was unmistakably astonished beyond all measure that the autopsy had been able to detect traces of strychnine in his wife's body. He had repeatedly asked if the doctor had been quite certain. Was the white powder really strychnine? Did strychnine really remain in the body?

The inspector assured him that it did and that the evidence was complete and confirmed. The only thing lacking in the case was the motive, but it would be quite possible to obtain a conviction without it. Why he had murdered his wife did not matter so much as the fact that he had, and this was a fact which the police were in a position to demonstrate conclusively.

As things now stood, the inspector pointed out, he would probably be hung for the crime. If, however, he made a confession and presumably was able to offer some extenuating circumstances or, at least, expressed repentance, he might save his neck.

De Beer thought this over and eventually came to the conclusion that there was much in what the inspector said. At his next session with the interrogators, he indicated that he was now prepared to make a statement on the murder and that he would like to make it directly to the inspector himself.

Taken to Inspector Brinker's office, he said that it was true, he had murdered his wife with a tablespoon of strychnine in the cup of herbal tea which she took every evening. The reason for doing this was that he wanted to marry their housemaid, a twenty-year-old, blonde girl who came from the village of Fort Beaufort and who had worked for the de Beer's since 12 October 1978.

The girl's name was Elsabe Loubser and de Beer said that they had been having an affair since 6 January 1979. Being a civil servant, he was extremely precise in his dates and details.

He had been attracted, he said, to the big, generously built, blonde girl from the moment that she came to work for them and had begun almost immediately to lay hands on her whenever the opportunity presented itself. She had raised no serious objections and, encouraged by this lack of resistance, he had progressed to greater intimacies until on the night of 6 January, he had gone to her room at approximately 11 o'clock in the evening after his wife had gone to sleep where he had found her lying naked on her bed. Cape Town being in the southern hemisphere, January is, of course, the middle of the summer and the weather was warm.

They had had intercourse and, to his surprise, Elsabe had turned out to be a virgin.

After that they had had sexual relations frequently, sometimes in Elsabe's room and sometimes with the girl bent over the kitchen table with her skirts raised.

By the middle of April 1979, he had fallen so deeply in love with the housemaid that he could not bear the thought of life without her and he had asked her to marry him. He would, he said, divorce his wife.

Elsabe had not refused to marry him, but she had pointed out that divorce was not a simple matter. South Africa is conservative and divorce is frowned upon. For a man in his position, a divorce, probably contested and followed by a marriage to a housemaid, could cost him his job and certainly his social position.

De Beer had realized the truth of this remark and, without being too clear as to what he had in mind, had muttered that there must be some other way. He insisted that he had not, at that time, been thinking of murdering his wife.

On the following day, however, Elsabe had taken advantage of a moment when they were alone together and had pressed into his hand the little bottle of white crystals. She did not say what it was for, but she did say that it was a deadly poison and that it left no traces in the body.

De Beer, ravished by what he believed to be a demonstration of reciprocal feeling by Elsabe regarding their relationship, had proceeded to poison his wife that same evening.

He now recognized the folly of his act and regretted bitterly what he had done. It had been a sort of temporary insanity brought upon by an infatuation with a woman twenty-five years younger than himself. He was not, he pointed out, the first to find himself in such a situation.

This was perfectly true and it not only explained the motive of the murder, but constituted a basis for establishing the extenuating circumstances which would, perhaps, save de Beer from the gallows.

Healthy, successful men who have passed forty are often highly vulnerable to very young women and the courts recognize that their actions under such circumstances are not always completely rational. There would be precedents enough for de Beer's attorneys to draw on.

At the same time, however, de Beer's confession made Elsabe Loubser an accessory before the fact to murder and, possibly, even an accomplice. If she had procured the poison and had given it to de Beer with the hint that this could safely solve his marital problems, then she was as much of an instigator as he.

She was promptly taken into custody and brought to police headquarters where she was confronted with de Beer's tape-recorded confession.

Having listened to it, she said that there was not a word of truth in what de Beer said. She had never been intimate with her employer. She had entertained a great respect and even affection for Mrs de Beer and she had neither given de Beer any poison nor even suspected that he was in possession of any. The only explanation that she could suggest for his statement was that he was trying to pass the responsibility for the crime off on to an innocent housemaid in order to save himself.

Inspector Brinker was not convinced. De Beer's confession had been too precise, too detailed to be a pure fabrication, and it was the only reasonable explanation of his motives. Thinking that the young housemaid might not stand up well under a direct confrontation with her former employer and alleged lover, the inspector arranged for one.

The results were disappointing. De Beer went all to pieces, pleading with Elsabe to tell the police the truth and admit that they had been lovers and that she had given him the poison.

Elsabe was demure. 'I don't know what you're talking about, Mr de Beer,' she said. 'I have always tried to give good service while I was working for you. I don't know why you should want to harm me with these lies.'

De Beer was taken back, raving slightly, to the detention cells and Elsabe Loubser was released. There was not the slightest evidence other than the unsupported word of Petrus de Beer which would permit her to be held.

She had not, however, convinced the inspector. He still thought that de Beer was telling the truth. Otherwise, there was no logic to his actions whatsoever, and he had already been examined by a psychologist who reported that he appeared to be sane. De Beer was not hallucinating; he was telling the truth.

Whether he was or not made little difference to the inspector's case. Although he personally believed that Elsabe Loubser was at least as guilty of the crime as was de Beer, there was nothing in the world that he could do about it.

For de Beer the difference was a matter of life and death. With the refusal of Elsabe to support his statement, his hope for clemency as a result of extenuating circumstances had vanished. South Africa has the death penalty and uses it. Barring miracles, his next stop would be the gallows.

The inspector, therefore, instructed the sergeant to assign a man to keep an eye on Elsabe Loubser to see whether anything suspicious might turn up in her behaviour. He was afraid nothing would and he was quite right. One of the de Beers being dead and the other in jail, she had, of course, lost her job, but it did not take her long to find another equally satisfactory one in a house only a few blocks away from where the de Beers had lived. Good housemaids are as hard to find in South Africa as anywhere else.

Elsabe Loubser, therefore, continued, rather placidly, her housemaid's career, although nearly everyone who had had anything to do with the case suspected that she was as guilty of the murder of Doreen de Beer as was Doreen's husband. The de Beers being prominent, the newspapers had printed an enormous amount on the case and had speculated concerning Elsabe's role in the matter as much as they dared without inviting a libel suit. Elsabe herself had not given any indications concerning possible libel suits and had cooperated enthusiastically with newspaper reporters wanting interviews, but the city was full of lawyers who knew exactly how much could be extracted for any such unfounded assertations.

In the meantime, Petrus de Beer remained in the detention cells at police headquarters and clung stubbornly to his story. He was no longer being subjected to interrogation, partially because he had confessed to the murder and no further evidence was needed, and partially because the inspector was inclined to believe his story.

Nothing whatsoever of interest or significance having taken place with Elsabe Loubser, her surveillance by the detective was terminated and Sergeant Shryker only made an occasional check to see whether she was still in Cape Town and still working in the same place. The inspector did not want to lose track of her altogether because he had been striving for the past six months to determine the source of the strychnine with which Doreen de Beer had been poisoned.

If Petrus de Beer's story was to be believed and the

inspector did believe it, then it was Elsabe Loubser who had obtained the strychnine and given it to him.

If the inspector could find evidence of this, it would prove Elsabe's complicity in the crime and tend to confirm de Beer's account. This, in turn, could have an effect on the severity of his sentence.

The inspector had thought that tracing the origin of the strychnine might not prove too difficult. Most commercial strychnine is in the form of rat poison, but that which had been administered to Doreen de Beer consisted of chemically pure crystals. These were not as easy to obtain as rat poison and, as a matter of fact, were less suitable for murder.

Pure strychnine is exceedingly bitter, so much so that the bitterness is perceptible in the proportion of one part strychnine to 700,000 parts of water. Had Doreen de Beer not been in the habit of drinking a herbal tea which was also very bitter, she would almost certainly have noticed the taste.

As a matter of fact, she probably had, but it had been too late. As little as one half to one grain of strychnine is enough to cause death, and de Beer had laced the drink very liberally with the poison. A single swallow had, probably, been more than adequate. Almost instantly the typical abnormal irritability of the reflexes would have set in. The body would have arced painfully backward, the limbs begun to tremble, the neck to stiffen unnaturally and the muscles of the face to contract into a hideous sort of grin. Doreen would, however, have remained conscious. It would be only the stiffening of the chest muscles which would terminate her breathing and result in death by asphyxiation.

As the contortion of the body and the grimace caused by the contracted facial muscles closely resemble the symptoms of tetanus poisoning, the family doctor had been unable to make a definite diagnosis. Dr Hampton, however, trained in forensic medicine, had immediately recognized the signs of strychnine poisoning.

The inspector's efforts were, in the end, doomed to failure. He was not able to show that Elsabe Loubser had bought or otherwise obtained crystalline strychnine and, as he was a thorough man who overlooked no possibilities, he was also unable to find any evidence that Petrus de Beer had either.

De Beer had still not been brought to trial although nearly a year had passed as his attorneys were delaying matters as much as possible in the hope that some substantiation of the extenuating circumstances that he claimed could be obtained. The public prosecutor, like Inspector Brinker, inclined to believe de Beer's statements even though he could not prove them and anxious to give the accused the benefit of the doubt, was not pressing very hard for an early trial either. The newspapers, having found other and more interesting things to entertain their readers, had practically forgotten Petrus de Beer and Elsabe Loubser.

The homicide squad had not and towards the end of January 1980 Sergeant Shryker came into the inspector's office with the news that love had come to the housemaid.

'At least, it looks that way,' he said. 'The fellow's been driving over from Port Elizabeth two and three times a week and that's close to seven hundred miles round trip. Miss Loubser must have something about her that is mighty attractive to some men.'

'She had something that was mighty attractive to Petrus de Beer,' said the inspector. 'Who's this one? Also an older man?'

'Young,' said the sergeant. 'One year older than she is. The name is Marthinus Rossouw. Big, blond, athletic, good looking. He works in the diamond business in Port Elizabeth. No information as to how he came into contact with Miss Loubser, but he's been coming over to see her regularly since about the middle of this month. When he's here, they spend the night at the Rochester Hotel.'

'Second-class hotel,' remarked the inspector. 'Maybe it isn't true love after all.'

'Think of the seven hundred miles round trip,' said the sergeant.

Neither of the officers attached any particular significance to Elsabe Loubser's new friend. She was a young, attractive woman and it would have been more strange for her not to have a boyfriend than to have one. The only fact of any interest which turned up was that she was apparently concerned about her reputation for, although Rossouw registered at the Rochester Hotel under his own name, she gave her name as Barbara Carrington.

'She's probably publicity shy,' said the inspector. 'She had the newspapers buzzing around her so much at the time of the de Beer murder that she doesn't want to have the whole business start all over again. She must have been aware at the time that practically everybody thought that she was implicated in the murder or even directly responsible for it.'

'Well, I'll continue to keep an eye on her from time to time,' said the sergeant. 'You never know what may turn up.'

This was a prophetic observation, but it was going to be seven months before it became evident. The date was August 1980, a Saturday, and the middle of the South African winter. Business at the Rochester Hotel was slow and desk clerk, twenty-eight-year-old Ian Fielding, was peacefully reading a magazine behind the admissions desk in the lobby when he was startled nearly out of his wits by a piercing scream coming from somewhere on the first floor.

A slight but physically courageous man, Fielding dropped his magazine and went running up the stairs. One of the chambermaids was standing in the long hall a dozen doors down from the staircase and yelling her head off. When she saw Fielding, she fainted.

Fielding ran forward to where she lay and, looking through the open door of the room just beyond her, was astounded and horrified to see the naked body of a young, blonde woman sprawled across the bed with her knees bent over the edge of it and her feet touching the floor. Because of the circumstances, the scream and fainting of the chambermaid, he immediately jumped to the conclusion that the woman had been the victim of a rapist.

Conscious of his responsibility for a guest at the hotel, he dashed into the room and attempted to revive the woman, but soon realized that she did not appear to be breathing at all.

Nor could he find any trace of a heart beat. Although he could see no marks of injuries on the body, the woman's face was badly distorted, the eyes starting from their sockets and the tongue protruding from the mouth, and he thought she might have suffered a heart attack.

Picking up the house telephone on the table beside the bed, he told the switchboard operator to call the emergency ambulance service and, after a moment's hesitation, added that she had better also notify the police. He was not certain that the woman was dead, but, if she was, then it did not look to him as if it had been from natural causes.

He was out in the hall trying to revive the chambermaid when the telephone in the room rang. Going over to pick it up, he found himself speaking with the duty officer in the Criminal Investigations Department at police headquarters. The officer wanted to know if there really was a dead woman in the hotel as the switchboard operator had impulsively reported.

Fielding said that there was the body of a woman in the room, but he was not certain whether she was dead or not. He was afraid she was and she certainly looked it. He had called the ambulance.

The officer told him he was to remain where he was and not to allow anyone to enter the room until the police arrived. He wanted to know whether Fielding could identify the body.

Fielding said that he could not without checking the register. He was excited and confused and the dead woman's features were so distorted that he could not recognize her.

The duty officer then asked him if he knew the name of Elsabe Loubser and Fielding replied that he did not. He could not recall ever having had a Elsabe Loubser registered at the hotel.

In the meantime, Inspector Brinker and Sergeant Shryker were driving at a normally illegal speed to the Rochester Hotel. Off duty on that Saturday, they had been alerted over the telephone by the duty officer at police headquarters that a man identifying himself as Marthinus Rossouw had surrendered to the police and had stated that that he had strangled to death a Miss Elsabe Loubser in the Rochester Hotel. Confirmation that a woman, either dead or unconscious, had been found in one of the hotel rooms had just been received from a hotel employee. As Miss Loubser had been involved in the de Beer murder case, Inspector Brinker and Sergeant Shryker were being called in.

Arriving at the hotel only shortly after the ambulance, they found that Elsabe Loubser was very definitely dead as the result of manual strangulation and that Fielding had not been able to recognize the name because he had known her only as Barbara Carrington. He had, by now, collected his wits and not only remembered the girl, but also her companion with whom she had been coming to the hotel for over a half year now.

As there was little that needed to be done, the body of Elsabe Loubser was immediately removed to the ambulance and taken to the police morgue. An autopsy, subsequently carried out by Dr Hampton, was able to determine only that Elsabe had been engaged in sexual intercourse very shortly before her death and that it was the result of manual strangulation by a very strong man who had used great force. The girl's larynx was completely crushed.

Having viewed the corpse at the hotel and having taken a statement from Ian Fielding and the chambermaid who had discovered the body, the inspector and Sergeant Shryker hurried to police headquarters where Marthinus Rossouw was waiting in the detention cells. So far his only statement had been to the effect that he had strangled Elsabe Loubser to death, and he had not yet been sent for interrogation.

Actually no interrogation was necessary. Rossouw willingly volunteered a detailed account of the crime and the events leading up to it.

He had met Elsabe Loubser, he said, in a dance hall in Grosvenor Street on 16 January 1980. They had been immediately attracted to each other and, on that same evening, had had intercourse in Rossouw's car.

They had made a date for the following weekend and from that time on had seen each other as often as Rossouw could manage to get over from Port Elizabeth.

He had, he said, fallen deeply in love with Elsabe and on 15 July he had asked her to marry him.

Elsabe had replied that there was nothing that she wanted more in the world, but she had seemed confused and nervous and she had not given him a definite reply. He had thought that she wanted time to think it over before committing herself.

By that Saturday, on 2 August, she had still not given him a reply to his marriage proposal, and he began to press her gently. They were in the room at the Rochester Hotel which they always occupied and they were both naked as they had just engaged in intercourse.

Elsabe had hesitated, appeared to be on the verge of tears and then seemed to come to a decision. There was, she said, something that he had to know. Her name was not really Barbara Carrington.

Rossouw had been surprised and puzzled. When he had met her she had told him that her name was Barbara Carrington and he had never had any reason to doubt it. What was her name then, he wanted to know?

Elsabe had said that her name was Elsabe Loubser and, when this produced no reaction, she had asked him if he remembered the de Beer murder case.

Marthinus Rossouw remembered the de Beer murder case very well. Like everyone else in South Africa, he had been practically smothered under the masses of copy churned out on the case by the newspapers. There were few people in the country who did not remember intimately the details of the de Beer murder.

The mention of de Beer immediately made the connection in his mind and he recalled that the housemaid had been named Elsabe Loubser. As far as he could remember, however, she had not been implicated in anything other than the unsupported charges by the murderer himself. Why had she seen fit to give him a false name in that case?

Elsabe looked embarrassed and said that, if they were to be married, she did not want to start off by having secrets from him. What de Beer had said was true. She had deliberately tricked him into murdering his wife with a poison that she knew could easily be detected in the body.

The thunderstruck Rossouw demanded to know why she had done such a thing, and Elsabe said that she had done it because she hated de Beer. She had been a virgin when she came to work in the de Beer home and he had practically raped her. She had been unable to resist or complain because she was afraid of losing her job, and it was a very well paid one.

She had, therefore, put up with de Beer's sexual demands on her and had bided her time waiting for an opportunity to revenge herself.

The opportunity had come on 14 April 1979 when de Beer had asked her to marry him and, when she pointed out that divorce was impractical, had muttered that there must be some other way.

Elsabe, according to what she told Rossouw, knew a sort of faith healer and quack doctor from her own village of Fort Beaufort, and she had approached him asking him for a deadly poison which would leave clear traces in the body of a corpse. He had given her the little bottle of strychnine. She had not known that it was strychnine, only that it was deadly poison and that any competent doctor could easily detect it.

The following day she had given the bottle to de Beer with the assurance that it would leave no traces in the body of a corpse. De Beer, filled with love and blind trust in what he deemed to be his future wife, had said that he would take care of things and he had.

The final step in this diabolical plan which involved the cruel murder of a woman who had never shown her anything but kindness, was to deny the intimate connection between herself and de Beer; deny all knowledge of the poison; deny all knowledge of the murder and leave de Beer to hang for his crime without a trace of an extenuating circumstance.

It was the way she had planned it and it was the way it had worked, but, if she was now going to marry Rossouw, she could not do it without making a clean breast of the whole matter.

Having made her confession, she snuggled up to her lover, apparently expecting his approval.

She did not get it. Rossouw, it seemed, was anything but modern and progressive in his ideas on sex. Flying into a screaming, insane rage, he had grasped his proposed bride by the throat and had strangled her so violently and fatally that

148

she had been dead before she hardly had time to realize what was happening to her.

The very memory of the event excited Rossouw so much that he began to yell even in the inspector's office. She had tricked him the same way that she had tricked de Beer, he roared! She was no decent, respectable girl. She had been sleeping with de Beer for months. He would never believe that she had not enjoyed it. What she had told him was all lies. She had thought herself that the poison would leave no traces in the body and that she could then marry the rich, socially prominent de Beer. It was only when the scheme had not worked that she had treacherously abandoned her lover. He did not regret killing her! She deserved to die!

Rossouw was taken off, more or less foaming at the mouth, to the detention cells to cool down. He left behind him, however, a statement which would save Petrus de Beer from the gallows. There had been extenuating circumstances in the murder of Doreen de Beer and the late Elsabe Loubser was, if anything, more responsible for the crime than he.

As neither de Beer nor Rossouw were completely responsible for their actions and as Elsabe definitely was for hers, neither murderer was hung, but received life and twenty-five-year jail sentences respectively.

It was reported, however, that Petrus de Beer nearly paid the supreme penalty upon hearing of Elsabe's death.

He almost died laughing.

Civil servants are not, however, noted for their sense of humour.

11

A FORTY-POUND VICTIM
EIGHT FEET LONG

The cases of the murders of Doreen De Beer and Elsabe
Loubser represent what might be termed the garden variety
of homicidal madness. De Beer was driven to madness by the
belief, common among older men, that copulation with
young females will result in a return of youth. Rossouw was
reduced to insanity by sexual jealousy and deception in the
character of his beloved. If the human race had evolved with
only one sex instead of several, there would probably be close
to ninety per cent fewer homicides. This would result in
severe overpopulation.

Overpopulation means, among other things, that housing
is going to be in short supply or, rather, in even shorter
supply because in many places housing is in short supply
without any overpopulation.

Belgium is not a particularly overpopulated country and
yet housing is often something of a problem. It was, therefore, with considerable rejoicing that thirty-four-year-old
Erik Aertbielen took possession of the cottage at 21 Wolstraat
in the suburbs of the Belgian city of Antwerp on Monday, 16
August 1980. The previous tenant had moved out a week
earlier and, as he had left the place exceptionally clean and
tidy, there was little for Aertbielen to do other than to arrange
his own affairs and make a survey of the house and garden.

This took him most of the week, but, by Saturday, 23
August, he had completed his arrangements inside the house
and was preparing to lay out the garden.

It was, of course, too late in the year to do very much
planting, but he could at least mark out some paths and spade

up the flowerbeds and, on that sunny, warm afternoon with a cheery sea breeze blowing in from off the port, he set out to do so.

The first of the flowerbeds gave only cause for gratification. Although the preceding tenant did not appear to have put much effort into the garden, neither it nor the house were new and it had obviously been well cultivated over a long period of time in the past. The soil was rich, moist and comparatively loose.

Beginning with the second flowerbed at approximately a quarter past four in the afternoon, however, Aertbielen soon encountered a difficulty. He was spading deeply, the full length of the blade, and less than a foot beneath the surface of the earth something was preventing the spade from entering. It was not, however, hard like a stone, but something yielding.

Aertbielen, suspecting buried plastic sacks full of garbage, muttered a swearword and began to clear away the earth over the mysterious object.

An instant later, he dropped his spade and ran off a dozen yards. Whatever it was that lay buried there, it was sending up the most hideous stench that had ever invaded his nostrils.

Bitterly cursing the previous tenant whom he had, up until now, praised for having left the house in such good order, Aertbielen returned to the house, soaked a small towel in cologne, tied it around his mouth and nose and returned grimly to his task. Whatever this absolutely foul rubbish was, it had to be dug up and disposed of. Until it was the garden was unusable.

Aertbielen did not get very far with his project. The rubbish appeared to be wrapped in an old quilt, but as he got the spade under one edge and lifted it up, he dropped, for the second time, the tool he was using and ran off even further than before.

Looking up at him from the folds of the quilt was a hideously decayed human face. The cheeks had rotted through to expose the yellowed teeth. The nose was a small mound of putrefaction and the eyes swam like glazed marbles in the stinking liquid which filled the eye sockets. Despite its terrible condition, the face appeared astonishingly lifelike and he had had the impression that it was looking directly and sorrowfully at him. For an instant he was filled with a feeling of horror that it was about to climb out of the hole in the ground.

Although the sky was still cloudless, the August afternoon had suddenly gone a great deal less bright and it was obvious that there was going to be no more gardening that day. Afraid to turn his back on what lay in the hole in the earth, Aertbielen backed into his house, his nerves so shaken that he locked the door behind him, and went to telephone the police.

He was very impatient for them to come and do something about the corpse in his garden and, when the first patrolcar arrived, he was sitting on the curb in front of the house.

Although old and famous, Antwerp is not a terribly large city. Its population is only in the neighbourhood of 200,000 inhabitants. It does, however, have a sufficiently high crime rate that several homicide squads divide the duty around the clock. On this Saturday afternoon, it was the turn of Inspector Jean van Bulcke, chief of Homicide Three.

At that moment, the inspector was still sitting in his office waiting for confirmation from the patrolcar that the object in Erik Aertbielen's garden was actually a human corpse. As in any modern city, Antwerp has its share of psychopaths, alcoholics, drug addicts and practical jokers who account for a great many more homicide reports than there are homicides. If the squad was to go out on every report received, they would be almost continuously underway and mostly to no purpose.

In this case, however, confirmation was quickly received, the officers walking up to the hole while holding their breath and then making a hasty retreat to the patrolcar. It was, they reported over the radio-telephone a human body and a very dead one.

The inspector, sitting with the telephone receiver held to his ear, pointed his finger at his assistant, Detective-Sergeant Leopold Haan, who immediately jumped up and ran off down the corridor to summon the medical expert and the technicians from the police laboratory. Confirmation that there was a human corpse in the garden at number 21 Wolstraat was the stimulus which would touch off the homicide investigation.

Not much later, Inspector van Bulcke and Sergeant Haan arrived at the scene accompanied by Dr Jerome Beekman, the duty specialist in legal medicine. The detachment from the police laboratory was on the way, but had not yet arrived and, until it did, there was little the investigators could do except to go and peer into the hole while holding their noses.

Eventually it would be up to Dr Beekman to make an examination of the rotting corpse, but he could not do this until it had been brought up out of the shallow grave in which it lay, and that was a job for the laboratory technicians. They would not only have to extract the corpse, but also determine what potential clues might have been buried with it. These potential clues fell under two headings. One, they could be clues leading to the identification of the corpse. Two, they could be clues leading to the identification of whoever was responsible for the corpse being buried there. It could not yet be said that there would be clues leading to the identification of the murderer because there was, so far, no evidence that a murder had taken place. It was possible that death had occurred through natural causes and, until proved otherwise, no offence other than illegal burial of a corpse was a certainty.

However the question was not resolved by the doctor's examination of the body after it had been brought up, laid on a plastic sheet and the quilt surrounding it removed.

The quilt had not been tied, but merely wrapped around the body which, according to Dr Beekman, was that of a female, probably under the age of forty who had been dead and buried for close to six months. Decomposition was very advanced and the doctor was not at all confident that he would be able to establish the cause of death.

This preliminary examination having been completed, the corpse was enclosed in a plastic bag and lifted into a metal coffin for transport to the police morgue. There Dr Beekman would carry out the complete autopsy with the assistance of a team from the police laboratory who would search for clues to the woman's identity and attempt to recover identifiable fingerprints. Although the hands were very badly decayed, there was a possibility that enough skin remained on the fingertips to make an impression. The probability of other clues was remote. The corpse was entirely naked and bore no jewellery, except a small crucifix attached to a silver chain around the neck. The crucifix, also silver, carried no jeweller's mark and looked as if it might have been home-made.

In the meantime, the laboratory squad set about putting the earth at the bottom of the grave through a screen in the hope of recovering something that might be of value to the investigation.

The inspector, a bulky man with a rather oval figure and high complexion, stood watching them thoughtfully and silently. Presently, he was joined by the sergeant who had been taking a statement from Erik Aertbielen.

Aertbielen, said the sergeant, knew nothing about the matter. He had only moved into the cottage less than a week earlier and he did not know the name of the previous tenant although he understood that he had been a single man.

'I have the name of the real-estate agent that handled the rental of the house,' said the sergeant. 'He'll probably have the last tenant's name and, maybe, a forwarding address. You want me to go get it?'

'Yes,' said the inspector. 'Find out who the previous tenant was and if he was here for less than six months, find out who the one was before that. Beekman says she's been dead for six months or more, but I think we'd better extend that back for at least eight months. The condition the body is in, I don't think that Beekman can be too certain either.'

The sergeant nodded in silent acknowledgement and went away, a short, dark, rather slightly built man with a serious, busy sort of manner. He was conscientious and hard working, but, like all European police officers, he was basically a civil servant and he handled his work in the manner in which a civil servant would.

After a time, the technicians finished sieving the earth and came over to report that they had found a button, a throwaway-type cigarette lighter, some small pieces of wood and four cigarette butt filters. Whether any of these things had any connection with the corpse could not be said. They and the quilt in which the body had been wrapped were being taken to the police laboratory for further examination, evaluation and analysis. A report on the laboratory findings would be available on Monday morning.

The inspector nodded, went in to tell Erick Aertbielen that he could resume digging in his garden and returned to his office at police headquarters. There was nothing to do now other than to wait for the reports, one from the sergeant, one from Dr Beekman and one from the police laboratory.

He had hardly got settled in his office, however, when he received a frantic call from Erik Aertbielen. He had gone to get some earth from a sort of mound near the fence around the garden to fill in the hole where the woman's body had been buried and had come upon another corpse. This one smelled even worse than the first.

Aertbielen having established his credibility with the inspector, he did not wait for a confirmation, but notified the laboratory technicians and hurried back to 21 Wolstraat alone. Dr Beekman was still involved with the autopsy of the first corpse and the sergeant had not yet returned from his visit to the real-estate agent.

Aertbielen was quite right about the smell. It was worse than had been that of the dead woman, but he was mistaken in believing that there was only one corpse.

When the laboratory technicians had finally completed carefully opening up the mound of earth, they found not one body but seventeen – six boa constrictors and eleven rats. The rats were, of course, no more than skeletons.

'Boa constrictors?' said the inspector incredulously. 'Six boa constrictors and eleven rats? In Antwerp?'

'Well, they could be pythons,' said the technician in charge of the squad. 'Whatever the species, they're big snakes. The biggest one must have been about eight feet long when it was alive.'

'But what does it mean?' said the inspector. 'There must be some connection between the dead women and the dead snakes, but what . . .? And what about the rats?'

'They probably represent food for the snakes,' said the technicians. 'Offhand, it looks as if somebody has murdered a snake charmer and her act with her. Sounds crazy, I'll admit, but I suppose that snake charmers get murdered the same as anybody else.'

'Yes, I suppose so,' said the inspector. 'I just wish they wouldn't do it during my duty period. Snake charmers and that sort of thing are carnival people. They're continually travelling around to the little local fairs and they're the very devil to trace. They're an international lot, too. For all we know, the woman may not have even been Belgian.'

'The snakes definitely weren't,' said the technician.

Once again the laboratory specialists carefully sieved the earth in which the snakes and rats had been buried. Once again they recovered a number of miscellaneous objects which might or might not have some connection with the person who had buried them and, presumably, killed the snakes and rats.

It appeared that the snakes' heads had been cut off with something sharp and heavy, possibly an axe, and the rats seemed to have been crushed, for there were many broken bones in the skeletons. Whether this crushing had been carried out by the person who had killed the snakes or by the snakes themselves could not at the moment be said.

The killing of snakes, however large, not being classified as homicide or even a felony, the bodies were left in Aertbielen's garden and the technicians returned to police headquarters, taking with them only a few samples of the snakes' skin for the purpose of identifying the species.

The inspector too returned to his office and, although it was by now late in the evening, found his assistant waiting for him there. He had not been able to obtain very much information from the real-estate agent in charge of renting the cottage at 21 Wolstraat. The name of the previous tenant was Guy Baptist and he had moved into the cottage on 1 November 1979. The real-estate agent described him as an enormous man close to six feet six inches tall and extremely muscular. He had a long, black moustache, thick, black side whiskers and looked almost too fierce to be real. His manner had, however, been gentle and soft-spoken, although he had a somewhat dramatic way of expressing himself.

'November, December, January,' said the inspector, counting on his fingers. 'Over eight months. He was occupying the house when the body was buried there. I suppose there's no forwarding address?'

'None,' said the sergeant. 'However Baptist was alone when he rented the house and he doesn't appear to have had any female visitors. I went back out to Wolstraat after I had talked to the real-estate agent and questioned the neighbours. They say that he was very quiet, had no contact with anyone in the street and was hardly ever home. No one reported ever having seen him with a woman or having seen a woman come to the house.'

'They didn't mention anything about boa constrictors, did they?' said the inspector. 'Or rats?'

'What?' said the sergeant, slapping the side of his head as if he thought there was something wrong with his ears. 'I thought you said . . .'

The inspector explained. 'Actually, there's a sort of connection there,' he said. 'The woman was apparently a snake charmer and, from your description, this Guy Baptist sounds like the sort of person you might find working around the carnivals and fairs. Could have been billed as a strong man or something like that. In any case, that's the direction we'll start looking. With an appearance like that, he shouldn't be too difficult to identify even among the carnival people.'

'It's definitely homicide then?' said the sergeant. 'Has Beekman already reported on the autopsy findings?'

The inspector shook his head. 'Not yet,' he said, 'and I don't expect him to before Monday morning. The condition the body was in, he'll have his work cut out for him. However, it's very difficult to imagine how a snake charmer, her snakes and rats all ended up buried in that garden if it wasn't homicide. Whatever Beekman reports, I think that we want to have a talk with Mr Baptist.'

'Maybe it would be easier to begin by trying to identify the snake charmer,' said the sergeant. 'I can't believe that there are all that many snake charmers in Belgium. After all, it's a small country. People like that must have booking agents for places other than just the fairs. If one suddenly turned up missing, it should be possible to trace her through the booking agents.'

'That's not a bad idea,' said the inspector. 'Go ahead and see what you can do about locating a snake act that failed to meet her bookings after November of last year.'

As the inspector had anticipated, there was no report from Dr Beekman until nearly noon on Monday and then it was inconclusive. As was customary, the doctor came to the inspector's office to make a preliminary verbal report on such findings of the autopsy as were of importance to the investigation. The official, written report, which would go into exhaustive detail, would follow later.

'Well, to begin with,' said the doctor, dropping into the chair beside the inspector's desk and accepting one of his cigarettes, 'there's no positive proof of homicide. I don't know what killed her. It wasn't anything that left a large wound in the torso or that broke the skull or any of the other bones. She could have been strangled, smothered, poisoned perhaps or she could have bled to death. On the other hand, she could have choked on a piece of toffee or suffered a burst appendix. The fact is, decomposition is too advanced to say anything with certainty. I can't even fix the time of death closer than within a month or so.'

'Any suggestions as to what she may have looked like when she was alive?' said the inspector.

'Five feet six inches tall,' said the doctor. 'Live weight would have been around one twenty or a little more. She was generously built. Black hair, not dyed. Black or dark brown eyes. Around thirty years old, give or take five years in either direction. You know that the identification section failed to recover any identifiable prints?'

The inspector nodded. 'I hardly thought they would,' he said. 'It doesn't matter. They would only have been useful if she had a police record, and there's no particular reason to believe that she did. You're not classing it as homicide then?'

The doctor shook his head. 'Cause of death for reasons unknown,' he said. 'Of course, considering the circumstances and where the body was found, I personally have no doubt but that it was a homicide. There's no evidence of it on the body though.'

The inspector had not expected anything more from the autopsy report, and he was not surprised when the laboratory also turned in a negative report later that day. None of the items recovered at the scene with the exception of the quilt in which the body had been wrapped could be shown to have any connection with the corpse. The only conclusion that they had been able to draw was that the woman and the snakes had apparently been buried at about the same time.

In the meantime, however, Sergeant Haan had been busy and had come up with a tentative identification of the victim. She was twenty-eight-year-old Monique Verstrepen, and she was not a snake charmer, but a striptease artist.

'She did erotic dances under the stage name of Nikki Lee,' said the sergeant. 'The snakes were part of the act. She came on to the stage with the snakes draped over her strategic areas and then, as she did her dance, the snakes crawled away one by one into a big basket and she ended up nude. Supposed to have been a great act. She was very much in demand and not just as a dancer.'

'What do you mean by that?' said the inspector.

'Part of her job was being friendly with the customers,' said the sergeant. 'It seems that she was very friendly. If the price was right, you could take her home and she'd spend the night. Must have happened pretty often. She was a very pretty girl. Here. I brought along a picture for you. It's one of her publicity shots.'

The inspector looked at the large, glossy photograph which the sergeant handed him. It was the picture of a beautiful, voluptuously built woman with long, black hair and dark eyes. She was dressed rather carelessly in one or two snakes which were not covering the strategic areas quite as conscientiously as they were supposed to.

'She matches Beekman's description from the corpse,' said the inspector, handing the photograph back. 'She's disappeared, I take it?'

'Not seen since November first of 1979,' said the sergeant.

'She had a dozen or more bookings and she didn't show for any of them. The booking agent said he couldn't understand it. Normally, she was extremely reliable. A real professional.'

'If it wasn't for the snakes,' said the inspector, 'I'd say that she simply went home one night with the wrong guy, but I can't imagine her taking her snakes along on a one-night stand like that. The things were heavy. It would have been a problem just transporting them around. I suspect that we're going to find that there was a more profound relationship between Miss Verstrepen and Guy Baptist than a simple pick-up in a nightclub. See what the booking agents have to say about Baptist. Have you checked to see if there was ever a missing person report on Verstrepen?'

The sergeant had not and the inspector picked up the telephone and asked for a check. The answer came back shortly. Monique Verstrepen had been reported missing by her sister in May of 1980. The missing woman's husband had been contacted where the couple lived at 21 Wolstraat, and he had said that his wife had gone on tour to England and was going from there to the United States. The sister had been satisfied with this explanation. Monique, it seemed, often went off on tour for extended periods, although she had never before gone overseas.

The inspector asked the husband's name and was not at all surprised to hear that it was Guy Baptist. He was, it seemed, fifteen years older than Monique and they had been married on 18 December 1976. There were no children. The missing person report gave no profession for Baptist, but the officer who had gone out to investigate the disappearance said that he had had the impression that Baptist was in some kind of theatrical business.

Equipped with this information, it did not take the sergeant very long to determine that Guy Baptist appeared at carnivals, fairs and in nightclubs, sometimes with his wife and sometimes alone, as Samurai Khan, a magician, juggler, fire-eater, sword-swallower and fakir who supported his huge bulk on the points of twelve sabres while a young and pretty assistant stood on his stomach.

Unlike his wife, Baptist had been appearing regularly at his various commitments and was thought to be, at the moment, in Brussels, thirty miles south of Antwerp.

The Brussels police were immediately contacted with a request to locate Baptist and take him into custody. This, however, proved difficult as, like all of the carnival people, Baptist moved almost constantly and, having been in the business for a great many years, did not always make use of booking agents. Eventually, however, he was traced and taken into custody at the Railway Fair in Brussels.

Despite his size and appearance, Baptist offered no resistance and meekly accompanied the arresting officers to police headquarters where he was held until a slightly nervous Sergeant Haan and a detail of three detectives came down and brought him back to Antwerp.

As Baptist was not wanted by the Brussels police he had not been questioned there, but upon being asked by Inspector van Bulcke at police headquarters in Antwerp where his wife was, he replied that she had gone on tour to England and the United States.

The inspector then informed him that her corpse had been dug up from the garden of the house which they had occupied. He added that the bodies of her snakes had also been recovered.

Baptist sighed deeply and said that it was true, he had murdered his wife. He had not wanted to, but having done so, he had tried to conceal the fact as he did not want to spend his few remaining years in jail.

The inspector did not understand exactly what he meant by his few remaining years, but suggested that he begin at the beginning.

Baptist said that he and Monique had first met in 1971 when she had attended one of his performances. He was, at the time, divorced and had had an unfortunate experience with his first wife.

Although he had been trained as a pastry cook when a young man, he had not liked the profession and, following his compulsory military service, he found work as a truck driver. In 1958 he had had to deliver a carnival ride to a new owner, and had been propositioned by the ride operator to stay on and work with the carnival. He had done so and had taught himself all the various tricks of his act. The life suited him perfectly and he could not imagine working at any other profession.

Monique, too, had started out quite differently. She had been undergoing training as a dress designer, but she had been so impressed by Baptist's performance that she had come to see him after it was over and had asked if he would hire her as his assistant.

He had hired her and, very shortly thereafter, they had become lovers and had begun living together. Five years later they had married.

Their happiness, said Baptist, had lasted for two years and had then been destroyed by an act of infidelity. He did not know how much the inspector knew about carnival people, but their morals were, he said, very rigid. Marriage was for life and no extra-marital affairs were permitted.

The inspector, who knew that Monique had shared beds with a veritable army of customers from the nightclubs, raised his eyebrows involuntarily and Baptist, seeing and correctly interpreting the gesture, hastened to explain.

Monique's sexual activities with the customers, he said, were not infidelities. They were a part of the profession and a means of earning money. Monique was not emotionally involved.

It had not been Monique who had been unfaithful. It had been he. After Monique had worked out her routine with the snakes, she had become very popular in her own right and they had often booked separately. On one of these occasions when he was appearing in another town, he had had a brief affair with one of the other female performers. Unfortunately, another girl who knew Monique had also been part of the troupe and she had told Monique what her husband had done.

From that moment on, Baptist's life had been sheer hell. They were at that time living at number 14 Borsbeekstraat in the little town of Bergerhout halfway between Antwerp and Brussels, and they had usually managed to be home on those nights that they were not actually performing.

Monique, hot-tempered and insanely jealous, had been in an almost permanent frenzy of rage. She had smashed everything that they owned, had scratched and bitten her unresisting husband and had thrown wine, food and worse things into his face.

Guy, conscious of his guilt and unable to offer any defence, had accepted it all patiently up until the night of 1 November 1971. They had been due to move the following day to the cottage at 21 Wolstraat in Antwerp and all of their things were already packed.

Monique had been in a worse rage than ever and his patient acceptance of the abuse seemed only to goad her into greater excesses. Finally, she had seized one of the rats which she kept to feed her snakes which were, at this time in a large basket in the dining room, and had thrown it into his face. The terrified rat had bitten him on the cheek and this had been the final straw which snapped his patience.

He could not recall having seized her, but he was an enormously strong man and when he came to his senses again he was holding a dead body between his hands.

There being obviously no further employment for the snakes. He had chopped off their heads with one of his swords and had crushed the rats with his bare hands. When he moved the following day, his household effects had included eighteen corpses which he had then buried in the garden two days later.

'I'm sorry,' he said, clasping his huge hands between his knees. 'I didn't want to kill her. I loved her. But then, I didn't see any reason to go to jail for these last years. I wanted to die on the stage like any good trouper.'

The inspector still did not understand his reference to dying on the stage and his last few years, but following a physical examination and an interview with Baptist's doctor, the situation became clear.

As a professional fire-eater, Baptist suffered from a terrible occupational hazard. Every time he performed, the flame which he drew in and then blew out his mouth attacked his lungs and stomach. One lung was almost completely non-functional and the other was gravely affected. The condition of his stomach was such that an internal haemorrhage could carry him off at almost any moment. In the opinion of the doctor, he had, at the most, two years to live.

It turned out to be somewhat less.

Indicted for the murder of Monique Verstrepen in September of 1980, Guy Baptist or, as he preferred to be known, Samurai Khan died in the detention cells on 16 March 1982 without ever coming to trial.

12

SOMEONE COULD BE WAITING WHEN YOU COME HOME TONIGHT

Poor Samurai Khan was, perhaps, insane, but it was only temporary insanity and, had he ever come to trial, it would, no doubt, have been so recognized by the court. Having rats flung in your face is an experience to unhinge the reason of even the most stable-minded.

Monique was, if anything, crazier than her husband. Although a comparatively young woman, she had apparently never heard of the sexual revolution and did not realize that Samurai Khan's mistep was without significance. Her actions and end, once again, demonstrate clearly the dangers of conservatism and a refusal to accept the tenets of the New Morality.

Alas! Monique Verstrepen is not alone in her unreasonable attitude. There are others, many others, and their actions are sometimes even more violent than hers. Monique's reprisals were directed against her own husband, but there are persons who are so incensed by the New Freedom that they do not hesitate to take action against total strangers.

And, for the fullest blossoming of the New Moral Freedom, there is no place like the Spanish Balearic Islands. Not among the local Spaniards, of course, who still look upon Queen Victoria as a radical libertarian, but among the tourists who tend to confuse 'vacation' with 'non-stop orgy' and who greatly outnumber the local Spaniards in any case.

The largest number of tourists in the Balearic Islands and also the largest number of converts to the New Morality are the West Germans. Indefatigable tourists and well-heeled, they overrun the islands to the point where the uninformed might believe themselves in Hamburg or Frankfurt. Married or not, they come with the conviction that they are going to encounter an endless number of willing, able and not too hideous sex partners, and they do. This makes places like the island of Ibiza exciting.

Surprisingly enough, however, not for everyone or, at least, not in that way. Germany also has romantic souls for whom sex is not everything.

When Doris Erika Renate Heidemann came to the island of Ibiza in June of 1978, it was like the realization of a dream. A diplomaed hotel administration technician, the twenty-one-year-old girl from the German city of Düsseldorf had particularly wanted a job on one of the Spanish Balearic Islands and Ibiza was, without question, the most colourful of them all.

However, unlike the tourists, Doris thought Ibiza exciting for reasons that had nothing to do with sex, drugs, alcohol or the other standard forms of entertainment. It was warm. It was exotic. It was a place where she could practise her Spanish and gain experience in her profession.

An attractive but not pretty girl with a build that was more athletic than seductive, she was serious, hard-working, intelligent and highly efficient, all virtues formerly associated with the German character but now considered by some to be old-fashioned.

These old-fashioned characteristics were not, however, looked down upon at the Penta Club Bungalow Hotel in the resort city of San Antonio Abad where she was regarded as a most valuable employee who, by the beginning of August 1979 was already known to the often hard-pressed tour group leaders as a girl who could get things down when all else failed.

She would be sorely missed because Doris Heidemann would not be completing the season at the Penta Club Hotel this year.

Equally sorely missed would be Dr Don Luis German Perez de la Fuente, a thirty-two-year-old Spanish nobleman who was employed as a toxicologist at Guterrez Ortega Hospital in the city of Valdepenas.

Valdepenas is a very long way inland somewhere between Malaga and Madrid on the Spanish mainland. On the face of things, it seemed unlikely that Don Luis and Doris Heidemann would ever meet, and it was beyond the bounds of all probability that they would meet under the circumstances which they actually did.

However, even doctors and noblemen take vacations and, beginning 1 August 1979, Don Luis took his, setting off for the Balearic Islands of Majorca, Menorca and Ibiza, none of which he had visited before.

The highly educated and cultured descendant of an ancient family with a fondness for food and drink, he arrived in the city of Palma on the island of Majorca on that same day, 1 August and, finding it not to his liking, left the following day on the ferry for Ibiza. His vacation was for two weeks, but, as it was going to turn out, he would not be taking all of it.

On Ibiza, the doctor found accommodation at a first-class hotel in the largest town, also called Ibiza, and there he remained until the afternoon of 5 August when an unfortunate incident resulted in his departure.

In the meantime, in San Antonio Abad, on the western side of the island and less than eight miles from Ibiza with which it is connected by a modern highway, Doris Heidemann was having greater problems in finding accomodations for guests who had fallen victim to the common European practice of overbooking.

If this were not enough, there was also the social side of her job to consider and for the night of Saturday to Sunday, she was personally booked solid with dinner to be followed by a visit to one or more discotheques.

She was not looking forward to this very much. Like many Germans, she cared little what she ate as long as there was enough of it, and she regarded discotheques as a waste of time. However, her dinner companions were all important tour operators and travel-agency owners and the entertainment was of importance to the affairs of the hotel.

Before setting out for the evening, she performed one last service which might, under the circumstances, have been the most significant act of her life. A guest who through over-booking had no place to lay his head that night had appealed for her help. He was a fellow German and she was anxious to help him, but she knew with certainty that there was no bed free in San Antonio Abad that night and probably not in all Ibiza.

Except one. Her own.

Or rather two, for Doris had a small, spare bedroom in her ground-floor apartment at 12 Can Puig des Moli where she lived when she was home, seldom enough during the season. The rooms at the Penta Club Bungalow Hotel were too precious to be occupied by employees.

'Listen,' she said. 'I can't get you a room tonight, but you can sleep at my place. I don't know if I'll get home at all tonight, but, in any case, there's a spare bedroom. I'll leave the keys to the apartment at the desk.'

This last was necessary because Doris was on the point of leaving for dinner and the man had telephoned from the other side of town. She had no idea what he looked like even, but she wanted to make clear that all she was offering him was the bed.

The vacationer was grateful. He was coming immediately to pick up the keys.

Doris hung up the telephone, became involved in a half-dozen other matters simultaneously, got them more or less straightened out and left with her group for dinner and the discotheques.

She had forgotten to leave her keys at the desk. It was an oversight which proved fatal.

Monday morning is no more of a joyous occasion for the police in resort towns than in less exotic places, and Inspector Luis Hernandez of the Criminal Investigations Department of the San Antonio Abad police groaned slightly as he sank into the chair behind his desk and lit the first cigarette of the day.

In a normal town the size of San Antonio Abad, there would have been no criminal investigations department and few members of the uniformed branch, but San Antonio Abad was anything but normal in the summertime and their criminal investigations department was, if anything, seriously overworked.

As the inspector reached for the first file the telephone rang. A cultured voice speaking perfect, educated Spanish said, 'I have rid the island of the spirit of the Great Shark. You will find the vessel at twelve Can Puig des Moli.'

There was a sharp click as the conversation was terminated.

'Another hop-head on a bad trip, Pedro,' said the inspector, dropping the telephone back into the cradle. 'Twelve Can Puig des Moli. You want to take a look?'

On the opposite side of the office Detective-Sergeant Pedro Algernas raised his narrow dark face from the file he was processing and smiled. He was pleased to be getting out of the office, even if only for a short time.

'Any instructions?' he said. 'Should I bring him in? Or is it a her?'

'A him and a Spaniard,' said the inspector wearily. 'You'll have to play it by ear. He sounded completely crazy to me. Something about a great shark.'

The sergeant left the office and San Antonio Abad being a relatively small place, arriving in Can Puig des Moli within a matter of ten minutes on foot. It was, as might be expected in Ibiza at the height of the summer season, a gloriously sunny, warm day. The sea was blue. Flowers were everywhere. The streets were packed with vacationers. It was gay.

Doris Heidemann was not.

The sergeant, having rung the bell at number twelve and having received no answer, tried the door which he found unlocked and went in.

Doris was lying completely naked on the cold tiles of the living-room floor. She was sprawled on her back, her arms widespread and the sergeant's jaw dropped in horror as he saw that where her eyes should have been were only empty, bloody sockets. In a manner which he could not imagine, her eyes had been literally torn out of her head.

It was not all. The breasts were nearly ripped away and

were covered with enormous bite wounds, the marks of the teeth clearly visibile.

The genitals were a mass of dried blood and something was sticking out between the lips of the vagina.

The entire body was so covered with cuts, scratches and black bruises that, for a moment, the sergeant thought the woman was a negro.

Her race was, however, of minor importance. What mattered was that he was confronted here with what was unquestionably the worst homicide that he had ever seen or heard of.

Even though he realized that the woman must be dead, he knelt and automatically felt for a pulse or signs of respiration. There were none, of course, and he got to his feet relieved. It would have been even more horrible if this tortured mass of flesh were still alive.

Although there was a telephone standing on a side table not far from the body, he did not make use of it, but ran as fast as he could go back to headquarters where he reported the details of his discovery to a startled and apprehensive Inspector Hernandez.

The fact was this sounded like something that the inspector had long feared. With the ever-increasing number of drug addicts coming to the island each summer, he had often thought that it was only a matter of time before one of the grisly crimes common in such circles elsewhere took place.

Now it seemed that it had and, sending the sergeant to pick up the town's coroner and the entire staff of the small police laboratory, he hurried personally to the scene.

The sight which greeted his eyes was worse than the sergeant had described it, if anything, and the inspector, a short, stout, round-faced man who was perhaps a little too soft-hearted for criminal investigations work had to go outside and have another cigarette before he could begin the investigation.

In the meantime, the sergeant had arrived with Dr Felix Bastando, the tall, thin and slightly haggard-looking coroner, and the four members of the laboratory staff, and while the doctor proceeded to an examination of the corpse, the laboratory men set about attempting to identify the victim.

This presented no difficulty as Doris Heidemann's pass-port was in the drawer of a desk less than six feet from her body and, although the mutilated face on the floor bore little resemblance to the girl looking gravely out of the passport photograph, the height, weight and other general character-istics were enough to make reasonably certain the identifi-cation of the murder victim as the young German woman.

Also found in the desk was a rental contract for the apartment in Doris Heidemann's name, a number of letters from her family and friends in Düsseldorf and close to a thousand dollars in cash.

'Well, it was already obvious from the body that the motive was not robbery,' said the inspector. 'He must have been totally insane or drugged out of his mind. I wonder if this could be Angel Dust, that stuff we've been reading about?'

'According to her papers, she was working at the Penta Club Hotel,' said the sergeant. 'Do you think I should go over there and tell them?'

'Yes, do,' said the inspector, 'and question anybody you can find who knew her. Maybe they'll know who she was with last night.'

The hotel did, of course, know who Doris had been with the night before, and as the tour operators and travel-agency owners were all staying at the hotel the sergeant had no difficulty in contacting them.

They were not, however, of much help. They had parted from Doris at approximately three-thirty in the morning and had come back to the hotel in a group. It had been their understanding that she was going home.

By this time the news of the murder had spread through the hotel, and the desk clerk who had been on duty the previous evening came forward to report a curious and, as he thought, significant incident.

A man, he said, had come to the desk roughly a half-hour after Doris and the group of travel agents and tour operators had left and had asked if Miss Heidemann had left anything for him. On being told that she had not, he had looked at the desk clerk strangely and had asked for Doris Heidemann's private address.

The clerk had refused to give it to him and he had gone away looking angry.

He had been, said the clerk, a man with a frightening appearance, being very big and beefy with a heavily pock-marked face and slitted green eyes. He had been either totally bald or had had his head shaved. The clerk estimated his age to be around twenty-five.

To the sergeant, who knew nothing of Doris Heidemann's kind offer to let a vacationer whom she had never met sleep at her apartment, the matter was clear. The man had obtained the victim's address elsewhere, had gone to her apartment and had murdered her upon her return at approximately three-thirty in the morning.

As it was obviously important that the man be located and taken into custody before he had had time to leave the island, or kill someone else, the sergeant hurried back to the scene to tell the inspector of this development.

There he found that Dr Batando's estimate of the time of death agreed closely with this theory. Doris Heidemann had died at sometime between four and five o'clock that same morning or, as the doctor said, she would have been dying between four and five o'clock. Her murderer had taken his time about the business.

'As far as I can determine now,' said the doctor, 'she was trampled to death. He must have jumped up and down on her body until he broke practically every bone in it. All her ribs are broken, her collarbone is smashed, her breast bone is caved in, her internal organs are reduced to a pulp. Her eyes seem to have been gouged out with bare fingers, whether before she was dead or after, I can't say. One of them is lying on the floor there, but the other is missing. He may have taken it with him or even eaten it. The breasts . . .'

He was interrupted as one of the laboratory technicians turned pale green and made a rush for the door.

'There were bites taken out of the flesh of the breasts,' continued the doctor, looking as if he was inclined to join him, 'and I think the labia major of the vagina have been bitten through. The thing sticking out of it is a large, blood-smeared, ball-point pen of the kind sold for souvenirs.

There's another ordinary ball-point pen sticking between her ribs and I suspect he may have been trying to kill her by pushing it through her heart. If he was, he didn't succeed.'

'Is that all?' said the inspector, tight-lipped.

'Probably not,' said the doctor. 'There's what looks to me like semen spattered over the body, but I can't tell whether she was actually raped until I've done the autopsy.'

By now, every off-duty police officer, whether plain-clothes or uniform branch, had been called in, and the inspector rushed men to the airport at La Canal and to the ferry dock at Ibiza with orders not to allow any male to leave the island until he had been positively identified and his destination recorded.

At the same time, patrolcars were put to cruising the streets of San Antonio Abad broadcasting over loudspeakers the description of the man who had called at the hotel desk the night before to ask for Doris Heidemann's address and appealing for help from the public.

There were, however, some puzzling aspects to the report which the sergeant had brought back. The anonymous telephone call reporting the crime that morning had been from a Spaniard, but the desk clerk stated that the man with the green eyes and the bald or shaven head was a foreigner; a German, he thought.

He was, of course, quite right and by eleven o'clock the broadcasting operation bore fruit when the big man with the green slitted eyes was spotted by local residents lying on the beach.

He was arrested and brought to police headquarters where he identified himself as a twenty-three-year-old tourist from Munich and said that he had never laid eyes on Doris Heidemann in his life.

He told the inspector of her offer to let him sleep in a room in her apartment and said that, when he had gone to the hotel to pick up the keys and had found none waiting, he had come to the conclusion that she had merely made the offer to get rid of him and had had no intention of letting him sleep in her apartment.

Desperate for a place to sleep, he had provided himself

inadvertently with a solid alibi. He had simply picked the oldest, ugliest and therefore, cheapest prostitute he could find and had made a deal with her to spend the night in her bed.

As he knew the address and the woman's first name, the police had no difficulty in corroborating his story and he was released.

By this time, news of the murder had spread over the entire island and a forty-seven-year-old cab driver named Juan Castro reported to police headquarters with an important clue.

He had, he said, taken a fare to Can Puig des Moli at six-thirty on Saturday night. The man had said that he was looking for a German girl named Sonya and his behaviour had been extremely odd.

According to the cab driver's description, so had his appearance. He was, he said, a huge man, round-faced and very fat but not old. He had spoken high-class Spanish with a mainland accent.

This detail rang a bell with the inspector. The anonymous telephone call reporting the murder had been made in just such a voice.

The entire staff of the Criminal Investigations Department descended upon the district in which the street Can Puig des Moli was located and, armed with the description of the suspect, soon found another person with whom he had spoken, an elderly gardener.

The gardener's description tallied precisely with that of the cab driver as did the manner of speaking and his request for information. The fat giant had been looking for a German girl named Sonya.

The gardener, knowing that there was only one German girl living in Can Puig des Moli and not knowing what her name was, had told him number twelve was the address he was seeking.

The man had thanked him and had gone off in the direction of Doris Heidemann's apartment where he had, it now seemed probable, remained, waiting for the girl to come home.

It had not been a boring wait. Ample evidence of what the man had been doing during this time had been found at the scene and had puzzled the investigators because it had not been realized that he had spent over six hours in the apartment.

He had spoken to the gardener at approximately seven o'clock and had, presumably, entered the apartment shortly afterward by the simple expedient of leaning against the door until the tongue of the lock tore through the wood of the door jamb. For a man of his weight, this would have been a practical means of entry as the apartment was not particularly solidly built.

Once inside, he had made himself very much at home and, the technicians thought, partially or entirely undressed. It was certain, at least, that he had not been wearing shoes at the time that he killed Doris Heidemann as the doctor reported that she had been trampled to death with bare feet.

Lying about the living-room floor were twelve empty beer bottles which represented all of the alcoholic refreshments in the apartment and a large book in English entitled *The Joys of Sex*. This, it seemed, had been the property of Doris Heidemann who, it was known, had spoken fluent English.

Whether the fat giant had spoken or been able to read English was not known, but the book was liberally sprinkled with traces of semen, the same, according to Dr Bastando, as they found on the body of the victim.

The course of events from the time that the suspect had arrived in Can Puig des Moli was now clear and, being in possession of a good physical description, the police set about trying to trace the identity of the suspect.

Juan Castro had reported that he had picked up his strange fare at a bar called Calle Sta Ines and questioning of the owner and an employee there produced further reports of abnormal behaviour and expressed interest in a German girl named Sonya.

He had entered the bar at around six o'clock and had said to the bartender, 'You are from Madrid.'

The bartender had politely replied that he was not from Madrid but from Grenada.

This response had made the fat man furious.

'I am a nobleman and a doctor!' he had screamed. 'If I say you are from Madrid, you are from Madrid, you scum!'

The owner of the bar had come over to calm the customer who had immediately changed the subject and begun to talk about a German girl named Sonya whom he had known in Madrid. He said that he had been informed that she was living in San Antonio Abad and that he had taken a cab over from Ibiza to visit her.

He had also said a great many other strange things concerning the influence of the Great Shark and how it was causing Ibiza to become a second Sodom of sex and nudity.

The owner had politically agreed with him, but had said that there was nothing that he could do about it and his main concern was his business. As far as he was concerned, the customers could drink as well naked as clothed.

He had added that there had been a German girl named Sonya living in the Can Puig des Moli some years earlier, but that he thought she no longer lived there.

The man had then asked to have a cab called and had left in it.

The bar owner had not thought that he was a doctor or a nobleman, although he spoke very refined Spanish, but some sort of a madman. He had never heard of Doris Heidemann and he did not know that there was a German girl living in Can Puig des Moli. He had only told his unwanted customer the story about the mythical Sonya to get rid of him.

'It's as if some mysterious power had doomed that girl to be murdered in the manner in which she was,' said the inspector. 'If she had left her keys at the desk or if the desk clerk had given the German tourist her address, he would have gone there and would have run into the fat madman. He might have been murdered, although he's big enough to have taken care of himself, but Miss Heidemann certainly wouldn't have been.

'Then, again, if the bar owner hadn't picked that street name out of thin air, the murderer would never have gone there.

'And finally, if he hadn't run into the gardener who

knew that there was a German girl living in the street but didn't know her name, he would not have gone to number twelve.

'There were an incredible number of coincidences that conspired to bring about that poor girl's horrible death.'

'It seems strange to me that a man as obviously insane as this one would be wandering around loose,' said the sergeant.

'Probably escaped from some institution,' said the inspector. 'These fantasies about being a nobleman and a doctor . . .'

He was soon to learn that they were no fantasies.

Continuing to follow the trail backward from the Calle Sta Ines bar, the investigators took up the remark made by the suspect that he had come over from Ibiza in a cab and, his appearance being unforgettable, soon found the driver.

Like all of the other persons with whom the man had been in contact, this cab driver had found him strange and had thought that he was probably on hard drugs of some kind.

He had said that he found the influence of the Great Shark very strong on the island and that he was going to San Antonio Abad to visit a German girl named Sonya whom he had met in Madrid.

The cab driver had not seen fit to comment, but he had heard things said at the Hotel Corso in Ibiza where he had picked up his fare that led him to believe that the man had been in some kind of trouble there.

Minutes later, the police were at the Hotel Corso where they received confirmation that the suspect had, indeed, been in trouble.

Although Ibiza is an informal sort of place, particularly during the tourist season, the manager of the hotel reported that his bizarre guest had gone too far, wandering up and down the hotel corridors stark naked and knocking on doors. When a person of the opposite sex opened, he made suggestions for sexual recreation and demonstrated physically that he was fully prepared.

A three-hundred-pound maniac not being everyone's idea of a suitable sex partner, there had been complaints and the manager had asked him to dress and leave. He had immediately done so.

Not long thereafter, a dumbfounded Inspector Hernandez stood looking at an entry in the hotel register. Written in a fine legible hand was: 'Dr Med. Don Luis German Perez Casanova de le Fuente. Toxicologist. Guterrez Ortega Hospital, Valdepenas, Spain.'

'He wrote this himself?' demanded the inspector. 'Did you check his identity?'

'He wrote it himself,' said the desk clerk. 'He insisted on writing it himself. He had a valid, Spanish identification card and it carried the same information.'

The inspector still could not believe it and he placed a long-distance call to the hospital in Valdepenas. Did they have a Dr Don Luis German Perez Casanova de le Fuente there? And, if so, where was he?

Yes, indeed, said the hospital. Dr de la Fuente was their toxicologist, a man from a noble family. At the moment he was on vacation in the Balearic Islands.

The telephone receptionist in Valdepenas wanted to know if something had happened to Dr de la Fuente, but the inspector was too stunned to reply and simply hung up the telephone.

With a precise description and the knowledge of the name and origin of the man who, it seemed, was the murderer of Doris Heidemann, the police had little difficulty in locating him in another hotel in Ibiza, particularly as he had made no effect at concealment and had simply registered in his own name again.

From the point of view of the mad physician, there was no reason why he should not have used his own name. He did not expect any trouble from the police and was sincerely amazed that they did not praise him for having, as he said, rid the island of the influence of the Great Shark.

'I could see that it was the Shark as soon as I arrived here and saw the girls showing their breasts and all the little short skirts with nothing under them . . . Then, I knew it was Sonya and that I must find her.

'She had hidden well, but I found her hiding place and I

waited. When she came, I was waiting naked as one must wait for Sonya and I said: "Sonya, I know that you are a man. I shall rid this island of the Great Shark."

'Then, I put the pen between her ribs, but she was, of course, abnormal and I could not find the heart. So, I took out her eyes with my thumb and finger. It is easy if you know how. And then, of course, I jumped on her . . .'

There was a great deal more to Dr de la Fuente's confession, or rather his proud recital of the manner in which he had dealt with the Great Shark, but actually no confession was necessary.

In the pocket of his shirt at the time of his arrest was a small tube which had contained sleeping tablets.

Inside the tube was Doris Heidemann's right eye.

There is no possibility that Dr de la Fuente will ever stand trial for the murder of Doris Heidemann. He is, in the opinion of the psychologists who have examined him, hopelessly and dangerously insane and it is believed that it will be necessary to keep him under close security for a very long time, probably the rest of his life.

What caused the doctor to go insane is not known. There was no reason to believe that he was mentally disturbed at the time that he left Valdepenas. Nor had anyone in his circle of friends, colleagues and relatives ever heard him refer to anyone named Sonya or to any German girl he had met in Madrid. It was, as a matter of fact, at least four years since he had been in Madrid himself.

The only clue to his behaviour is the fact that he was known to harbour conservative views on sexual morality and had often remarked that, although the German and other Nordic tourists brought money into Spain, the damage they were doing to traditional Spanish values exceeded the benefits.

13

THE BUTCHER SHOP MURDERS
WERE THE WURST

Dr Don Luis German Perez de la Fuente may have been mad,
but he was, at least, morally motivated. Anxious to rescue his
country from the malevolent influence of the mythical Great
Shark and the equally imaginary Sonya, his mind apparently
broke at the sight of the vast hordes of tourists overrunning
the Balearic Islands and the result was the incredible butchery of a young woman whose conduct and morals the doctor
would, in all probability, have found beyond reproach had he
met her under different circumstances.

The entire case has the unreality of madness to it. The
murderer thought he was killing someone who did not
apparently exist. His motives were incomprehensible to the
ordinary person. The *modus operandi* was horrible beyond
belief. And he made no effort to conceal his act nor to escape
the consequences of it, but was, in fact, obviously proud of
it.

Others, more calculating, go to great lengths to conceal
their guilt, kill as efficiently as any employee of a slaughterhouse, have all too understandable motives and pick on the
most prosaic of victims. They are not mad because they are
illogical. They are mad because they are too logical. They
want money. Someone has money. They kill them and take
it. A very direct way of thinking, but not as moral as the good
doctor's confused thoughts.

On Friday, 4 January 1974, fifty-four-year-old Roman
Rauch disappeared without trace in the city of Graz, Austria.
Foul play was immediately suspected.

And with good reason. Rauch was a money postman.

In Austria, there are two kinds of postmen, one who comes around and drops mail in your box and another who brings you money. This money could be your pension, a win in the national lottery or simply a sum sent you by some individual or firm for any reason whatever. The money is paid out on your doorstep in cash. A money postman, therefore, carries very considerable sums of cash in small bills, and he carries them into every section of the city from the toughest to the most exclusive and this every working day of the week. In some ways it is rather remarkable that any of these men survive at all.

Roman Rauch had survived for a long time and he had never been robbed or attacked during his entire career as a money postman. He had been married and the father of two children, now grown up and away from home, and he had been fond of his job.

'I never see anything but happy faces,' he had often remarked to his colleagues and his wife. 'Everybody is happy to see the postman with the money coming to them.'

Now, however, Roman Rauch was missing and there was no telling what had happened to him. He should have concluded his route by eleven-thirty and returned to the post office. When he had not appeared by noon, the supervisor called the police. The post office is fully aware of how tempting targets its money postmen are.

So are the police. Within less than thirty minutes, the bluff, hearty, pipe-smoking chief of the investigations section, Inspector Arnold Kirschner, arrived at the post office with his assistant, Detective-Sergeant Joachim Bukovsky. The two men had been having lunch at a small restaurant near police headquarters. It was patronized almost exclusively by the members of the Criminal Investigations Department, and, although they had rushed away leaving the food standing and without stopping to pay, the patron had not been disturbed. He was quite accustomed to it.

Quick as the police reaction had been, the supervisor at the post office was ready for them and had already drawn up a route of the places that Rauch should have covered that morning. He had then telephoned all those persons on the route having telephones and had narrowed the list to a half-dozen parties.

'They're all pensioners,' he said, 'and they don't have telephones. I've been able to trace Rauch up to this point. He paid out to a Mr Johann Fiedler at approximately ten o'clock and he should have paid out to Mrs Catherine Grobius here at around ten-forty-five, assuming that he wasn't held up. I've talked to her on the telephone and he hasn't been there. So, he disappeared somewhere between Fiedler and Grobius which covers six persons, but none of them have telephones so I can't pinpoint it any more exactly than that.'

'Any idea of how much he was carrying?' said the inspector.

The supervisor consulted the sheet of paper on his desk. 'A thousand six hundred and forty-two dollars and twelve cents after he left Fiedler,' he said. 'Minus anything he paid out after that.'

'Right,' said the inspector. 'All right, here's the location of the area, Boo. Bring out a half-dozen men from the station and have them check the addresses: the last place he visited and the first one he failed to visit. Then, throw everything we've got into the area and comb it.'

The sergeant nodded in comprehension and dashed out of the post office to telephone from the policecar parked in front of the building. He was an intense sort of young man, thin, harassed-looking with straight, rather long, blond hair and a very prominent nose. The inspector considered him to be one of the best assistants that had ever had.

An hour later, the police knew exactly where Roman Rauch had disappeared, but, despite the great number of officers thrown into the search, they could find no trace of him.

'It's a business district,' said Sergeant Bukovsky. 'Stores, shops and so on. He paid out a hundred and two dollars to Simon Landauer here in Buelow Street at approximately ten-twelve, and he should have paid out one hundred and six dollars and thirty-four cents to Leon Preis at roughly ten-twenty, but he didn't. So it was somewhere between those two places that he turned up missing. Assuming that he took the shortest route from one place to the other, he would have come right down Schoenau Street and that's practically all business. There's not even an alley where he could have been waylaid.'

'Any possibility that Landauer or Preis might have been a little greedy?' asked the inspector, chewing on the stem of his pipe.

'Greedy, maybe,' said the sergeant, 'but capable, not. Landauer is eighty-four, and Preis is seventy-six and nearly blind. Either one of them can just about make it to the front door. There's no possibility that they had anything to do with it.'

'Strange,' said the inspector. 'How in hell can a postman in uniform disappear in the middle of a busy shopping street like Schoenau? Have you found anybody who saw him there?'

The sergeant shook his head.

'And I don't think we will either,' he said. 'You know how it is with a postman or any other uniformed public servant. People just don't see them. They're an accepted part of the scenery, like lamp posts or dustbins. If we do find anybody, it will be some one who knew Rauch personally.'

'What about money deliveries in Schoenau Street itself?' said the inspector.

'Rare,' said the sergeant. 'It's mostly business places and they handle their transactions through the bank. The supervisor wasn't able to find any record of anything for the past six months.'

'Well, keep searching,' said the inspector. 'It's impossible that a hundred-and-seventy-pound postman in full uniform can vanish into thin air. He's somewhere in that area, dead or alive. All we've got to do is find him.'

But that the police could not do. The entire district was combed house by house, alley by alley and cellar by cellar. Not the slightest trace of the missing postman or the some fifteen-hundred-odd dollars that he had had on him when he disappeared was found. It was as if Roman Rauch, the balding, good-natured postman, who had liked his job and

183

who had enjoyed bringing their pensions to the old people, had never existed.

Reluctantly, the post-office supervisor assigned a new man to the route. His name was Gerhart Rosenberger, he was twenty years old, and he had only very recently gone to work for the post office.

'I can't understand it,' said the sergeant irritably. 'If there'd have been a mouse hidden in Schoenau Street, we'd have found it. We've practically gone through the people's drawers. He's got to be there, but he isn't.'

'Desk drawers, I presume, you mean,' said the inspector. 'Well, we apparently have to accept that he isn't there and the only explanation that occurs to me is that he left voluntarily. Simply took the money and beat it. Doesn't often happen with a postman, but men of that age sometimes go all to pieces, get mixed up with a young girl or something like that. He may be sitting on the French Riviera at this moment.'

'With fifteen hundred dollars?' said the sergeant. 'He had over five thousand in his savings account and it's still there. He would have taken that too.'

'Yes, of course,' said the inspector wearily. 'So he didn't abscond and he's still in Graz which means that he must be dead. Somebody murdered him for that money.

'However, it's obvious that they must have got rid of the body immediately because we were in the district less than three hours after he was last seen alive. It's possible that it was a truck or a delivery van. The murderer persuaded him to get into it, killed him and simply drove away with the body.

'That, in turn, would mean that Rauch knew him personally and trusted him.'

'If that's true, it would make the case a lot easier,' said the sergeant, 'but what makes you think so?'

'He was an old, experienced money postman,' said the inspector. 'Do you think he would have got into a truck with a total stranger?'

'I wouldn't have thought he would get into one with his mother,' said Sergeant Bukovsky. 'You want to concentrate the investigations on the circle of his acquaintances then?'

The inspector nodded. 'Acquaintances, friends, colleagues, relatives even,' he said. 'It has to have been some-body he knew.'

But it seemed that it was not. Although the investigations continued on through January, February, March and into April, no likely, or even possible, suspect was uncovered and, after the first of April, there was an even greater mystery for, on that date, Gerhart Rosenberg, the young postman who had taken over Roman Rauch's old route, disappeared as suddenly and mysteriously as had his predecessor!

The post-office records showed that Rosenberg had had approximately seven thousand six hundred dollars on him at the time!

'Exactly the same thing!' said the inspector in astonish-ment. 'He paid out to Lindauer and not to Preis. In short, he disappeared at precisely the same point in his route as Rauch did. Somebody in that district has worked out a scheme for robbing and murdering the money postmen. We've got to solve this and quick. There are God knows how many thousands or even millions of people who depend upon the post office to bring them their pensions and other payments and, if this fellow gets away with this, it's going to spread all over Austria and the whole system of postal payments will be disrupted.'

'Someone in the district,' repeated Sergeant Bukovsky. 'You don't think any more that it was delivery truck or something like that?'

'I don't know what to think,' said the inspector. 'But we can check on the delivery-truck angle if we assume that the driver was known to the victims. It would be a person who was known to both Rauch and Rosenberger and, considering the difference in their ages and length of service with the post, that couldn't have been too many people.'

It was none at all. The investigations showed that Rauch and Rosenberger had not even known each other and that they had had no common acquaintances. Several of the other employees of the post office had known both men as col-leagues, but all of these could account for their time very exactly on the days of the disappearances. They had, as a matter of fact, all been working.

'Well, scratch that theory,' said the inspector. 'It wasn't a delivery van and it wasn't anybody who knew both Rauch and Rosenberger. It was somebody right there in the district.'

'Maybe it was,' said the sergeant. 'But I don't know who. All the pensioners who got their money through the post knew Rauch and Rosenberger by sight, of course, and so did some of the business people along his route, but we always come back to the same thing; he paid out to Lindauer and not to Preis so he disappeared in that relatively short stretch between sixteen Goethe Street and one-forty-four Chlodwitz, going almost certainly by way of Schoenau. I've walked over that stretch a hundred times. We've interviewed every person living there. We've searched the buildings and we searched the businesses on the day of the disappearances and afterwards. We haven't found the slightest trace of either man.'

'There probably isn't any to find,' said the inspector. 'Now, that it's happened twice, it's apparent that whoever is doing this is working to a carefully conceived plan and they're not going to leave any traces. None the less, we're going to have to continue the investigations whether there's anything to investigate or not. The post office is refusing to put money postmen on that route and the pensioners are having to come down to the post office to get their pensions. We're getting a lot of bad publicity over this. The papers have been running interviews with old, sick pensioners who have to crawl to the post office because the police can't provide security for the mailmen.'

'Couldn't we assign a man to accompany the postmen?' said the sergeant. 'The post office should be satisfied with that.'

'We could, of course,' agreed the inspector, 'but for how long and what happens if the fellow changes his area? We can't put a cop permanently with every money postman in the city.'

'I see,' said the sergeant. 'All right. What do we investigate when there's nothing to investigate?'

'Every person living or working along that stretch of street which Rauch and Rosenberger must have travelled in going from Simon Lindauer to Leon Preis,' said the inspector. 'And every person who had any reason to be anywhere along that route between the hours of ten and eleven on any day.'

'Already done,' said the sergeant promptly. 'Five times over, There are twenty or thirty people who could conceivably have killed the postmen and taken the money, but there's no evidence that anyone of them did or that any one of them had any particular reason to do so. If the motive was money, then that excludes no one because almost anybody can use money.'

'Some more than others,' said the inspector. 'You've got your lists of the people living along there. I want you to put people to checking on whether they've been making new purchases or paying off pressing debts or anything like that. Then I want you to make up a separate list of the houses where the housewife or some female was home alone at the time that Rauch and Rosenberger disappeared. Those two men weren't killed on the street. They were lured into a building and the female of the species is still the best lure going.'

The sergeant obediently took up these less than promising lines of investigation and pursued them with his customary vigour, but his daily reports remained monotonously void of interest.

'There were a few ladies who were home alone,' he said, 'both on the morning of January fourth and April first, but they're hardly the type to lure anybody, although a couple of them, at least, could have strangled both postmen to death with their bare hands and, maybe, simultaneously. None of them have shown any sudden affluence recently.'

'And the businesses?' said the inspector.

'There are nine,' said the sergeant. 'Schmitt's Grocery Store, Hold's Butcher Shop, the Sunshine Café, Ziegler's Second-Hand Book Store, Beisel's Stationery and Newsstand, Hann's Real-Estate Office, Foerster's Bakery, Huber's Dry Goods and Brink's Café. All small, owner run businesses with the exception of the Sunshine Café which is part of a chain. As you know, business is nothing extra this year and Hold, Ziegler and Huber are all having trouble. However, none of them has paid off any debts and both Ziegler and Huber have some pressing ones.'

'And Hold?' said the inspector. 'How can a butcher be in trouble with meat the price it is?'

'Living too high apparently,' said the sergeant. 'He only took over the shop from his father two years ago, and he's now got a luxury apartment on Schiller Street and a luxury girlfriend to live in it with him. Name's Christa Pfeifer. Twenty years old and looks like she would be a pretty expensive girl to have around. Hold's twenty-six. He has a few debts with the tax people and the slaughterhouse.'

'But he hasn't paid them,' said the inspector. 'When did he get the luxury apartment? Before the postmen started disappearing or after?'

'A year and a half ago,' said the sergeant. 'Almost as soon as he took over the shop. However, we know for a fact that he's clear. There's no back entrance to the shop and we've got witnesses who can testify that Hold never left the shop at all on the mornings of January fourth and April first. The reason they know that is that he's all alone there. If he went out, he'd have to close the shop and he didn't.'

'And you searched the shop on the day of the disappearances?' said the inspector.

'That's right,' said the sergeant. 'It's a small place. Just the butcher shop itself and a very small sort of sitting room behind it. No back entrance. No back window. No basement. Large refrigerator, of course. It contained sausages and a tray of sausage sandwiches which he sells to the school children. Not bad. I tried one.'

'Well, if he didn't leave the shop and if there's no place there to hide a body, then Hold couldn't have done it unless he quickly chopped the postmen up and sold them as steaks and roasts to the customers,' said the inspector. 'Besides, what would a postman be doing in a butcher shop? One of the cafés, possibly, but not the butcher shop.'

'And now?' said the sergeant.

'Continue the investigations,' said the inspector grimly.

The sergeant continued, but he did not get anywhere.

Three days later both Roman Rauch and Gerhart Rosenberger were found; Rauch accidentally and Rosenberger because the police had been given an indication from the discovery of Rauch where to look.

Both men were dead and partially dismembered. Each was neatly packed in a large cardboard carton tied with twine and left standing, in the case of Rauch, on a public dump and, in the case of Rosenberger, at the edge of a flooded gravel pit which was often used as a dump. The weather having been cool at that time of the year, neither body was very badly decayed.

'Which is fortunate,' said Dr Peter Findel, the dark, hook-nosed police medical expert, peering at the inspector over the tops of his gold-rimmed glasses.

He had come to the inspector's office to report personally on the result of the autopsies as it would take time to have the official versions typed and the doctor had reason to believe that the investigators were, to say the least, impatient.

'Both men died as a result of a single hatchet blow to the back of the head, delivered with great force and, I suspect, some skill,' said the doctor. 'The bodies were also dismembered with skill. This was not the work of an amateur.'

'You think it was a doctor?' said the inspector in astonishment.

'No,' said the doctor. 'A butcher. Moreover, in both cases, the last food taken, and that very shortly before death, was a sausage sandwich. Does that tell you anything?'

'Hold!' said the inspector and the sergeant in one voice.

'Almost surely Hold,' said the doctor, who was fully informed on the results of the investigations up to the present. 'Although how you're going to prove it when you searched the shop and didn't find anybody, I don't know.'

'It's my fault!' exclaimed the sergeant. 'It must have been there all the time and I didn't find it. There's just one place those bodies could have been and that's in the deep freeze behind the counter. Hold was serving his customers out of it while we were there: steaks, chops, things like that. The bodies must have been there underneath the meat. How

189

could I have been so stupid! He made a fool of me twice in a row!'

'Well, don't let it bother you, Boo,' said the inspector. 'I doubt that there are very many persons who would have thought of such a thing either. One thing for certain, Hold is going to have some pretty upset customers if this ever gets out.'

'You mean it may not?' said the doctor in astonishment.

'I hope it will,' said the inspector, 'but you have to remember that, although Hold is undoubtedly our man, we have no evidence that would convince an examinations judge. We are not in a position to go for an indictment and, if we make our suspicions public without proof, it'll ruin Hold's business and he'll sue us. What we need is physical evidence.'

'You'll get it,' said the smarting sergeant grimly. 'Even if I have to spend the rest of my life finding it.'

As it turned out, the sergeant did not have to spend the rest of his life or even any very substantial amount of it in obtaining further evidence of the guilt of Karl Hold, the young, luxury-loving butcher.

The first break came with a sworn statement by a twenty-four-year-old employee of the real-estate company located opposite Hold's Butcher Shop. From her seat in front of the window, Gertrud Falschegger had an unobstructed view of the entrance to the butcher shop and she testified that she had seen Gerhart Rosenberger go into the shop, but not come out again. Although she could not remember anything about Roman Rauch, she had noticed the young and handsome Rosenberger on more than one occasion and was apparently in the habit of watching for him as he passed.

'Both Rosenberger and Rauch went into the butcher shop every morning,' said the sergeant. 'It's astonishing how things fall into place when you know what to look for. Now, in addition to the Falschegger statement, I've located a dry-cleaning place where Hold sends his things and on both January fifth and April second, that is, in both cases, one day after the disappearances, Hold sent the carpet of the little sitting room behind the shop in for dry-cleaning. The dry-cleaners no longer remember what it was in January, but in

April, there were bloodstains on it. They, of course, know that Hold is a butcher so they thought nothing of it. Finally I have located a customer of Hold's who says that the shop was closed briefly on the afternoon of April second. He was presumably cutting up the body of Rosenberger then and packing it in the carton. In the case of Rauch, he wouldn't have had to close because the day following was a Sunday. Do you think it's enough?'

The inspector thought so and, following his arrest and a few hours of interrogation, so did Karl Hold.

'It was the money,' he said. 'I needed money. Rauch had a habit of coming in to buy a sausage sandwich every morning when he was passing so on that morning I asked him if he would like a cup of coffee with it. I said I'd made some fresh coffee in the back room. He came in and while he was having his sandwich and cup of coffee, I hit him on the back of the head with the hatchet. He died instantly, of course. Then, I took him out and put him into the deep freeze behind the counter and covered him over with the meat. It wasn't too risky. Most of my customers are regulars and I know what time they come in. In any case, it's hard to see over the counter what's going on behind. Unfortunately, Roman didn't have much money on him so I had to give the new man the same treatment.'

The treatment which Karl Hold received from the court was more compassionate than that which he had accorded his victims. Although found guilty of premeditated homicide on two counts, he escaped the death sentence and, on 23 August 1974, was sentenced to life imprisonment. He will be eligible for release in about twelve years.

14

NOTHING HALF BAKED ABOUT
THE GIRLS OF DOLENJA VAS

Although not only a citizen of a nominally capitalist country,
but a businessman as well, Karl Hold did not make very
efficient use of his victims. Granted, he cleaned them out of
what money they were carrying, but, as a butcher, it should
have occurred to him that he was in possession of a considerable quantity of fresh meat which, if not suitable for
roasts or chops, could be turned into excellent sausage or
hamburger.

It was a thought that had occurred to others in the past and
will, no doubt occur to others in the future.

But not, of course, in Socialist countries such as Yugoslavia. If, as good Socialists must, you so love your fellow men
that you are prepared to sacrifice your own interests for the
good of society, you can scarcely be expected to turn them
into sausage for private sale.

Unfortunately, however, even in the best of Socialist
systems, incidents do take place and one of these was on 17
October 1977 when Vida Menas suddenly disappeared and
was never seen again.

As she was eighteen years old and very pretty, this would
not have been unusual in some parts of Europe, but Vida
lived in Dolenja Vas, a very small village in the heart of
Yugoslavia. Young girls did not normally disappear in
Dolenja Vas. Vida was, in fact, the very first to have ever
done so.

Her parents were, naturally, greatly puzzled and concerned and, after they and the rest of the adult population of
Dolenja Vas had searched everywhere for her in vain, they

notified the police in Kocevje which was ten miles to the southeast and not a very large community either, but large enough to have a police force and even a criminal investigations department.

Inspector Marko Skolik, a heavy set, muscular man with a normally expressionless face, and his assistant, Detective-Sergeant Pyotr Brodnik, who was much younger, more handsome and less phlegmatic in his expression, came up to Dolenja Vas and investigated. The only thing that they could determine was that the girl had disappeared; something that the villagers already knew. She had not, as yet, had any steady boyfriend among the local youths and she had last been seen by her own parents when she left the farmhouse at a little before two o'clock in the afternoon. No one could be found who had seen her after this time, and this was very strange because in such a small community as Dolenja Vas it is very difficult to avoid being seen no matter where you are going or what you are doing.

'She probably ran off to Ljubljana,' suggested the sergeant. 'They say that she was a pretty girl and there are more opportunities for pretty girls in Ljubljana than in Dolenja Vas.'

'It is forty miles to Ljubljana,' said the inspector, 'and there is only the one road. As she has no means of transportation, she must be walking. We shall, therefore, telephone the police in Ljubljana and ask them to look for her. She could not have arrived yet.'

Ljubljana is, of course, the capital of Yugoslavia and a comparatively large city. It is true that there were more opportunities for a pretty young girl in Ljubljana than in Dolenja Vas, but Vida, it seemed, had not gone there. Although a watch was kept, the girl never turned up and a policeman travelling over the road failed to spot her.

'Then she must have gone east to Karlovac, or west to Rijeka which is on the sea and would be an interesting place for a young girl, or even to Trieste which is, unjustly, not in Yugoslavia any longer,' said the inspector.

'Are you going to contact all of these places?' said the sergeant,

'Yes,' said the inspector and he did, but none of them ever reported finding any trace of Vida Menas.

This failure troubled the inspector quite a lot. He did not like having young girls disappear within his administrative district and he was, therefore, even more concerned when, on 4 May 1978, only slightly more than six months after the disappearance of Vida Menas, a second girl was reported missing.

This girl was nineteen, one year older than Vida, but also very pretty. She came from the village of Ribnica, less than two miles to the northeast along the road to Ljubljana from Dolenja Vas and even smaller than that community. Her name was Ljuba Smarovas.

The farmers in Ribnica knew, of course, of the disappearance of Vida Menas from the neighbouring village and, this time, the police in Kocevje were notified immediately.

A very large-scale search operation was organized, contingents of volunteers coming in from all the surrounding farming communities and a special tracking dog being brought down from the capital with its trainer.

The dog failed to pick up the girl's tracks, possibly because she had been, at one time or another, almost everywhere in the village and there was no clear trail for the animal to follow. As in the case of the disappearance of Vida Menas, the search parties found nothing.

The inspector returned to Kocevje a very worried man. Two girls had disappeared without trace in his administrative district and he should be investigating the disappearances. There was, however, nothing to investigate. The girls simply and suddenly disappeared. There were no witnesses, no clues, nothing which could be taken as a lead. There was not even any indication as to what had happened to Vida Menas and Ljuba Smarovas.

'The villagers say that a vampire is loose in the district,' said the sergeant. 'He is carrying off young girls to suck their blood.'

'This is a Socialist, progressive country,' said the inspector. 'We do not have any vampires and, besides, there is no such thing.'

'My grandfather says that when he was a young man a vampire came and carried off several girls from a village south of Karlovac. He said that they were later discovered working in a house of prostitution in Trieste. They had made a great deal of money.'

'Your grandfather is an old man,' said the inspector, checking himself just in time from saying 'idiot'. 'When he was a young man we did not have Socialism in Yugoslavia. As a matter of fact, there was no Yugoslavia even. The girls were carried off not by vampires, but by procurers who wanted to make money from them. Such things happen in capitalist societies.'

'Exactly!' said the sergeant in triumph. 'As this is a Socialist country and there are no prostitutes or procurers, then the girls must have been taken by a vampire. Who else would have a use for young girls?'

The inspector could not think of any answer to this, but he still did not believe that Vida Menas and Ljuba Smarovas had been carried off by any vampire and he ordered the sergeant not to believe it either.

'The only possibility,' he said, 'is that the girls left of their own volition. Vida Menas ran off somewhere and, Ljuba Smarovas hearing of her success, imitated her. It is not impossible that other girls will attempt to do the same.'

The inspector's words were prophetic for by 21 August of that same year yet a third girl was reported missing. Her name was Schipka Postalnyi, she was twenty years old and the prettiest girl in her home village of Prezid, less than fifteen miles to the southwest of Dolenja Vas as the crow flies, but a good fifty miles following the road.

It took the inspector and the sergeant over two hours to get to Prezid which lies on a parallel road to the one where Ribnica, Dolenja Vas and Kocevje are located. The road passes through the mountains and there are a great many curves and steep grades.

Prezid is even smaller than Dolenja Vas and Ribnica, and the people there had not heard of the disappearances of Vida Menas and Ljuba Smarovas, but they had been so startled and puzzled by the sudden disappearance of the village's prettiest girl that they had immediately called the police.

This time there was a little more indication of the direction, at least, that the missing girl had taken. She had left her parent's home at approximately one o'clock in the afternoon to look for mushrooms in the forest to the east of the village. When she had not returned by five o'clock, her father had gone to look for her. He had been unable to find her and had eventually been joined by every other resident of the village, none of whom had been able to find her either.

Like the villagers further to the east, the people of Prezid thought that the girl had been carried off by a vampire and they wanted to know what the police were going to do about it.

There was not very much that Inspector Skolik could do. The villagers had already searched the area around Prezid and, as they knew it far better than anyone else, it was unlikely that bringing in a further contingent of police and volunteers would produce any greater results. In addition, he had already made the experience with the search for Vida Menas and Ljuba Smarovas. Neither had produced anything and he did not think that such a search would produce anything here.

He was, however, beginning to feel somewhat out of his depth and so he telephoned the National Gendarmerie Headquarters in Ljubljana to say that girls were disappearing in his administrative district, that he had been unable to discover the slightest trace of what was happening to them and that he did not feel that Kocevje could continue to accept the sole responsibility for the investigation. As the girls were, almost certainly, no longer in his district, they must be elsewhere in Yugoslavia and this made the cases a national rather than local affair.

The gendarmerie replied that they would arrange for a nationwide search and that he should send exact descriptions of the girls together with their photographs and, if possible, fingerprints to Gendarmerie headquarters where wanted circulars would be made up and distributed to all police units throughout the country. They thought that the girls had simply run away and would soon be found. Yugoslavia is not a place where it is easy to remain missing permanently.

Their estimate was going to turn out to be overly optimistic. Although Inspector Skolik and Sergeant Brodnik were able to obtain excellent photographs of the missing girls, precise descriptions and even, in the case of Vida Menas and Schipka Postalnyi, fingerprints, all of which were sent to Gendarmerie Headquarters in Ljubljana, no reports concerning the girls were received.

Or, at least, none had been received by 16 February 1979 when Lila Bratislav disappeared. Lila was twenty years old, very pretty and came from the village of Kocevska Reka, three or four miles to the southwest of Kocevje, cross country, but, again, much further by road.

The village people in Kocevska Reka knew all about the disappearances in Ribnica, Dolenja Vas and Prezid. By now everyone in the district did. Like the residents of the other communities, they thought that Lila had been taken by a vampire, and they thought that the vampire was living in Kocevje.

The inspector was inclined to agree with the second part of this theory, if not the first. All of the disappearances had taken place within the administrative district surrounding Kocevje and they had all been in villages so small that a stranger to the area would have been noticed. There had been no strangers reported at the times of the disappearances which meant that the murderer was someone who could be present in all of the little communities without attracting attention.

The inspector was, by now, of the opinion that it was murder and that the girls had not left of their own volition. One girl might have run away, either to some other part of the country or even outside it. Even two might have managed it. But not four.

If murder it was, then the motive was obvious. None of the girls had had any money or enemies. They had all been young and pretty. Some had, perhaps, been virgins, but they had probably not been obsessed with remaining in that condition.

A little force might have been necessary, but not murder. The killer would, therefore, be a sex psychopath.

This was a type of crime with which the inspector was totally unfamiliar. In the little farming communities of his district, there were, of course, occasionally crimes in which the motive was sex, but, so far, there had never been any homicidal sex deviates. As in most rural areas, there was a considerable amount of incest, ninety per cent of it unreported, some child molesting, also generally unreported, and a very occasional rape with violence.

The authors of such rapes were, however, nearly always normal farm boys who had taken by force what they had been unable to obtain through persuasion. Even so, he pulled out such records of sexual offences as he had and went through them carefully. There was no one in the records who could possibly be considered as a suspect in the disappearance of the four girls.

The National Gendarmerie, too, was becoming concerned over this startling series of disappearances from one small district, and a team of officers was sent down from Ljubljana to find out why nothing had been done about it. They reviewed everything that the inspector had done, talked to the people in the various villages from which the girls had disappeared and went back to Ljubljana no wiser than they had come. They were unable to suggest any new line of investigation to the local police.

Inspector Skolik was, therefore, doing nothing although he would have liked very much to do something. He would have liked to, at least, put out a warning to the people of his district that they should avoid leaving their daughters in the company of some specific person and that they should report the appearance of this specific person to the police. He had no doubt that there was such a person but, unfortunately, he had not the faintest idea of what he might look like or even where he came from, although he suspected Kocevje.

In the meantime, the villagers had more or less taken things into their own hands. Whether the person responsible for the disappearances of four young girls was a vampire or a sex psychopath made very little difference. The important consideration was that he be prevented from making off with any more girls and vigilante groups were spontaneously formed in all of the little villages throughout the district. Women went out of doors only in company with others, and at sunset the shutters of the houses were closed and the doors were barred. It would have been as much as a stranger's life was worth to knock on the door of one of the village houses at night anywhere in Kocevje district.

And yet, despite all of these precautions, on the afternoon of 5 December 1979, nineteen-year-old Mira Kosecki disappeared from the village of Stari Log less than five miles to the north of Kocevje.

Actually, Mira, who was, of course, very pretty, did not disappear from Stari Log itself, but from somewhere along the road connecting it with Kocevje. This was a perfectly straight, unencumbered stretch of secondary road with little traffic, and even Mira's parents had not objected to her walking into Kocevje in the middle of the afternoon. It seemed completely impossible that anything could happen to anyone on a public thoroughfare such as this.

Nonetheless, Mira, who had been planning to spend the night with her aunt in Kocevje, had been strictly instructed to telephone back to Stari Log immediately upon her arrival at her aunt's house. Her parents did not have a telephone in the farmhouse, but she could call the post office in Stari Log and the post master, who was her father's nephew, would come and tell them that she was all right.

When she did not call, her father, who could estimate very exactly how long it would take his daughter to walk to Kocevje, went to the post office and telephoned the aunt.

Mira had not arrived and her father set off down the road at a dead run, followed by most of the adult population of Stari Log, many of them carrying pitchforks, axes or clubs.

They ran all the way to Kocevje. They did not find any trace of Mira Kosecki. The fifth disappearance had taken place.

This was too much. The entire district was in an uproar, a contingent of soldiers from the Yugoslavian army was sent down to comb the forest and mountain valleys, and several persons travelling along the public roads were set upon and beaten by local villagers on the simple grounds that they did not know them.

Aside from a degree of excitement, all of this produced nothing. The girls were gone. There was no indication as to where, why or by what means.

Several men already having been beaten at various places in the district, the inspector was embarrassed but not surprised when a German tourist named Klaus Hochbauer appeared at police headquarters in Kocevje to report that he had been beaten badly by a strange man.

Hochbauer, who was forty-six years old and who had been touring Yugoslavia in his Volkswagen, had stopped to ask directions of a man walking along the road between Dolenja Vas and Kocevje. The man had not only failed to provide him with directions, but had, without any hesitation, dragged him out of the car and beaten his head so violently against a large stone lying beside the road that he had lost consciousness. When he had come to, the man was gone.

The inspector thought, at first, that this would probably have been one of the villagers from Dolenja Vas or some other local community who, not understanding German, had taken Hochbauer for the Vampire, as the person believed responsible for the disappearances of the five girls was commonly known throughout the district, and had thought to put an end to him. It was only when Hochbauer reported that he had also been robbed of all his money, a sum of a little over $600, that the theory became untenable.

The villagers of the Kocevje district were angry, frightened and dangerous. They were quite capable of violence to the person of such an obvious stranger as the German tourist. But, even if murderous, they were basically honest. None of them would have robbed him.

This meant that Klaus Hochbauer had been attacked, not by a suspicious and infuriated husband or relative, but by one of the few known criminal elements in the district. As they were so few as to make this practical, the inspector ordered them all arrested. They were interrogated, their whereabouts at the time of the attack on Klaus Hochbauer determined and, within something less than a day, the inspector knew that none of them could have done it.

Moreover, Hochbauer's description of the man who had beaten and robbed him did not correspond to any of the potential suspects. He was, he said, not very tall, but strongly built and muscular. His age was estimated to be around thirty and he had black hair, black eyes and a two or three days' growth of black beard. Hochbauer had thought him to be exceptionally handsome.

In a more heavily populated area it would have been difficult or impossible to identify a person from such a vague description, but traffic along the roads in the Kocevje area is not heavy. The inspector thought that others might also have seen the man who had robbed Hochbauer and, if they had and if he was local, they would know him.

A criminal investigations department detachment under Sergeant Brodnik, moved out into the countryside and in a surprisingly short length of time a tentative identification of the robber was obtained.

He was, it seemed, thirty-two-year-old Metod Torinus, a bachelor who lived alone on a small farm just outside Dolenja Vas.

Torinus had no police record, had never attracted attention previously and was remarkable for nothing. He was merely one of the small farmers in the district among hundreds of others.

None the less, he answered to the description of the man who had attacked Klaus Hochbauer and he and no one else resembling him had been seen in the area at the time in question.

A police party, led personally by Inspector Skolik, proceeded to Torinus's farm where they took Torinus into custody, began to interrogate him and made an intensive search of the premises for the stolen money which had been mostly in German currency and was, therefore, easily identifiable.

Torinus denied the attack on the German tourist and said

that he knew nothing about the disappearances of the girls other than what everybody in the area knew. They had been carried off by a vampire. He appeared, however, to be highly nervous and, presently, the inspector noticed that he was most nervous when the searchers were near to the baking oven.

This was an old-fashioned construction, not inside, but outside the house, constructed of stone and mortar and with its own chimney. Such ovens were once standard for most of Europe, and many still remain in rural areas although they are no longer in use. They are large, massive blocks of masonry intended to hold heat sufficient for the baking after the fire which has been built in them has been drawn out and replaced with the bread.

'Look in the oven,' called the inspector. 'That is where he has hidden the money.'

'No, no!' cried Torinus. 'It is not true! I confess. I robbed the tourist, but the money is not in the oven. It is in a glass jar buried in the manure pile. Come. I will show you.'

The entire police party followed him to the manure pile behind the stable and the jar was dug up. It contained the money that had been stolen from Klaus Hochbauer.

'Excellent!' said the inspector. 'Take him back to Kocevje and charge him with highway robbery with violence. He will undoubtedly receive a long sentence for this.'

The sergeant moved to carry out his orders, but, as he was leading Torinus away, the inspector stopped him.

'Why do you have such a silly grin on your face?' he asked the prisoner. 'Are you so stupid that you do not realize the trouble you are in?'

Torinus remained silent and looked down at the ground, apparently attempting to adjust his features to a more suitable expression, but without much success.

'Wait!' said the inspector. 'Don't take him away yet. There is something funny here. When was it that he started looking so pleased?'

'When we went to dig up the glass jar with the money,' said the sergeant.

'My conscience was relieved because I had confessed my

crime,' said Torinus hurriedly. 'It was that which made me happy.'

'No,' said the inspector. 'It was something else . . . Let me see now, we were . . . the baking oven!'

Metod Torinus turned suddenly white as a sheet and began to tremble.

The reason became clear moments later when the inspector opened the great iron door of the baking oven and shined his flashlight inside.

'What is this?' he cried. 'What are these bones doing in a baking oven? Oh my God! That is a human skull!'

As a good communist the inspector did not, of course, believe in God, and it was some indication of the state of his emotions that he should call upon the deity. Under the circumstances, however, even a good communist was justified in such an exclamation for it is not often that an inspector of criminal investigations solves five homicides and a robbery within less than an hour.

Dr Josef Hartounian, a large, bald and jovial expert in forensic medicine, came down from Ljubljana and, having examined the bones in Metod Torinus's baking oven, pronounced them to be those of young females not older than twenty-four. Two of them could be positively identified as they had had dental work. They were Ljuba Smarovas from Ribnica and Lila Bratislav from Kocevska Reka. Mira Kosecki from Stari Log was tentatively identified from having suffered a broken collarbone as a child.

It did not matter, in any case, as Torinus had, by now, long since confessed to all five murders. Having nothing to lose, he also confessed to the five rapes that had preceded them.

Although sufficiently handsome that he would have had little difficulty in finding compliant female companions, Torinus suffered from an emotional abnormality which made sex with violence carried out on an unwilling partner necessary for the satisfaction of his desires.

According to his statement, all of the girls had accompanied him willingly and unsuspectingly to his farm, which was not doubted, although opinions varied as to why. Torinus said that they had gone there for sex. The girls' relatives said that they had been virgins and, if they had gone willingly to Torinus's farm, it had been for nothing more than cakes and coffee. It was pointed out that all of the victims had been killed during the time of the afternoon when they could be reasonably expected to have tea.

Whatever the case, upon their arrival at the farm, Torinus had leaped upon them, torn their clothing from their bodies, tied them hand and foot and, apparently, subjected them to sexual torture, this continuing, in some cases, so long that the girls' relatives were already searching for her before she was dead.

In the end, his sexual desires satisfied, Torinus had simply strangled the girls to death and had then cremated bodies and clothing in the baking oven.

He had, he said, been planning to clean the bones out of the oven and bury them somewhere else, but he had been busy and had not got around to it.

If he had, it is very probable that Inspector Skolik's case of the five missing girls would never have been solved and might very well have become the case of the ten missing girls or the fifteen missing girls or any given number.

Communist countries are not very liberal in their attitudes toward criminals and on 10 December 1980, after a relatively short trial, Metod Torinus was found guilty of multiple murder, sentenced to death and four days later executed.

15

YO-HO-HO AND
A BOTTLE OF SCHNAPS

The abrupt end of Metod Torinus, doubtedlessly quicker
and less painful than those of his victims, was, demonstrably,
a failure of Socialism. If he had been in an agricultural
commune, as he should have been, it would have been
possible to keep an eye on him and perhaps prevent this
wholesale destruction of useful workers and potential
mothers, to say nothing of the damage to the tourist industry.
Alas! Yugoslavian Socialism is not yet pure. Many farmers
still till the soil without proper supervision from public
servants and this is the result of it. A serious loss to the state
and a sordid, shameful business all the way around.

Not that things are handled a great deal better in the West,
but they are, at least, sometimes glamorous and filled with
the thrills and excitement of adventure and the always news-
worthy escapades of the international jet set.

Of course, not everyone is as fascinated by the jet set as its
own members and those persons who make their living
writing about them. For the sailing crowd, jet-setters are
mindless milksops. What is 'in' is a yacht, the bigger the
better – transatlantic crossings, cruising in the Caribbean,
the South Seas or, for the timid, the Mediterranean.

Such a way of life builds hard men and courageous women,
a spirit of independence, the ability to rely upon one's self and
upon trusted shipmates, the keen eye in the bronzed face, a
slightly enhanced roll in the gait and a tolerance for startling
quantities of alcoholic beverages. It can also be dangerous.

On the morning of Saturday, 19 December 1981, when the
sailing yacht *Apollonia* out of Bremen, West Germany, made

landfall in the lovely harbour of the island of Barbados she was flying the signal flags for 'doctor needed on board' and the port physician hurried to the dock as she was being tied up.

The harbour master had come with him and they found only four persons aboard a sailing yawl which would normally carry a crew of six. One of these four was a young man lying in the cabin below decks and, having examined him, the doctor expressed amazement that he was still alive. He had been shot completely through the body from chest to back with a heavy calibre gun some considerable time earlier, but the bullet appeared to have missed all vital organs and blood vessels and had simply exited out his back near the spine.

He was, however, in an understandably serious condition and he was rushed by ambulance to the hospital for treatment.

In the meantime, the harbour master had summoned the police who began by establishing the identities of the four persons on board. They were forty-two-year-old Paul Termann, the navigator, his companion thirty-six-year-old Dorothea Permin, twenty-nine-year-old Dieter Giesen, an owner of a bar in Constance, a city in the south of Germany, and twenty-five-year-old Michael Wunsch, who was a student and the man who had been shot through. Wunsch also came from Constance and was a friend of Giesen's.

Speaking for all of the party, Termann, a strongly built man with a full, black beard, recounted a tragic story of death and madness on the high seas. Not only had Michael Wunsch been wounded, the captain and his mistress had both been lost overboard and it had to be presumed that they were dead.

The ill-fated voyage had begun nearly a month earlier in November when Termann and Dorothea Permin had made the acquaintance of thirty-five-year-old Herbert Klein in a bar in Las Palmas in the Canary Islands. Klein came from the city of Krefeld, West Germany, as did his twenty-five-year-old mistress, Gabriela Humpert. He had only recently bought the *Apollonia* which was registered in Bremen, and was looking for a crew to sail her to the Caribbean where he planned to charter the boat out for day trips.

Termann was an experienced navigator and, as he and Dorothea were interested in spending the winter months in the Caribbean, they had immediately signed on.

Unfortunately, while they were ashore celebrating the new association, someone had broken into the *Apollonia* where she lay in the harbour at Pasito Blanco and had stolen $3500 in cash and a number of valuable navigation instruments.

This had been a severe blow for Klein who, Termann thought, had been rather short on money, but Termann, who was not short on money at all, had offered to loan him $12,000, an offer which was promptly accepted.

Finances, captain, navigator and feminine company now being settled, there remained only the signing on of a couple of deck hands and these were quickly found in the persons of Dieter Giesen and Michael Wunsch who wanted to go to the Caribbean to practise skin-diving there.

On Saturday, 26 November 1981, the *Apollonia* had put to sea in excellent weather and with the crew in high spirits. Neither Klein nor Gabriela had had much experience in sailing, but the others had and things went smoothly.

Until Thursday, 3 December, when a vicious storm suddenly blew up out of nowhere and the crew of the *Apollonia* found themselves fighting for their lives and for the life of their ship. Fortunately, they had been sailing with reefed sails at the time but, even with a reef in, the boat was knocked down flat and, for a moment, it seemed doubtful that she would be able to right herself. Green water came pouring in over the lee railing, into the cockpit and down the companionway into the cabins. The storm had blown up so suddenly that nothing had been battened down.

For a short time, all was fear and confusion, but then the heavy, lead weight of the yawl's keel pulled her back upright. The wind dropped as suddenly as it had risen and the crew flopped down wherever they were and drew deep breaths of relief.

Only then was it noticed that Gabriela Humpert was missing.

For twelve hours they had sailed up and down, criss-crossing the area, hoping against hope that the girl had managed to keep herself afloat, but they had found no trace of her. She had been wearing heavy seaman's boots which had presumably filled with water and pulled her down like a stone.

Klein had gone wild. As the search continued and hope of finding the missing girl dwindled, he became more and more unhinged and finally began ordering the others about with a .357 Magnum revolver in his hand.

Michael Wunsch, the young student, had made the mistake of attempting to reason with him and Klein, losing all control of himself, had shot him at practically point-blank range. Wunsch had collapsed and the other members of the crew, fearing that Klein would kill them all, had rushed him.

Klein had fired two more shots, but had missed and, stepping back to escape the charge of the crew, had caught his foot on the low coping along the roof of the cabin and had fallen overboard.

Termann had thrown him a lifebuoy attached to a rope, but Klein had refused it and had swam away from the ship. The others were afraid to jump into the water after him because he was clearly mad and they feared that he might try to drown them. He had already shot Wunsch and had attempted to shoot the others so he was, obviously, capable of anything.

The ship was, therefore, brought around with the idea of coming up to him and fishing him out of the water with a boathook, but bringing a sailing ship around takes time and, by the time that the manoeuvre was completed, Klein had disappeared. The impression that the others had was that he had not wanted to live and had gone to join his drowned mistress voluntarily.

With Klein and Humpert lost, the most urgent matter was to get Wunsch to a doctor as quickly as possible. He was still alive, but obviously in a very serious condition and, as the radio had gone out of order several days earlier, they could not call for help. They had, therefore, set sail for Barbados, their original destination, and had made landfall after six days.

This statement was made in the presence of the Barbados police, but repeated a second time before the German consul general. All of the persons involved were German citizens and they had requested that their consul be present.

As Herbert Klein could now be presumed dead, the *Apollonia* represented a part of his estate and was impounded by the authorities until such time as the question of his legal heirs could be cleared up. Paul Termann, Dorothea Permin and Dieter Giesen were all flown back to Germany by commercial airline and two weeks later Michael Wunsch followed them. The young man had had what the doctors describe as a truly miraculous escape. The heavy, .357 Magnum slug had passed between his lungs, touching neither of them, had come within a quarter of an inch of his heart, had struck no bones, had severed no major blood vessels and had passed out his back between the ribs a fraction of an inch from his spine. He had had a hole straight through him which, although exceedingly painful, was not really dangerous and, assuming that there was no infection, would heal itself.

By a second miracle, there had been no infection and Wunsch was already partially healed by the time that he had arrived at the hospital. Physically, that was. Mentally, he was a nervous wreck.

In the meantime, a copy of the statement made by Paul Termann, speaking for the crew of the *Apollonia*, in the presence of the Barbados police and the German consul general had been forwarded air mail to Bremen where it eventually landed on the desk of Inspector Johann Bauer of the Bremen Criminal Investigations Department. Bauer, a lean, muscular man with close-clipped, blond hair and very bright blue eyes, was chief of the squad assigned to investigating crimes along the Bremen waterfront. According to the statement a number of crimes had taken place aboard the *Apollonia* and, although eight hundred miles out in the Atlantic was something of an extension of the Bremen waterfront, it still fell within his jurisdiction for Bremen was registered as the ship's homeport.

The inspector began to process the case in a routine, matter of fact manner. It was, by no means, the first time that such things had landed on his desk and, in some cases, the actual events had taken place further away than the drama which had played itself out on the *Apollonia*, Bremen, with a population of six hundred thousand, is one of West Germany's large seaports and there are many vessels of all kinds registered there.

If the inspector's handling of the case was routine, it was also thorough and having read twice through the copy of Paul Termann's statement, a minor discrepancy caught like a burr in his mind.

'Take a look at this, Peter,' he said, tossing the statement over to his assistant, Detective-Sergeant Peter Bergmann, who sat at the desk facing his own. 'Fellow here says that the storm blew up so suddenly and unexpectedly out of a clear blue sky that they didn't even have time to batten down the hatches. Then, he says when the girl went over the side she was wearing sea boots which filled with water and dragged her down. If the weather was so good before the storm and it came up so suddenly, where did she have time to put on sea boots before getting washed overboard?'

The sergeant read silently through the report. He was a young man, blond like his chief, but round-faced, cheerful looking and pleasingly egg-shaped, being noticeably thicker in the middle than on either end.

'The same question applies to the reef in the sails,' he said, tossing the statement back. 'What do you intend to do?'

'Well, for starters, let's bring the lot of them up here and take separate statements,' said the inspector. 'This one was made by just one man speaking for all of them. Could be that the others will have different versions. In the meantime, I see that they've sent the log of the *Apollonia* along and you might check her location on 3 December and then ask the weather bureau just how bad that storm was out there in the Atlantic on that day.'

The sergeant nodded and went about carrying out his

instructions. Some forty minutes later he put down the telephone and said, 'There wasn't any storm within a thousand miles of that location on that date.'

'Huh?' said the inspector who was, by now, working on something else.

'The *Apollonia*,' said the sergeant. 'She wasn't hit by any storm on 3 December unless she managed somehow to get over into the Pacific. The weather bureau has satellite photos of the whole area for 3 December and there wasn't any storm.'

'Wrong date?' suggested the inspector. 'The second? The fourth?'

'I thought of that,' said the sergeant. 'Nothing for three days earlier and nothing for two days later. It couldn't have been more than two days later or they wouldn't have had time to reach Barbados when they did.'

The inspector sat silently and thoughtfully looking at his assistant for several minutes. 'I wonder what really did happen out there,' he said finally.

'Maybe I should take a run down to Krefeld and have a talk with the people there about Herbert Klein,' suggested the sergeant.

'I think you should,' said the inspector, 'and before we get the others up here for the reconstruction. This whole business is beginning to smell a little strong.'

The police had already arranged with the Winkler Shipyard on the River Weser to the north of Bremen for a reconstruction of the event on 3 December aboard the *Apollonia* on a ship of her approximate size and construction. Paul Termann, Dorothea Permin, Dieter Giesen and the now largely recovered Michael Wunsch had all been summoned to appear on 22 January to carry out this re-enactment of what had supposedly taken place, and the police had reserved hotel accommodation for them for that night.

The sergeant went down to Krefeld, a large, industrial city on the edge of the Ruhr district a few hundred miles to the south. When he returned, it was with the news that Herbert Klein had not been the wealthy, international yacthsman that he was supposed to be.

'He was the manager of a trucking firm,' said the sergeant, making his report to the inspector. 'Last year he went all to pieces, divorced his wife, sold everything he owned and bought the *Apollonia* for ninety thousand dollars cash. It must have taken every cent that he had. He then acquired the twenty-five-year-old mistress and set sail for the Canary Islands. His wife is thirty-three and still goes by the name of Birgit Klein. Her only comment was that she would have been better off if he had drowned himself before she met him. Fortunately, there were no children.'

'Another seeker of adventure in a world where any real adventures are either illegal or painful,' commented the inspector. 'Did he have insurance and, if so, who was the beneficiary?'

'I didn't think to check on that,' said the sergeant, embarrassed. 'You think maybe he isn't dead and that this is some kind of a deal to swindle the insurance company?'

'Could be,' said the inspector. 'There have been weirder schemes and Klein sounds like the type.'

'I'll check with his bank,' said the sergeant. 'They should know his financial situation.'

The bank knew more. They knew, for example, that Herbert Klein was alive and well and had been travelling extensively in Europe. He had cashed traveller's cheques in the south of France, in Italy, in Switzerland and in several places in Germany. The last had been cashed less than a week before in Hamburg.

'The man must be mentally retarded,' said the inspector. 'Doesn't he realize that, if he goes around cashing his cheques, they're going to come back to the bank and constitute positive proof that he's still alive. What in the devil is he trying to do and where's the girl?'

'In my opinion, an even greater question,' said the sergeant, 'is where is he getting the money to pay Termann, Permin, Giesen and Wunsch to keep their mouths shut. He has to be paying them because they're obviously lying and what other reason could there be for it?'

'What about the insurance?' said the inspector.

'He wasn't insured,' said the sergeant. 'He cashed in his insurance when he bought the boat.'

'Well, then what . . . ?' exclaimed the inspector. 'Get me Hamburg on the telephone immediately. We've got to get our hands on this Klein and the sooner the better. Let's just hope he stays in Hamburg long enough to cash another cheque.'

The inspector's wish was going to be granted. A physical description of Herbert Klein and a picture obtained from his parents were sent to the Hamburg police where they were made up into a wanted circular to be distributed to the tellers of all the banks in the city. If Klein turned up to cash one of his cheques, the teller was to signal one of his or her colleagues to summon the police and stall until they could arrive. This would normally not be very long. The Hamburg police are highly efficient and the city swarms with patrol-cars.

On Monday, 18 January 1982, the trap snapped shut. A man appeared at the teller's window of a downtown bank, handed in a traveller's cheque for $100 and presented his personal identification card. It was in the name of Herbert Klein and carried the Krefeld address.

The teller gave the appointed signal, knocked a tray of coins on to the floor and began picking them up while the customer waited impatiently.

He did not have long to wait. The officers from the patrolcar had been advised that Klein might be armed with a .357 Magnum revolver and they walked quietly up behind him on either side, pressed the muzzles of their service pistols into his ribs and advised him not to move.

A search produced no weapon but more traveller's cheques, and Klein was taken to police headquarters to explain what he was doing in Hamburg when he was supposed to be at the bottom of the Atlantic.

He promptly offered an excellent explanation. He was not Herbert Klein.

Perhaps forty-one-year-old Hans Kruger might have been less frank with the Hamburg police were it not for the fact that he had a police record and his fingerprints were, therefore, on file. In any case, he would eventually have been brought back to Krefeld to explain what had happened to Gabriela Humpert if nothing else, and there he would certainly have come into contact with someone who had known the real Herbert Klein whom Hans Kruger resembled not at all. Klein had been tall and rather skinny with a good deal of hair and moustache and not much chin. Kruger was balding, broad-shouldered and had a jaw like the bow of a harbour tug.

In fact, he looked very much like a cartoonist's idea of a burglar and that was precisely what he was. Kruger was a thief, a burglar and a break-in artist. It was he who had broken into the *Apollonia* at Las Palmas, and it was this break-in which had netted him, in addition to the cash and the navigational instruments, the traveller's cheques and identification card of Herbert Klein. A man with considerable experience in such matters, he had had no difficulty in reproducing a reasonable facsimile of the yachtsman's signature.

Kruger had been arrested many times before and did not resent such actions on the part of the police. Transferred to Bremen to see if he knew anything about the mystery of the *Apollonia*, he assured Inspector Bauer that he did not, but volunteered the information that he had been able to take his time about plundering the *Apollonia* because he had received a tip that there would be no one on board.

The tip had come from an old friend, Paul Termann.

This was a valuable piece of information, although it did nothing toward solving the question of what had taken place aboard the *Apollonia* in mid-Atlantic, and the inspector put his assistant to checking yacht owners on the Bremen waterfront to see if any of them had any information about the black-bearded navigator.

And, indeed, several did and none of it was favourable. The most critical of all was his most recent employer but one, fifty-four-year-old Captain Guenther Lohse, owner of the sailing yacht *Orion X*. Captain Lohse had such strong feelings about Paul Termann that he sat down and wrote a seven-page statement in which he said, among other less flattering things, that Termann was a madman, a violent character and a gun nut. Although too poor to afford more than a rowboat, he was obsessed with the ambition to own a yacht, and was prepared to do anything to get one. While serving on board the *Orion X* he had talked of nothing but drug- and gun-running which he believed would get him into the big money.

Termann had no sooner been shipped as navigator than he unilaterally declared himself captain, although Lohse both owned and captained the boat. This being pointed out to him, he compromised and appointed himself second captain, a position which does not exist on a ship. This led to such violent quarrels with the rest of the crew that Lohse had been forced to discharge him as everyone else on board had threatened to walk off if he remained.

Termann, concluded Captain Lohse, was also a bum navigator whose reckoning had the ship in the wrong ocean half the time.

'Call up the hotel and cancel the reservations for Termann and his girlfriend,' said the inspector to Sergeant Bergmann when he had finished reading this report. 'They'll be putting up in the detention cells here and they won't need them.'

'What about Giesen and Wunsch?' said the sergeant. 'Whatever happened, they had to be in on it. They signed the protocol of Termann's statement in Barbados.'

'It looks like it,' said the inspector, 'but, for the moment, I'm prepared to give them the benefit of the doubt. Constance reported that they were clean, didn't they?'

As the case had progressed and become more mysterious, the sergeant had contacted the police in Constance with a request that they check out the backgrounds of Dieter Giesen and Michael Wunsch. This had been done and the Constance police had reported that both men were exactly what they had said they were. Giesen was a respectable businessman and the owner of a high-class bar. Wunsch was a student and the son of a well-to-do Constance family. Both men were passionate fans of skin-diving and both belonged to a skin-diving club on Lake Constance, the large body of water which separates the southern end of Germany from Switzerland.

None of the parties involved had known, of course, that

they were being investigated and all appeared promptly on Friday, 22 January 1982, in Bremen for the re-enactment of the event. This re-enactment was, however, going to turn out a little different than anyone had anticipated.

To begin with, Paul Termann, Dorothea Permin, Dieter Giesen and Michael Wunsch never reached the hotel where they believed that rooms had been reserved for them, but were met at the railway station by an impressive contingent of criminal investigations department plain-clothes officers under the command of Sergeant Bergmann, were taken into custody and brought to the interrogation rooms at police headquarters. The inspector had, in the meantime, changed his mind and had cancelled the hotel reservations for Giesen and Wunsch also.

And it was Giesen and Wunsch on whom the questioning was concentrated. Both were apparently respectable, young men who were not known to have ever been involved in anything illegal and the inspector felt that they were the ones most likely to break down and reveal the truth.

His assumption was correct and, after little more than a few moments of interrogation and a warning that continued silence could result in charges of concealing a felony or acting as an accessory after the fact, both men made separate but identical statements of the events on board the *Apollonia*, not on 3 December but on the 13th, the only difference being a gap in Wunsch's account as he had been unconscious part of the time.

According to Giesen and Wunsch, the *Apollonia* had barely set sail from Las Palmas when Termann began to display the strange behaviour which had made him so unpopular on the *Orion X* and other vessels. Appointing himself captain, he had reversed any orders given by Klein and had begun commanding the others about like galley slaves. This included Dorothea Permin who not only supported him, but was so subservient to his will that she allowed him to accompany her to the toilet, apparently to make certain that she did not get into any mischief there.

Klein and his mistress, Gabriela Humpert, had attempted to resist, but they had been no match for the physically powerful and aggressive Termann. Giesen and Wunsch, unwilling to become involved, had tried to avoid taking sides and had contented themselves with hoping that the voyage to the Caribbean would be a swift one, and that they would soon be able to leave the most uncomfortable ship they had ever set sail in.

Both had thought that Termann was more than a little mad, but not actually dangerous up until that Sunday, 13 December, when he had produced the .357 Magnum and had advised Klein that he was not only taking over the command of the *Apollonia*, but the *Apollonia* herself. He, Termann, was now owner and captain and everyone was to obey his orders instantly and without question.

Foolishly, Klein had attempted to argue and Termann had gone into a hysterical rage, screaming that he would now kill both of them, meaning Klein and Gabriela.

There was no doubting his sincerity and the couple had thrown themselves on their knees and pleaded for their lives. Instead of killing them, Klein suggested, they could be set adrift in the ship's boat.

Termann would not hear of it, but he did not kill them immediately either. Instead, almost the entire day of 13 December was spent in a sort of macabre argument with Klein and Gabriela pleading and arguing for their lives and Termann sticking to his original plan of murdering them.

Finally, he had said that he would agree not to kill them, but only if they committed suicide themselves. Producing a second pistol, he had loaded it with two bullets and laid it on the seat in the cockpit. They could take turns in shooting themselves or one could shoot the other and them commit suicide. Termann then went below to the cabin to relax and wait at the foot of the companionway.

Another man might have picked up the pistol lying on the seat in the cockpit and shot Termann through the head as he sat there, but Herbert Klein, whatever his failings, was not a killer. Instead of murdering his enemy, he attempted to overpower him and, in so doing, lost his life and the life of his young mistress.

Klein had picked up the iron handle of the bilge pump

lying in the cockpit and, reaching down through the opening of the companionway, had swung it at Termann's head. He had hit him, but it was only a glancing blow and with not enough force to even throw Termann off balance.

The black-bearded killer who was holding the .357 Magnum in his hand had swung around and had fired instantly.

Unfortunately for Michael Wunsch, who was also sitting in the cockpit, he was no better a shot than a navigator and the bullet missed Klein and struck Wunsch in the chest. Wunsch fell to the floor of the cockpit unconscious and was not a witness to any of the acts which followed.

Giesen was, but he would have much preferred not to be. Following the failure with the pump handle and the shooting of Wunsch, Klein had run forward to hide himself in the bow compartment of the boat, but Termann had forced him out at gunpoint and brought him crawling back to the cockpit. There he was ordered to stand with his back to the railing and Termann fired a bullet at close range into his chest, the impact tipping him over the railing and into the sea.

Turning around from this accomplished murder, Paul Termann found himself staring into the fear-widened eyes of Gabriela Humpert. The second bullet passed directly between them.

Giesen had, of course, considered himself to be a dead man, but Termann also had his practical side. The *Apollonia* was too big to be sailed safely by himself and Dorothea Permin alone. Advising Giesen that he had connections in Germany and that, if he revealed so much as a word of what had happened upon their return, he would arrange for a killer to come down from Frankfurt and eliminate him, he wrote up the statement to be presented to the German consul and the police in Barbados and forced Giesen to sign it. When Michael Wunsch recovered consciousness, he was given the same warning and, overjoyed to learn that he was not to be executed immediately, had sworn silence and signed as well.

Giesen and Wunsch insisted that they had been simply too frightened of Termann to say so much as a word while they were still in Barbados. He was, they thought, quite capable of whipping out a pistol in the very presence of the German consul and shooting them down on the spot. The man was violently insane and even after their return to Germany they had been afraid to say anything before Michael's wound had healed enough that they could clear off if necessary.

The statements of Dieter Giesen and Michael Wunsch were flatly contradicted by Termann and Dorothea Permin who stuck to their original version and said that Giesen and Wunsch were trying to get them into trouble because they had quarrelled with them on the ship.

However, separation in the detention cells from Termann had a beneficial effect on Dorothea's character and, after a week of interrogation, she broke down and verified in all details the accounts given by Dieter Giesen and Michael Wunsch.

Paul Termann was indicted on two accounts of voluntary homicide and one count of piracy on the high seas, an unusual charge even for Bremen. Dorothea Permin was indicted on two counts of acting as an accessory after the fact to homicide and on one count of acting as an accessory after the fact to piracy in return for her cooperation with the police.

She was sentenced to only five years' imprisonment with three years suspended on 21 January 1983.

A month later, Paul Termann was given the maximum sentence of life imprisonment. Rather surprisingly, the psychologists who examined him expressed the opinion that he was sane.

16

HOMICIDES PERFORMED, QUICK SERVICE, REASONABLE RATES

The temptation arises to wonder who, if not Paul Termann, is insane. Or is it that, in a paranoically egalitarian society, even the logic of madmen is to be respected?

Termann was logical. He wanted a yacht. Klein had a yacht. Ergo, he killed Klein and took his yacht. A trifle simplistic, perhaps. After all, the yacht was registered in Klein's name and, without a bill of sale, Termann could scarcely hope to change the registration. However, it may be that he was planning to have a bill of sale made out and signed by his friend, Hans Kruger, who owed him a favour in any case. Perhaps, the psychologists were right. Paul Termann was sane, but rather more direct in his dealings than most of us.

Such directness crops up rather frequently in our modern societies, particularly in connection with the transfer of wealth. Those who do not have it feel that they are entitled to it and take steps accordingly. Homicide becomes a sort of social adjustment, and for those who are incapable by reason of lack of strength, resolution or technical training to carry out the sticky parts, there are skilled, reliable experts.

The acts committed by these experts fall into a curious category. They are homicides because someone is killed by the expert, but are they murder?

The hired assassin has no motive for his crime other than the fee he is paid. He does not dislike the victim; frequently has never before laid eyes on him or her. Had it been the victim who employed him, he would as cheerfully have executed his current employer. He is simply paid to kill.

So, too, are official executioners, soldiers, agents of the world's secret services and terrorists or freedom fighters. Granted, not all of these are paid in cash, but there is compensation of some sort, and terrorists who survive to bring about a successful change in the ruling group usually do rather well for themselves.

It would appear that, if the direct way of thinking of a Paul Termann is to be regarded as sane, then the direct homicides of the professional killers cannot be described as murder. There is a demand for the service. They fill it.

Such crimes are difficult for the police to solve as it is necessary to establish the motive of not the killer himself (or herself, in deference to woman's equality, although there are few female professional killers as yet), but of the person who hires him. This can be unclear. Murders are often committed for trifling motives.

But because a man makes lousy pizza?

For a time, it looked it, although pizza was about the last thing on the mind of thirty-year-old Walter Bronheim as he came riding his bicycle down Dolberger Street in the West German city of Hamm and entered the bicycle path leading through the small forest known as the Schafbusch.

Some two hundred yards to the west of the Schafbusch, the main highway running from Hanover to Cologne is intersected by a secondary road into which the bicycle path opens and, just before reaching this intersection, Bronheim came upon the body of a man lying on his back at the edge of the road.

The man was wearing dark blue trousers, black shoes, a black, cord jacket and a rose-coloured shirt with frills down the front and at the cuffs. The front of the shirt was no longer rose-coloured, but red with fresh blood.

Hurriedly dismounting from his bicycle, Bronheim ran forward and knelt down beside the man. He assumed that this was the victim of a hit-and-run driver and he was relieved, but also horrified to see that blood was still welling out of the man's chest which rose and fell with his laboured breathing. His eyes were closed and he appeared to be unconscious.

Although Bronheim had had some experience in first aid, he grasped instantly that the man's injuries were too serious for anything that he might be able to do and he ran back to the bicycle and pedalled off in the direction of the village of Uentrop, the nearest community, to summon help.

As he rode he turned his left hand on the handlebars and looked at his wristwatch. The time was exactly ten minutes past nine.

It did not take Bronheim long to reach Uentrop nor to find a public telephone there, and he dialled the number of the emergency ambulance service in Hamm, reporting that there was a severly injured man lying in the road near the Schafbusch forest and saying that he would now return to where the victim lay and wait for the ambulance.

Hamm is a city of some 180,000 population and its emergency ambulance service has ample opportunity for practice because of the vast numbers of automobile accidents. Bronheim had had barely time to pedal back to where the man lay when the ambulance arrived.

The victim, a slender, dark-haired and olive-skinned man in his late thirties or early forties, was still alive but unconscious, and he was lifted quickly on to the stretcher, slid into the ambulance and taken away in the direction of Hamm.

The victim having been reported as still alive, the duty emergency doctor had come out with the ambulance and, as it raced through the streets with flashing, blue, warning lights and screaming siren, he began cutting away the blood-soaked shirt for the purpose of determining the nature of the injury and stopping the flow of blood.

The ambulance had covered less than half the distance to the hospital when he leaned over the partition, tapped the driver on the shoulder and said, 'Call the hospital. Tell them we have a gunshot wound. Multiple thorax. The police should be informed.'

The driver carried out his instructions over the radio-telephone and increased his speed, but, even as the stretcher with the wounded man was being carried through the emergency entrance, a long, violent shudder passed over the body and was followed by a cessation of all movement.

'Into the operating room!' snapped the doctor. 'There may still be a chance to . . .'

There was none. The man was dead and, as later examination would show, from four heavy-calibre bullets fired into the chest with such accuracy that a child's hand could cover the entry wounds. The damage that they had inflicted had been such that the victim had been doomed from the instant of impact and it was only remarkable that he had continued to live as long as he did.

This having been determined, the body was transferred to the police morgue for an autopsy to determine officially the cause and time of death. As there was little question but that the case was one of deliberate homicide, it would also be necessary to recover the bullets and any other indications which might be of value to the investigation which would follow.

This autopsy was carried out by Dr Oscar Wittauer, a relatively young assistant coroner with a long, sad face and a drooping blond moustache. Although the autopsy was routine, he took quite a time about it, causing Inspector Heinz Wagner of the Hamm police Criminal Investigations Department to fidgit irritably. A busy man with a near military haircut and a carefully clipped moustache which was beginning to go grey, he was anxious to get on with the investigation.

While he paced about the autopsy room, peering over the doctor's shoulder and generally getting in the way, his assistant, Detective-Sergeant Kurt Kettenmyer, went impassively through the dead man's pockets in search of identification. He was a young man who wore his wavy brown hair down to his collar and tended to scowl a great deal, not so much because he was bad-tempered but because he believed this to be a suitable expression for an investigations officer.

There were a good many things in the pockets and, as he removed them, he laid them out in a neat row on the edge of the table. First came a crumpled pack of cigarettes with four cigarettes of a popular brand in it, then an expensive-looking cigarette lighter, followed by four keys on a souvenir keyring from the city of Berlin, the equivalent of $64.22 in small bills and coins, a collection of scraps of paper, mainly restaurant bills, a small penknife, a leather folder containing a personal identity card and a driver's licence and, finally, two photographs, one of a very pretty, young woman and the other of a little girl of about ten.

The inspector pounced on the case with the papers and was soon able to determine that the victim was forty-year-old Vincenzo Sapuppo, married, the father of one child, an Italian national from the city of Palermo, Sicily, and a pizza baker by profession. His local address was listed as 24 Brandenburg Street and the inspector sent the sergeant there immediately to notify the widow, arrange for the official identification by the next of kin and attempt to learn whether there were any obvious suspects in the murder.

In the meantime, the inspector having decided that nothing of any great significance was going to come out of the autopsy, he went off to view the scene of the discovery of the body and, presumably, the scene of the crime.

Two patrolcars had been sent by the dispatcher at police headquarters and they had blocked off a section of the road where traces of blood showed that the body had lain. Sitting in one of the cars was Walter Bronheim who was being held until someone took his statement.

The inspector did so and, having determined that he knew nothing of value to the investigation, sent him off about his business. The only information that he was able to provide was the exact time of the discovery, which the inspector thought might give some indication of the time of the shooting. Having seen the wounds, he did not believe that the man could have lived very long after receiving them.

Although it was obvious that nothing would be found at the scene, he was a thorough man and he called headquarters over the car's radio-telephone and arranged for a detachment from the police laboratory to come out and go over the area.

He did not wait for them, but returned to headquarters. It was unlikely that they would find anything at all, and the best he could hope for was an opinion as to whether the shooting had taken place there or elsewhere. The road was hard-surfaced so there would be no footprints or tire tracks to be connected with the shooting. The laboratory report was, however, necessary for the records.

The fact was, the inspector had already formed an opinion of his own, and that was that this was a gangster-type execution. He had thought so the moment he saw the bullet wounds, and his suspicions had received support with the knowledge that the victim was a Sicilian.

There were a great many Italian guest workers, as they were called, in the great industrial and mining complex of the Ruhr and they came mainly from southern Italy. Hamm was technically not in the Ruhr, but it was only twelve miles to the east of it and there were a great many Italians there, too.

Like ethnic groups everywhere, they had brought their traditional societies with them and one of these was the Mafia. There had been kidnappings, extortions, protection-racket violence and a gang killing or two.

Actually, the police had not concerned themselves very much with this local branch of an old organization as their activities had been confined largely to their own compatriots. The local Germans were seldom involved and, in any case, the crime rate in the Ruhr was at a level to make the efforts of the Mafia seem insignificant.

What the inspector thought the investigations would show, if they showed anything, was that Vincenzo Sapuppo might have started life as a pizzario, but that it had been a long time since that had been his primary source of income. Rather, he had been working in a small-time capacity as a leg man or collection agent for some group in the Underworld. He had, however, been more greedy than smart, had held out more than permitted and had been punished when his employers put out a contract on his ears.

The inspector would not have been surprised if Sapuppo had had a police record, but the records section said no, they had no Sapuppo in the files. As far as they were concerned he was clean.

Clean and remarkably lucky or unlucky, depending upon how you looked at it. According to the final autopsy report,

Sapuppo had been hit with four nine-millimetre slugs in the immediate vicinity of the heart and had been killed by none of them. Despite expert shooting, not a vital organ had been touched; not a major blood vessel severed. Had he been found in time he would have survived, but, according to Dr Wittauer, he had continued to live for as much as seven hours following the shooting without anyone coming to his aid. The only favourable aspect to the matter was that he had apparently been unconscious the entire time.

The four slugs had been recovered from Sapuppo's body and sent to the Ballistics Department which reported that they had been fired from a Beretta automatic and that there was no record of the gun.

This did not surprise the inspector in the least. A nine-millimetre Beretta was a killer's gun, and professional killers did not go around with guns that had a record with the police.

The inspector had already decided that the only possible direction which the investigation could take was to try and determine whom Sapuppo had worked for and then get them deported on some pretext as an example. There was obviously not going to be enough evidence to convict anybody of the murder.

Having thus cleared matters up in his own mind, the inspector was irritated when Sergeant Kettenmyer returned from his interview with the victim's widow bringing information which cast considerable doubt on his theories.

Mrs Sapuppo, said the sergeant, had been quite positive. Her husband had had no connections to the Underworld or, she had added, to anything that brought in money. He had been exactly what his identity card said, a pizzario and not even a very good one.

'She suggest that he was murdered by one of the customers?' said the inspector sarcastically.

'She said he's had trouble with his employers more than once,' said the sergeant, forgetting to scowl. 'She's a very unfortunate woman. Only twenty years old and . . .'

'Sapuppo was forty,' said the inspector. 'This must be his second marriage. That child in the picture couldn't be Mrs Sapuppo's if she's only twenty.'

'Maybe she said twenty-two,' said the sergeant. 'It's her daughter all right. She may have married very young. Do you want me to take a look at her background?'

'Definitely,' said the inspector. 'If Sapuppo didn't have any connections to the Underworld and he didn't have any money, then Mrs Sapuppo is about the only possible motive, short of something weird like a mistaken identity. That twenty-year difference in ages makes a love triangle of some sort a good bet.'

An excellent bet, actually. The Sapuppos being well known in the local Italian community, the sergeant had little difficulty in finding out nearly everything there was to know about Magdalena Sapuppo who, it seemed, had married in Sicily at the age of fourteen.

'Not her idea and not even his,' said the sergeant. 'The families arranged it. They apparently thought there was more money in making pizzas than there is.

'Mrs Sapuppo immediately got pregnant and produced her only child when she had just turned fifteen. Three years later, they came to Germany and they've been here ever since.

'Sapuppo's held a whole string of jobs as pizzario and Mrs Sapuppo was apparently telling the literal truth. He didn't have much talent for the profession, and he didn't make much money. No trace of any connection to the Underworld.'

'And the name of her lover?' said the inspector cynically.

'Luigi Mosca,' said the sergeant. 'Thirty. Married. Two kids. Heavy-equipment operator for a construction firm. He and Mrs Sapuppo have been at it for about two years, which is double the time any of the others lasted with her so it must be true love.'

'Had lots of them, did she?' said the inspector. 'Did Sapuppo know?'

'About the others and about this one, too,' said the sergeant. 'He spoke of his wife's lovers as casually as if they were part of the family. Could be she was too much for him what with that twenty-year age difference and all.'

'Fine,' said the inspector. 'But then, why bother to murder him? That cost money.'

'Brought it on himself apparently,' said the sergeant. 'He was planning to return to Sicily and take his family with him next month. Mrs Sapuppo couldn't stand the thought of separation from her loved ones.'

'Or vice versa,' said the inspector. 'Well, that should do it. Bring in Mrs Sapuppo and Mosca and we'll see what interrogation can do. Normally, a couple like that gets nervous about the other one selling out and they both end up blabbing their hearts out. True love holds up fine until it's a question of who's going to take the rap.'

Unfortunately, true love held up somewhat better in this case, possibly because it was obvious that no one was going to take the rap. The suspects' alibis were as solid as the Rock of Gibraltar. Hours before the shooting and long after it, Luigi Mosca and Magdalena Sapuppo had been in the constant presence of large numbers of disinterested witnesses. They were so obviously in the clear that the inspector could not even hold them for questioning.

'We should have guessed that,' said the inspector. 'The job was professional so they hired somebody to pull it off while they arranged their watertight alibis.'

'So they get away with it,' said the sergeant.

'Not at all,' said the inspector. 'What we do now is find the bird who pulled the trigger and offer him a deal if he testifies against his employers. People like that are practical. He'll cooperate.'

The inspector was, undoubtedly, right in expecting cooperation from the killer, and the only flaw in his plans was that it proved impossible to determine who he was. The sergeant spent a great deal of time and effort on this project, and he did learn many things other than the identity of the murderer.

He was able to determine where Sapuppo had apparently been not long before he was killed. The pizzario's car, missing since the time of the murder, was found parked near the Silvermoon discotheque in the town of Ahlen, twelve miles to the north of Ham. It was a yellow Peugeot 104 and the owner of the Silvermoon, an establishment patronized by a somewhat older clientele than was customary, said that he knew Sapuppo well and that he had been in the Silvermoon with another Italian until three in the morning of 15 September.

This would have been an important lead had it not been for the fact that the autopsy had established that Sapuppo was lying in the road with four bullets in his chest twenty miles away at the time.

There were other flaws in the discotheque owner's testimony. He was unable to describe Sapuppo, seemed to think that he was blond, an unusual hair colouration for a Sicilian although not unknown, and confused the details of his murder with those of another case.

Whereupon the sergeant took a look into his background, found that he had spent more of his life in institutions for persons suffering from nervous disorders than out, and came to the conclusion that the lead was worthless.

There remained, however, the fact that Sapuppo's car had been parked near the discotheque. By whom? Possibly the murderer. It was one of a number of questions that would never be answered.

The question as to the price of the killing was. It had cost precisely three thousand dollars, the amount which Mosca had borrowed on a personal loan from the Hamm Savings Bank two weeks before the murder took place.

Asked what he had done with this money, Mosca said he had lost the entire amount playing roulette. Asked why he had borrowed it, he replied, 'To play roulette.'

At this point the official investigation ended by reason of having nothing left to investigate. There had been little mention of it in the press. Mrs Sapuppo would have provided wonderful pictures and text, but, as she was not charged with anything, even an insinuation could have resulted in a lawsuit. As for the victim, the death of an incompetent pizza baker was not a story to grip the imagination of the German public.

Not the imagination of the public, perhaps, but certainly the imagination of Inspector Wagner who fumed and fretted and was profoundly annoyed that anyone, however lacking in professional skills, could be murdered practically under his nose and that he could do nothing about it. He was utterly convinced that Magdalena Sapuppo and Luigi Mosca were guilty of the murder, and he was very disappointed when a check of the records showed no entry for the heavy-equipment operator.

As a matter of fact, the only thing which the investigation of Mosca had shown was that he was a harassed man who was in over his head financially. Although he was a good, steady worker, he had a wife and two children to support plus, now, Magdalena whose husband had died without insurance. In addition, he had the payments on the three-thousand-dollar loan and the total was more than his salary would cover.

Persons in Luigi Mosca's position often do something foolish and on the afternoon of Tuesday, 10 February 1981, he did.

Although it was mid-winter, the day was dry and compara-tively sunny if not exactly warm. On a country road outside Hamm, thirteen-year-old Dirk Reimann, son of a wealthy building contractor, was stolidly peddling his bicycle home from school as he did every weekday.

Presently, he was passed by a yellow Alfa-Romeo which cut in ahead of him, forcing him to stop.

Reimann, a stout youth with a deceptively sluggish appear-ance, got off the bicycle and stood staring phlegmatically at the three men in the car. Although two of them worked for his father, he had never seen them before and he did not know who they were or what they wanted.

The three Italians whose purpose it was to kidnap and hold for ransom the young contractor's son came boiling out of the car and all jumped on him simultaneously. According to their plan, he was to be quickly overpowered, dragged into the car and driven swiftly away to an abandoned farmhouse where he would be held until the ransom was paid.

This was a good plan, but it did not take into account the possibility that the victim might not be in agreement. Instead of meekly submitting to being overpowered, young Reimann began to take wild, roundhouse swings with his fists, kick with his feet and bellow like a bull with his tail on fire. One of the Italians was knocked sprawling with a punch in the nose.

Another doubled up and went hopping off with a savagely kicked shin. And the third, noting that the boy's roars were attracting attention and that passers-by were hurrying to the rescue, shovelled the casualties into the Alfa-Romeo and, taking the wheel, raced away at top speed.

But not fast enough. The indignant Dirk Reimann had noted the licence number and so had two of the approaching rescuers. A half-hour later, the police knew of the kidnapping attempt. Forty-five minutes later, they knew the identity of the owner of the yellow Alfa-Romeo. An hour after that, they had him in custody.

It was Luigi Mosca.

'Very good,' said the inspector, rubbing his hands together. 'Very good. Now, we have a bargaining position. Either he confesses to the Sapuppo murder, or we'll nail him with a short sentence for attempted kidnapping.'

The sergeant looked at him as if he would have liked to comment on his mental condition, but thought he had better not.

'You mean a long sentence, don't you?' he ventured.

'Short,' said the inspector. 'Followed, of course, by deportation to Sicily.'

'And that will cause him to confess to murder?' said the sergeant.

'Once I bring to his attention who will be waiting for him there,' said the inspector.

'The Italian police?' said the sergeant in obvious mystification.

'The Sapuppo family,' said the inspector.

The sergeant finally understood.

And so, too, did Luigi Mosca. After having given the matter only very little thought, he agreed with the inspector that he would be better off serving a sentence in Germany for murder than arriving a free man in Sicily to face the relatives of the man he had had murdered.

The actual murderer of Vincenzo Sapuppo, said Luigi Mosca, was thirty-five-year-old Vincenzo Madiri who lived in a village near Palermo and who killed persons on a contractual basis. Madiri, he added, was a cousin, but, even so, he had received no discount and had had to pay the full price including Madiri's round-trip air fare first class.

As the inspector had anticipated, Mosca concluded his statement with the assurance that the murder had been entirely Magdalena's idea and that he had opposed it from the start. She had, however, forced him by threatening to expose his infidelity with her to his wife.

This was not a very plausible excuse as Mosca had been living more or less openly with Mrs Sapuppo for close to two years and his wife not only knew about it, but so did everybody else in the Italian community in Hamm. It did, however, show that Mosca was still not thinking clearly.

Magdalena Sapuppo was. Taken into custody and advised of her lover's confession, she immediately branded it a lie from beginning to end. Luigi Mosca, she said, had had nothing to do with the murder. It was her husband, and it was she who had had him murdered. Mosca was merely trying to take credit so as to cheat her of the long jail sentence which she so richly deserved.

What had not occurred to Mosca had obviously occurred to her instantly. The first one out of jail would also be the first to arrive in Sicily.

Later, during the course of a confrontation between the two former lovers, the dispute reached near comic proportions.

'It was my husband. I alone am responsible,' said Magdalena.

'It was my cousin who killed him,' said Mosca. 'You had nothing to do with it.'

'You did not think of it,' said Magdalena. 'You did not have enough intelligence to even kidnap a thirteen-year-old boy. He drove the three of you before him like sheep. How could you plan a murder?'

'And who is still paying the payments on the loan from the bank?' howled Mosca in a frenzy of rage. 'It is my cousin. A top professional. All first class. It is my money. And who gets the long sentence? You? Hah! I demand justice!'

'I wouldn't be surprised but what he'll get it too,' remarked the sergeant after the confrontation was over. 'The thing that puzzles me is why nobody seems concerned about Madiri. He's the one who actually pulled the trigger. You'd think that he would be the one the Sapuppos would be after, but apparently not. He simply did the job and flew back to Sicily without a care in the world.'

'Maybe it's because he did it on a professional basis,' said the inspector. 'Nothing personal, so to speak. Or maybe it's because he is obviously not a good man to argue with. The Italian police may be able to tell us. I've asked for Madiri's arrest.'

The Italian police did not arrest Vincenzo Madiri, but they did send an officer around to take his statement, a copy of which was forwarded to Inspector Wagner in Hamm.

In it Madiri said that he did not know anything about the murder, had never heard the name of Sapuppo and had a great many cousins, one or more of whom might or might not be named Luigi Mosca. In any case, nobody had paid him to kill anybody and he had not. He was not in the killing business, but made his living doing small contracting jobs.

The police did not comment on the accuracy of the statement, but merely observed that the charges against Madiri appeared to be based on the unsupported statements of two confessed murderers. In any case, sovereign states do not extradite their own nationals and Mr Madiri had said that he was too busy to come to Germany voluntarily at the moment.

The inspector was not satisfied with this report and requested assistance from the German embassy in Palermo who sent one of the vice-consuls around to talk with Mr Madiri.

He found him up on the roof of his mother's house where he was carrying out certain necessary repairs to the tiles. There being no witnesses present, he confirmed that he was, indeed, a professional killer and that he had carried out the Sapuppo contract in Hamm. His understanding had been that he was being jointly employed by the widow and his cousin, but he was not prepared to put anything in writing. He was not worried about the Sapuppo family. They could hardly hold it against a man for practising his trade and, God knew, business was bad enough. Times were tough all over.

It was obvious from this that there was not very much that

233

could be done about Mr Vincenzo Madiri and Inspector Wagner proceeded to bring charges of incitement to homicide and acting as an accessory to the fact of homicide against Magdalena Sapuppo and Luigi Mosca indiscriminately.

At their trial, both cooperated enthusiastically and were rewarded, she with seven years' imprisonment and he with nine. Sentencing was on 4 September 1981. Normally, neither would serve much more than a third of these sentences before being parolled and deported to Sicily.

It is considered probable that they will be met at the airport.

17

WHO CAN I GET TO RAPE MY SON?

Magdalena Sapuppo and Luigi Mosca do not really belong in this book. There was nothing mad about them. In a world with no generally accepted standards of morality, they acted practically and reasonably.

Vincenzo Sapuppo was threatening their happiness. It was, therefore, necessary to eliminate him, but neither Magdalena nor Luigi possessed the necessary skills. They were in need of the services of an expert and, as they did not have the cash to finance the job, they took a convenient bank loan.

The only thing that went wrong was that the payments were too high. Had they been stretched out over a longer period, it is possible that they could have lived happily ever after with no necessity of visiting lovely, but dangerous Sicily.

Unless, of course, Mrs Mosca began to stand in the way of their happiness in which case there would have had to be another bank loan and another tiring trip north for Mr Madiri who does not care for air travel and sometimes suffers from motion sickness.

He would, of course, be subject to other discomforts if Inspector Wagner knew that he was coming, but that would be unlikely. For the inspector the case is closed, and he has gone on to other, less trying matters. At least, he hopes they will be less trying. European investigations officers have enough problems without suspects clamouring for longer sentences while known murderers go uncharged. Such investigations can be emotionally exhausting.

But not for Inspector Richard Rademacher of the Criminal Investigations Department of the Salzburg police. Inspector Rademacher was never exhausted and on this Sunday, 18 February 1978, it was going to be a good thing too.

A small man, slightly built with the long, wavy, brown hair and pale sensitive face of a poet, the inspector was as neatly dressed and shaved as if he had just risen rather than having been pulled out of bed at one in the morning; and it was six in the evening now.

'In all my twenty-six years of investigation work,' said the inspector, 'and in everything that I have ever read on the subject of crime, I have as yet to encounter anything resembling this mess.'

His voice was, like his character, at variance with his appearance: high, clear, hard and emotionless. Known to his colleagues as a ruthless driver, he was even formidable physically.

'It would help if he would talk,' said his assistant. 'First he was hysterical, and now this thousand-dollar-an-hour lawyer telling him to shut up.'

Detective-Sergeant Pitt Krimzsky sounded a little hysterical himself. A tall, powerfully built man with tightly curled, blond hair and a jutting jaw, he had not stood up as well to the seventeen-odd hours on duty as had his chief, although he was close to twenty years younger.

'Call the hospital again and see if they'll let us talk to the girl now,' said the inspector. 'She wasn't badly hurt. There's no reason why we shouldn't be able to talk to her.'

The sergeant picked up the telephone on his desk which stood back to back with the inspector's and dialled. There was a short exchange of conversation in a not too friendly tone and the sergeant hung up.

'Tomorrow morning at the earliest,' he said. 'They say she's physically all right, but the shock of seeing her friend murdered made it necessary for them to put her to sleep until tomorrow. According to her papers, she's only twenty-two.'

'With forty years' experience,' said the inspector. 'The girl's a professional. That's obvious. What does the vice squad report?'

'Nothing, so far,' said the sergeant. 'I'll go down and shake them up.'

He stood up from the desk, stretched and left the office. He could as easily have telephoned the office of the vice squad, some of whose members had been called in to check on the identity of witness and victim, but he was secretly anxious to get away from his chief for a few minutes. It had been a long day since had been pulled out of bed in the early hours of that Sunday morning and the inspector's typical worrying and forcing of the case was beginning to get on his nerves.

The inspector, who was not unaware of this, let him go without comment and, alone in the office, got up from his desk to go and stare at the snow-covered scene outside the window. Darkness had fallen and the street lamps were on. So were some of the lights in the shop windows, but there were few pedestrians in the street and not much vehicle traffic. Salzburg, on the border between Germany and Austria, is a quietly beautiful, historic city and its residents incline to peacefully spent weekends once the tourist season is over.

Although he could not see it from the office, he could visualize the River Salzach winding northward from the city and forming the national boundary. In that same direction and less than three miles away was Anthering, the village from which Klaus Winkler had come to Salzburg five years earlier. He had been seventeen at the time, a slight, effeminate, only child of rich parents, and he had registered as a student at the Salzburg Academy of Beaux Arts.

At the moment, that was all that the inspector knew about Klaus Winkler, that and one other thing.

He was a murderer.

Why he had become a murderer the inspector could not guess. The neighbours who had summoned the police to the chic, expensive apartment building at twelve Mozart Street had been dumbfounded. The witness who had survived with only minor injuries could, perhaps, have explained, but she was in a state of shock and the doctors at the hospital would not let him talk to her. Like her murdered companion, she was a German national and not Austrian. Her name was

237

Renate Braun and the inspector was convinced that she was a professional prostitute and an expensive one. Einrich Winkler, forty-eight-year-old owner of the Winkler Metal Forming Company in Anthering, and his handsome forty-four-year-old wife Frieda had assured him that they knew nothing of the affair, although the inspector was not entirely convinced of that and, of course, big, beautiful, twenty-one-year-old Helga Schmidt could tell him nothing because she was dead, her dark, lovely head crushed by the violent blows of something heavy and irregularly shaped. It was thought that this would have been the blood-smeared, bronze statue of a naked man which had been found near her body and which the technicians in the police laboratory were now examining.

The person who could explain it all was Klaus Winkler and the inspector had thought that he would soon do so under interrogation, but so far he had not. It did not appear to be so much a question of a strong character resisting the interrogators. Winkler was anything but a strong character. Rather, he appeared to be in such a state of shock himself that he could not discuss what had taken place rationally. He was, it seemed, not only afraid of being taken for insane; he was afraid of actually being insane and thought he had lost touch with reality.

He had not lost touch with reality to the point where he was willing to confess to the murder, although he had not denied it either. The inspector thought that he might have by now had it not been for the extremely expensive attorney whom his parents had brought with them upon learning of his arrest. All three were now waiting in the outer office and the inspector could estimate what it cost to keep an attorney like that sitting all day Sunday in a police station.

The attorney had shut young Winkler up like a clam, but there was too much physical evidence for him to gain his release and the inspector felt confident that he would eventually be able to pry the clam open again. Unless he was greatly mistaken, the main cause of Winkler's silence was simply embarrassment. He was obviously a sensitive young man and this was a case that reeked sex.

Freak sex, too. In appearance, Winkler was almost a caricature of a homosexual and the things found in his apartment confirmed it.

So, what had he been doing with two beautiful, naked, sexy, young, German prostitutes?

The inspector could quite simply not imagine. Maybe Winkler was bisexual, but he certainly didn't look it.

The inspector sighed, called the switchboard to report where he could be located, and left the building to go to the police morgue where he suspected the autopsy would be practically completed.

It was completed and Dr Egon Harz, a painfully thin man with sunken cheeks, a long, sallow face and straight, long, black hair hanging in locks about his mournful eyes, was engaged in washing his hands. The corpse, with the terrible cross of the autopsy cut from collarbone to pubes still gaping wide, lay on the marble table.

The inspector inspected it dispassionately.

'Well?' he said.

'Identical to my report at the scene,' said the doctor. 'She was killed less than an hour before we arrived. Cause of death was multiple fractures of the skull. Probably the statue.'

'Sex?' said the inspector.

'She had been having a good time,' said the doctor. 'Lots of lubrication. A little semen in the vagina. Not much. Trace in the mouth. Saliva in the public hair and on the external genitals.'

'What the hell!' said the inspector. 'The man's a homosexual.'

The doctor shrugged and said nothing.

'All right!' said the inspector in an annoyed voice and left the autopsy room, closing the door a little more firmly than necessary.

The sergeant had returned from the vice squad when he arrived back at the office. He reported that the two girls had not been officially prostitutes. They had been too high class; too expensive for that. Erotic entertainers, said the sergeant. Very good. Very costly.

'Then, how did they get mixed up in a mess like this?'

snapped the inspector. He was not a man who liked loose ends or unexplained motives and in this case there was nothing else.

The sergeant did not reply. There was nothing he could say. The inspector already knew everything that he knew about the case and he was not prepared to do any speculating.

He had seen immediately that it was a mess from the moment they had been called out that morning. The dispatcher who had not even been present at the scene personally had said so over the telephone.

'A weirdo, Pitt,' he had said. 'We've had a homicide report from twelve Mozart and I've got a car there now. They say that there's a dead woman, another one hurt and a guy who's either high on drugs or in shock. Everybody's stark naked. The inspector's already on the way. He wants you to join him.'

The sergeant had immediately left for Mozart Street and, having less distance to travel, got there almost as soon as his chief.

The emergency ambulance, first to be called away, had been even quicker and the injured girl was being carried to it on a stretcher. Her only visible injury was a small cut on the left shoulder and the beginnings of a massive bruise around it.

The dead girl lay on the carpeted floor of the bedroom, halfway between the door and the bed. There was a certain amount of fresh blood on the carpet around her head, but no marks on the body and she looked as if she were merely sleeping. The intern with the ambulance crew had, however, checked for signs of life and there were none.

Klaus Winkler had been sitting in one of the easy chairs in the salon, leaning forward with his face buried in his hands. The officers from the patrolcar said that he had gone to the chair after letting them into the apartment and had been there ever since.

Otherwise, there were only the neighbours who had called the police. They had been awakened by what sounded like a battle royal and some piercing screams, apparently from the girl who had escaped. They had come to the door and

Winkler had let them in without a word. After seeing the girl lying on the bedroom floor and jumping to the conclusion that she was dead, they had left hurriedly and called the police. Winkler had apparently shut the door after them. The injured girl had neither said anything nor attempted to leave and the neighbours had thought that she and Winkler were related.

Renate Braun having been taken away to the hospital, the inspector approached Winkler and asked him to make a statement.

Winkler had looked at him in bewilderment and had said that his name was Klaus Winkler, but seemed confused over what had taken place. He gave his parent's address and asked that they be notified.

The inspector had then cautioned him on his rights and had ordered him taken to police headquarters. He also called for a detachment from the police laboratory to try and discover what had taken place in the apartment. No statements having been obtained, he did not know whether Winkler was a suspect or a victim, but he was not taking any chances.

Winkler became a suspect shortly after the arrival of the technicians who took his fingerprints, compared them to those on the bronze statue and noted the blood with which it was smeared. It looked, they said, as if there had been some kind of a sex orgy which had become violent.

The inspector had already come to the same conclusion. What had apparently been the clothing worn by the two girls had been hung up neatly on the backs of two chairs and two totally transparent and extremely sexy nightgowns had been laid out in the bedroom. There were also two expensive overnight cases stuffed with sex toys and pornography, all of it heterosexual. Pornography found in the apartment, however, was homosexual. Also in the cases were the girls' personal identification papers which was how the inspector learned their names and nationality.

Curiously, there were no signs of refreshments, no glasses or dirty plates, but there were two wet towels in the bathroom indicating that two persons had taken baths. A T-shirt and a pair of men's jeans lay on the floor of the living room, and a pair of men's shorts, expensive, silk and peach-coloured, had been flung over the shade of a lamp. This clothing apparently belonged to Klaus Winkler as it matched other items found in the closets.

Winkler's clothing was not all that was in the closets. There was other clothing in a larger size and there were two sets of toilet articles in the bathroom. The young man had not, it seemed, lived alone.

Faced with such contradictory evidence, the inspector had come to the conclusion that Winkler and his room-mate were bisexuals who had brought in a couple of expensive call girls for an evening's entertainment. A quarrel had, however, arisen and had degenerated into a physical battle with fatal results. As the other man was missing, the inspector assumed that he was the more promising suspect.

The laboratory technicians and Dr Harz were inclined to disagree. Everything in the apartment, they said, indicated a purely homosexual relationship. The male couple would no more have thought of inviting in a couple of females than they would of entertaining a pair of king cobras.

And there the matter had remained throughout the day while the inspector fumed and fretted and attempted to pry some kind of information out of somebody.

He had had just one success. Klaus Winkler's apartment mate had been identified. His name was Leopold Floer and he had been able to prove beyond a shadow of a doubt that he had not been in the apartment at the time of the murder and that he had nothing to do with it.

In fact, he was not even willing to believe what the inspector told him. He knew Klaus Winkler well, he said, intimately even, and it was utterly impossible for him to have been consorting with females, prostitutes or otherwise. Klaus did not like women. There was only one woman in the world that he would tolerate within a yard of himself and that was his mother.

The inspector had not been pleased at this confirmation of the doctor's and technicians' theories and the rejection of his own and, now that the autopsy was complete and there was still nothing concrete, he decided on an interview with Winkler's parents who were still waiting with the attorney in the outside office.

Taking them separately and beginning with Winkler, he chose to be blunt.

'I presume you are aware that your son is a homosexual?' he said.

Winkler flushed. 'I am aware of it,' he said shortly.

'Do you believe him capable of a relationship with a woman?' said the inspector.

'Not any more,' said Winkler, paused and then burst out in a torrent of angry words.

'It was Frieda! She ruined the boy! Always wanted a daughter and she made one out of him. My God! she was still putting him in dresses and giving him dollies to play with when he was ten. It's not his fault!'

'You could have done something, Mr Winkler,' said the inspector.

'I did,' said Winkler. 'When he was sixteen, I packed him off to boarding school. I thought they might still make a man out of him, but it was too late.'

'Have you tried psychiatric treatment?' said the inspector.

He did not know exactly where the interview was leading, but his years of experience in criminal investigations were telling him that there was something wrong with Einrich Winkler's statements although what it was he could not say.

'He wouldn't cooperate,' said Winkler. 'Finally, I had to give up. He wanted to come down to Salzburg, study at the academy and have his own apartment and I let him. What else could I do?'

'You knew he was living with a man named Leopold Floer?' said the inspector.

'I know none of his friends and I want to know none of them,' said Winkler.

The inspector's interview of Mrs Winkler was shorter, but it was enough to confirm that what Winkler had said was essentially true.

Assured that there was no hope of Klaus being released that night, the Winklers and their attorney went home and, a little later, so did the inspector. He had finally accepted that he was not going to find out what had happened yet that evening.

This situation resulted in a near sleepless night for the inspector who was, in any case, a light and restless sleeper, but it had a more calming effect on Klaus Winkler in the detention cells and, on the following morning, he announced that he was prepared to make a statement.

The inspector was pleased, but less so once he had heard it for he did not believe a word of it. It was, in fact, the most improbable statement that he had ever heard, he told the sergeant, and the only explanation he could find for it was that Winkler's attorney had put him up to making it with the intent of offering an insanity plea.

'It was a little after eleven on Saturday evening,' said Klaus Winkler. 'Leo was not coming home that night and I was having a quiet time with some books.

'I was not expecting anyone so when the doorbell rang, I thought that Leo had changed his mind and was coming home. If I'd stopped to think, I'd have remembered that he had his own key and didn't have to ring the doorbell, but I didn't and I went and opened the door.

'There were two strange girls standing outside and, as I'd never seen either of them before in my life, I thought they must have got the wrong address.

'However, before I could say anything the biggest one, the one that got killed, said, 'Is Raymond Huncke here?'

'I said that I didn't know any Raymond Huncke and that they had the wrong address.

'She said, "Well, he used to live here and he gave us this address. Can we come in for a minute? We've come a long way and we're tired."

'I said, "Of course, Come in." and after they had come in, I offered them a drink.

'They laughed and said they didn't drink on the job and they were acting very funny, walking around the apartment and picking up things and looking at them.

'I didn't like that and I said, "You better go now. My friend is coming home any minute now and he is very jealous." I wanted them to know I wasn't interested in girls.

'They just giggled and the little one went into the bathroom. I yelled, "Hey! What are you doing in my bathroom?" and she came to the door and started taking her clothes off. She said, "I'm taking a bath. That's what bathrooms are for."

'I thought that she was completely mad and when I turned around, the other one was taking off her clothes, too.

'I couldn't believe what was happening and I sort of lost my head and started screaming at them to get out and some other things, but they didn't pay any attention and when they'd finished with their showers, they came into the living room and started walking around naked in an obscene sort of way.

'I was just sitting in a chair and wondering if I had gone crazy or if somebody had put some kind of a drug into my food. I couldn't believe what was happening.

'All of a sudden they both sort of jumped on me, and one of them kissed me on the mouth! I almost lost my lunch! I was really sick! They were pulling my clothes off and rubbing themselves on me. I couldn't do anything. You wouldn't believe how strong they were.

'I was fighting and yelling, but they got my clothes off and they got me down on the floor and they began to touch me all over, but mostly my private parts. They were laughing like crazy and they were excited, too. I think they were touching each other. I couldn't bear to look.

'The worst part was that they were getting me excited, not the real me, of course, but my body and I had a sort of orgasm. I was so disgusted and frightened, too, that I made a terrible effort and I broke away from them and ran into the bedroom. I thought I could lock the door and call out the window for help.

'They were too fast for me though and they pushed me onto the bed and started playing with me again. One was squatting over my hips and I think she'd taken me right in her. The other was sitting across my face and trying to get me to kiss her. I was nearly smothered.

'I think I may have bitten her. I was desperate, and when I

got one hand free I was feeling around for something to defend myself, and I got hold of my little statue of Adam and I hit the big one with it. I don't know how many times I hit her. I was out of my mind with fear and disgust.

'Then, I saw the other one running and I threw the statue at her and hit her on the shoulder. I guess it was right after that that the neighbours came.'

'The attorney couldn't have made that up,' said the sergeant. 'And if he did, Winkler couldn't have memorized it. It has to be true.'

'It can't be,' said the inspector. 'This is a crazy world, but we're not at the point yet where beautiful, young prostitutes rape homosexuals in their own apartments for free.'

The inspector was, however, wrong in every respect but one. Two beautiful, young prostitutes had raped Klaus Winkler in his own apartment. The only thing was, it had not been for free.

Later that same day Renate Braun recovered sufficiently from her experience to make a statement, and she confirmed in every detail the story which Klaus Winkler had told the police.

With the addition of one detail which provided the explanation to what had otherwise been a totally inexplicable performance on the part of herself and her dead friend.

'We were hired,' she said. 'Two thousand five hundred dollars and expenses. If I'd have known how it would turn out, I'd have thrown the money in his face.'

'Whose face?' said the inspector, already knowing the answer.

'Einrich Winkler's face,' said Renate Braun.

'I thought it would make a man of him,' said Einrich Winkler.

On 26 June 1978, Klaus Winkler pleaded not guilty to homicide by reason of legitimate self-defence. The jury, although sympathetic, decided that the fate with which he had been threatened was not so terrible as to warrant quite such such a vigorous reaction, found him guilty of manslaughter and sentenced him to seven years' imprisonment.

He is serving his sentence in a men's prison, of course.

18

COLD BUFFET

There are superficial parallels in the Sapuppo and Winkler cases, mainly the use of qualified professionals to carry out the dirty work. Mrs Sapuppo did not feel up to murdering her husband. Mr Winkler could not rape his son. Outside help had to be called in.

Curiously, however, the principals of the Sapuppo drama, who were all from the underprivileged sector of society, were more conventional in their outlook and more sane in their actions than the participants in the Winkler tragedy, all of whom belonged to the favoured class. Girls included. No pizzario nor professional killer either ever earned two and a half thousand dollars plus expenses for three or four hour's work.

If there was anything crazy about Mrs Sapuppo and her lover, it was merely the failure to realize that Mr Sapuppo's relatives might react violently to his death and, even here, they probably believed that they could conceal their responsibility.

By contrast, the Winklers and everyone connected to them appear to have been suffering from serious delusions.

Mrs Winkler tried to make a little girl out of a little boy and nearly succeeded. Mr Winkler tried to make him back into a boy again and failed. The two prostitutes set out to rape a man whom they knew in advance to be a homosexual. Klaus, in the face of all anatomical evidence, believed himself to be a girl. The jury showed prejudice. Had Klaus really been a girl and the two prostitutes men, he would probably have been acquitted. Even the police were a little confused by the time the case was over. The official mind is not constructed for the contemplation of such extremes in human behaviour.

A good many official minds are not constructed for the contemplation of anything which does not fit current ideology with regard to crime and its prevention. For the past fifty years or so, the predominant theory on crime and criminals has been that there are none. What has been called crime is the justified actions of persons who are not criminals but under-privileged members of society. By correcting the injustices of society, crime and criminals will be eliminated.

This an excellent theory and its only fault is that it does not work. Violent crime has increased steadily and continues to increase despite all efforts at rehabilitation and reinsertion programmes. The human being is predisposed to the use of force and only force will restrain the dangerous tendencies of a substantial part of society.

Crimes against property have also increased, but at a slower pace, although it would seem exactly here that the underprivileged would exert their greatest efforts. There is, however, a reason for this.

Compare the sentences handed down and actually served for murder and for bank robbery and it will be seen that the murderer is substantially better off. It is rare for him or her to serve more than seven years for the crime. A bank robber can expect to spend twenty years or more behind bars and, if necessary, he will be hunted to the ends of the earth, particularly if he managed to make off with a sizeable amount of cash.

This may seem unjust, but it is economically understandable. Murderers are caught by civil servants on fixed salaries with modest tax-supported means at their disposal. Bank robbers and the like are tracked by private as well as public agencies and the means at their disposal are exceeded only by what the bank or insurance company hopes to recover plus the value of the deterrent effect.

In short, there is very little to be gained in catching and punishing murderers. There is a great deal to be gained in catching and punishing bank robbers.

This attitude is not confined to capitalist countries. In Socialist countries, economic crimes will get you executed as swiftly as will murder. The crime rate in socialist countries is low, either because there are no underprivileged or because everyone is underprivileged.

Or, just possibly, because of those swift and pitiless executions.

In the Western world, executions seem to exercise a peculiar effect on the emotions of legislators and other persons in positions of power. Although these, theoretically, are the representatives of the citizens who have elected them, and although polls in nearly every country show substantial majorities in favour of capital punishment, the rights of the convicted are given precedence in almost all cases. Very little consideration is given to the rights of children and older persons to live without fear of rape, torture and death. The protectors of human rights protect unevenly.

This state of affairs has given rise in recent years to the strange spectacle of criminals more civic-minded than their prosecutors. Violent criminals, recognizing the danger which they pose to society have literally pleaded with the courts to sentence them to death.

Sometimes, the courts have listened, more often not. When they have not, the results have occasionally been tragic. The judges or others whose decision led to the tragedy are never held responsible. They are described as great humanitarians in the press.

Sometimes, however, even a great humanitarian finds himself confronted with a situation where mercy seems out of place.

The lean, distinguished-looking man with the prominent, slightly hooked nose had risen to his feet and a sudden hush fell over the courtroom of the Superior Criminal Court in the city of Troyes, France. It was known that there would be an appeal for the death sentence.

'Your Honour,' began the man in a deep, low and oddly tranquil voice, 'ladies and gentlemen of the jury, members of the press and fellow citizens. It is not my intent to entertain you with long speeches. There is little to be said. The accused in this case has freely admitted his guilt. He has murdered wantonly and deliberately three times. He has assured the court that, given the opportunity, he will kill again. This man must never again be released into society and, as long as he is alive, there is such a possibility. It is, therefore, the duty of this court to eliminate the possibility in the only manner in which it can with certainty be eliminated, and that is by sentencing the accused to die on the guillotine.

'That is all I have to say. Condemn the accused to death and see that he passes under the guillotine surely and at the earliest possible date.

'I thank you and I count upon you to do your duty as human beings and as citizens of France.'

Thirty-nine-year-old Claude Buffet who had just demanded his own execution sat down and quietly folded his hands in his lap. He was, without question, the most controlled person in the courtroom.

A few feet away, Buffet's fellow accused, thirty-six-year-old Roger Bontems, was sweating copiously, his swarthy face turned pale with concern. He was no killer and he did not see how he could be sentenced to death, but even the mention of the guillotine made him nervous. Privately, as he had publically, he cursed the day that he had been assigned to share a cell with this homicidal madman.

The hush which had lasted while Buffet was speaking had ended and there were savage cries of 'Kill him! Chop off his head!' from the spectators, many of whom were friends and relatives of the victims.

Buffet gazed at them dispassionately with a sort of mild curiosity and rose to his feet once again.

For a second time, there was a dead silence.

'I do not apologize to the relatives of the persons I have murdered,' he said coldly. 'I accept no responsibility.' He raised his hand dramatically to point at the official picture of the president of France which hung in that as in all French courtrooms. 'There!' he cried, 'is the man responsible for the deaths of Nicole Compte and Guy Giradot! Take your complaints to him!'

There was something to what he said and every person in the courtroom was aware that, were it not for President Georges Pompidou, Claude Buffet would now be dead and Nicole Compte and Guy Giradot alive.

France had the death penalty, but the last time it had been invoked was on 11 March 1969. General Charles de Gaulle had been president then and he was not a man to have much sympathy with violent criminals.

Pompidou, who replaced him, was more of a progressive and he immediately began commuting all death sentences to life imprisonment, something which only the president had the power to do.

It was not a popular exercise of that power and not even a wise one. If something went wrong, then, exceptionally, the responsibility was all too clear.

Now something had gone very wrong indeed, and President Pompidou found himself faced with a decision which he would rather have avoided. He had already saved Claude Buffet from the guillotine once. Would he dare to save him again?

Basically, the whole business was due to a misfortune in timing. Had Buffet chosen to murder Francoise Besimensky a year earlier, General de Gaulle would still have been president when he was convicted and his head would have rolled..

However, Mrs Besimensky, a twenty-seven-year-old fashion model who was married to a prominent physician, was murdered on 18 January 1967 and justice in France being no more swift and certain than it is in most other places, it was October of 1970 before the trial took place.

By this time, General de Gaulle was out of office and Georges Pompidou was president. It was a fatal difference.

The case had begun prosaically enough for a Paris murder with the discovery of Mrs Besimensky's body lying among some bushes in the great park of the Bois de Boulogne on 19 January.

Mrs Besimensky had been killed by two bullet wounds in the upper part of the chest. The bullets, recovered at the time of the autopsy, proved to be nine millimetre, and they had been fired at extremely close range.

There were certain indications of a sexual motive. The woman's underwear had been removed and there had been apparently some tampering with the sex organs, although no traces of semen or of actual penetration were recovered. It was, therefore, possible that the sexual indications were false and represented an attempt by the murderer to mislead the police.

This theory was strengthened by the fact that no identification was found with or on the body which had, however, been left in comparatively conspicuous view guaranteeing its early discovery.

Efforts by the police to identify the victim were immediately successful as her husband had reported her missing when she failed to return home the preceding evening. Efforts to identify her murderer were less so.

The chief difficulty was the motive. If it had not been sexual, and there was good reason to believe that it had not, what then? According to her husband, Mrs Besimensky would not have been carrying a sufficiently large sum of money on her to be murdered for it and, in any case, there would have been no reason for a robber to murder her once he had his hands on the money.

Unless, of course, she knew him, but Mrs Besimensky did not move in social circles that could be expected to include robbers.

There remained a personal motive of some kind. Mrs Besimensky had been a beautiful woman. A lover perhaps . . . ?

Or Dr Besimensky. In the murder of a married person, the spouse is always and automatically the primary suspect until proven innocent.

Dr Besimensky was very quickly proven innocent and so, for that matter, in another sense, was his wife. Francoise Besimensky had not had any lovers.

This left the police with only the alternative which they liked least. The murderer of Francoise Besimensky was neither a robber nor a disappointed lover nor an outraged husband. He was simply a killer.

True killers are not uncommon in modern society and they have not been uncommon in the past. Jack the Ripper was one of the more conspicuous, but there have been many others and in all countries. In a dismaying number of cases,

252

the true killers are not brought to justice and it is often not even known that a series of seemingly unrelated crimes is the work of a single individual. Motive is a very important factor in the solution of crimes, and the true killers have only their desire to kill, something which is not traceable.

This does not mean that the true killer has no motive at all. He does, but it is not one known to others. It is something inner, concealed and not apparent so that the killer appears a normal and, not infrequently, attractive member of society.

Confronted with what they suspect may be such a case, the police have little choice but to search the files for similar incidents, cling to any clues which may have been recovered at the scene and wait for the next murder.

Actually, they did not have long to wait, but what arrived was not a new murder but a lucky break, and it was provided by an attractive young mother of a five-year-old daughter.

Being rather careless in some respects, the attractive young mother was not married nor was she completely certain who the father of her little daughter was. This did not mean, however, that she was any less attached to her child, and when her current companion strangled the child unconscious while she was out shopping, she went to the police. She had, of course, severed relations with her violent friend, but she wanted to be certain that he did not return.

The police, to whom such reports were routine, ran a check of the files and found that the child-strangler was Claude Buffet, a man with a criminal record covering some sixty-odd offences, mostly theft or robbery.

Buffet, a man with an eventful if not, necessarily, distinguished career, had been born in the city of Reims on 19 May 1933, but, following the end of the war, the family had moved to Cognac where he had received his first sentence at age eighteen for the theft of a motorcycle.

The sentence had been suspended on the grounds of his youth and Buffet had gone off to join the French Foreign Legion where he had spent a good deal of time in the punishment cells for theft, fighting and similar offences. Sent to Vietnam, he had promptly deserted, but having no place to go, had turned himself in to the military police.

Having completed his service with the French Foreign Legion, Buffet had held a succession of jobs as a servant and waiter and was currently employed as a truck driver. He was not, however, popular with his colleagues who described him as arrogant, nor with his employers who said that he insisted on driving the truck while dressed in a starched, white shirt and deerskin gloves.

Such conduct was not criminal, but there were other indications that Buffet might have been involved in some of the numerous robberies of taxi cabs which take place continuously in Paris.

A little more effort was put into tracing his activities and, to the gratification of the investigators, it was possible to show that a nine-millimetre revolver which had been used in some of the cab robberies had been in Buffet's possession and presumably still was.

Up to this point, no one had thought of connecting Buffet with the Besimensky murder, but now a comparison of a bullet recovered from the upholstery of a taxi cab was made with all nine-millimetre bullets on record with the Ballistics Department and it developed that this bullet had been fired from the same gun that killed Francoise Besimensky.

The investigators were surprised. Buffet was an old customer, but they had always considered him to be rather small fry. Now, it seemed, he was one of their most sought murderers.

Taken into custody, Buffet, with his vast experience in such matters, promptly denied everything and claimed police harassment, but the nine-millimetre revolver was recovered from his apartment and so were some pieces of Mrs Besimensky's jewellery. After a valiant but unsuccessful attempt to place the blame for the killing on his current mistress, Buffet gave up and confessed to the murder of Mrs Besimensky whose name he had only learned from the newspapers.

According to Buffet's confession, he had not had anything against the victim nor had he even particularly wanted to rob her, although he had done so on the principle of 'waste not, want not'. The reason he had killed her was simply that he had been wondering for some time what it would feel like to kill somebody.

Now he was wondering what it would be like to be killed himself and, at his trial in October of 1970, he pleaded manfully for the death sentence, saying that he thought that the plunge of the heavy blade of the guillotine might prove to be quite exhilarating, even though for only a short time.

There was some speculation among the French, a cynical race in any case, that Buffet might be trying reverse psychology on the court in the hope of escaping the death sentence, but, if so, he was mistaken for the jury very promptly found him guilty as charged and sentenced him to die on the guillotine.

President Pompidou as quickly reversed the jury's decision and commuted the death sentence to life imprisonment.

Said Claude Buffet, 'You will be sorry.'

He knew what he was talking about.

Having been deprived of his exhilarating encounter with the guillotine, Buffet was taken off to the prison of Clairvaux in the east of France. It was a high-security prison with little chance of escape and early releases were not as common at that time as they are today.

There he was placed in a cell with one of the most luckless bank robbers in history, the thirty-six-year-old Roger Bontems, who was soon to provide the world with a crushing example of the dangers of keeping bad company.

Bontems was the more unfortunate in that he had little choice in the company he kept, but he and Claude Buffet got on well in any case. Both probably made an effort. Bontems was serving a twenty-year sentence for armed robbery and Buffet was in for life. They were obviously going to be together for some time.

Assuming that they did nothing about it, but on the morning of 21 September 1971 they made the fatal decision to attempt a unilateral reduction of their sentences and at a little before eleven o'clock the sirens throughout the prison began to wail. A break-out was underway.

It was something which did not happen very often, but the

prison personnel were prepared for it. Steel doors clanged shut. Guards along the walls slipped shells into the breeches of their riot guns and the machine-gunners in the corner turrets readied their weapons. It was not immediately known how many inmates were taking place in the escape attempt.

It was known that the attempt was taking place in the prison clinic and this sector was promptly blocked off from the rest of the prison. The situation, it appeared, was in hand.

Hurrying to the scene of the action, the warden found a group of armed guards under the direction of the chief guard in position before the closed doors of the clinic and one unarmed, badly shaken cell-block guard.

According to his statement, he had brought the cellmates Buffet and Bontems to the clinic because they had complained of having sore throats. With him had been another guard, twenty-five-year-old Guy Giradot, whose sympathies for the prisoners were well known and who was, consequently, popular with them.

The guards and the two prisoners had entered the clinic where they had been met by prison nurse Nicole Compte, an attractive, cheerful thirty-three-year-old mother of two little girls. She, too, was popular with both prisoners and prison employees.

Suddenly, Buffet and Bontems had whipped home-made but dangerous knives out of their clothing and, seizing Giradot and Mrs Compte, had put the edges to their throats.

The second guard, powerless to interfere without endangering the lives of the hostages, had run out the clinic door and had sounded the alarm.

In the opinion of the warden and the chief guard the situation was dangerous but not hopeless. It was true that the men were holding two hostages and Buffet, at least, had nothing to lose as he was already serving a life sentence. On the other hand, the clinic was deep inside the prison and, if Buffet and Bontems attempted to make their way out using the hostages as a shield, there would be opportunities for a sharpshooter to pick them off, even assuming that the many gates through which they would have to pass were opened for them. In addition, the prisoners could scarcely kill the hostages as they would then have nothing left with which they could bargain. It was the common situation of a stalemate where neither side could take action.

The prison authorities had an advantage, however. There was little or nothing to eat in the clinic and, eventually, Buffet and Bontems would get hungry. Unfortunately, so would Giradot and Mrs Compte, but there was nothing to be done about that.

Approaching the door of the clinic the warden identified himself, pointed out that the prisoners' situation was hopeless, and called upon them to release their hostages and come out. If they did so promptly and the hostages had suffered no harm, there would be no disciplinary action taken. The incident would be forgotten.

It was the maximum that he could offer, but it was not enough for Buffet.

'We want two machine pistols, a thousand rounds of ammunition and a fast car,' he called. 'We'll release the hostages as soon as we're clear.'

'That is beyond my authority to grant and you know it, Buffet,' said the warden. 'You'll never get out of this prison.'

'Then,' said Claude Buffet, 'we'll cut their throats.'

'You'll be guillotined,' said the warden unsteadily. He knew death in a man's voice when he heard it.

'That was my original request, I believe,' said Claude Buffet.

The warden withdrew, the sweat running down his face.

'What are we going to do?' said the chief guard in a hoarse whisper.

'Notify the next of kin,' said the warden. 'Tell them to come at once.'

The guard's face was appalled. 'You think it's that bad?'

'Not quite,' said the warden. 'Bontems is no killer. Maybe if Mrs Giradot and Mr Compte make an appeal, he'll protect them from Buffet until we can break in. I don't know what else we can do.'

There was nothing else to be done and the appeals by the next of kin of the hostages had no effect other than to nearly break the hearts of everyone present for they were answered by the hostages themselves.

'I am still alive and unharmed,' called Nicole Compte. 'Kiss my children and tell them I love them.'

'Jeannette, my darling,' cried Guy Giradot, married less than a year. 'Go away. Do not remain here. Everything will be all right.'

But everything was not going to be all right and all of the men present felt it in their hearts. Buffet was a killer and he had nothing to lose. Bontems was, apparently, completely under his influence. The hostages could expect no help from him.

Buffet had convinced the warden of his sincerity and the advantage had now turned to him. Taking the offensive, he demanded that food and drink be sent in to the clinic.

The warden, his face contorted with the agony of a decision that no man should be required to make, refused. If he once gave in to the prisoners' demands on any point it would only lead to still further demands.

'If there is no food within a half-hour, we will kill one of the hostages and throw out the body,' said Buffet, speaking as calmly and emotionlessly as if he were planning to discard a pair of old shoes.

The warden believed him, but he could not comply even if he so wished. He had, by this time, been in contact with the Ministry of Justice in Paris and no concessions were to be made to Buffet and Bontems regardless of the circumstances.

'We'll have to rush them,' said the warden. 'There's no point in waiting any longer.'

At eleven o'clock in the evening, twelve hours after the escape attempt had begun, the guards smashed in the door of the prison clinic with a fire axe and took into custody Claude Buffet and Roger Bontems, both of whom stood rigid with hands held high over their heads so as to avoid any pretext by which so many avidly yearning trigger fingers could have sent the machine-pistol slugs ripping through their bodies.

The warden ran past them through the admissions room and into the ward of the clinic itself and the men following at his heels heard him give a deep, agonized groan.

Lying on the floor of the ward were the bodies of Nicole Compte and Guy Giradot. Their throats were cut from ear to ear.

Once again there was a trial, and once again Claude Buffet pleaded guilty to premeditated, deliberate murder and requested his own execution on the guillotine.

Roger Bontems, who had been separated from his cell-mate, did no such thing. He had, he admitted, wanted to escape from the prison, but he had not killed anybody and he had never had any intention of killing anybody. He did not request his own execution and said that he regretted not having killed Buffet the first time he laid eyes on him.

Once again, a raging jury granted Claude Buffet's request and sentenced him to death on the guillotine. They went, in fact, even further and sentenced Roger Bontems to the same punishment, although Buffet had assured them that Bontems had had nothing to do with the murders and had not even been in the room at the time.

All eyes turned to the president of France. Would he once again save Claude Buffet from the guillotine?

It was thought certain that he would commute Roger Bontems' sentence. The man had, after all, harmed no one and had apparently not even known that Giradot and Mrs Compte were being killed.

The president maintained a majestic silence. There was to be a general election on 4 March 1973 and the opinion polls had shown roughly one hundred per cent of the electorate in favour of the death penalty.

French executions used to take place early in the morning. At ten minutes past four of 28 November 1972, a limp Roger Bontems was marched to the grim machine, laid face down-ward as prescribed by law and, an instant later, his head dropped into the basket. One of the few persons in modern times to be executed for a lesser crime than murder, he was a victim of a political system where popularity overrides principle.

It had taken three minutes to cut off Roger Bontems' head, and it took another seven to hoist the blade back up and set another basket for the head in place.

At four-twenty of that morning, Claude Buffet strode to the guillotine, his manner brisk and eager. He had, he said, a last request. Could he be permitted to lie on his back so that he could see the blade descending?

Executioners are men with strong nerves.

'I regret, monsieur,' said executioner André Obrecht, 'the law requires that you lie face downward.'

Claude Buffet had, it seemed, been quite sincere in his wish to rid society of a dangerous element in the form of himself so was he really mad?

Yes, indeed. Although the psychologists who examined him pronounced him sane and responsible for his acts, no really sane person can cut the throats of harmless persons when there is not the slightest benefit to be gained from it. As for wishing to die, this is so common that it can scarcely be described as abnormal. Most persons with the death wish take care of matters themselves, however, and do not expect the state to kill them.

Was the president of France mad for commuting the sentences of a whole string of murderers and then sending to the guillotine a man who had murdered no one?

Not at all. The president won the elections handily.

Were the people who elected him mad?

Not really. The alternative was the socialists and their first act upon arriving in power was to abolish the death sentence altogether.